LORD M.

or the Later Life of Lord Melbourne

also by David Cecil

Biography:

TWO QUIET LIVES
Dorothy Osborne and Thomas Gray

THE STRICKEN DEER
or The Life of Cowper

THE YOUNG MELBOURNE

Criticism:

POETS AND STORY-TELLERS

EARLY VICTORIAN NOVELISTS
Essays in Revaluation of Dickens,
Thackeray, the Brontës, Trollope,
George Eliot and Mrs. Gaskell

HARDY THE NOVELIST

LORD MELBOURNE in 1838

DAVID CECIL

LORD M.

or the Later Life of Lord Melbourne

CONSTABLE · LONDON

LONDON
PUBLISHED BY
Constable and Company Ltd
10-12 *Orange Street, W.C.*2

INDIA
Orient Longmans Ltd
BOMBAY   CALCUTTA   MADRAS

CANADA
Longmans, Green and Company
TORONTO

SOUTH *and* EAST AFRICA
Longmans, Green and Company Ltd
CAPE TOWN   NAIROBI

First published 1954

PRINTED IN GREAT BRITAIN BY THE CHISWICK PRESS
NEW SOUTHGATE, LONDON, N.II.

To
My Mother
who first told me about Lord Melbourne

PREFATORY NOTE

I OWE MY READERS an explanation. This book was originally intended to form part of a single volume covering the whole course of Melbourne's life, and divided into three sections. The first, extending from childhood into middle life, was to describe the formation of his character; the second was to give an analysis, illustrated by references both to his earlier and subsequent history, of this character when set into its final shape; and the third was to tell how this character exhibited itself in action during his later years. Owing to untoward circumstances, it was not possible to carry out this plan to its intended conclusion, and the first and second sections appeared together in a single volume. When, some years afterwards, I returned to my task, I found it impossible to make clear my interpretation of Melbourne's later history without recourse to the analysis of his character which concluded the first book. Merely to recapitulate it in different words seemed a futile waste of effort. I have therefore taken the liberty to include a section of the final chapter of *The Young Melbourne* in the Prelude to the present volume.

I must add some words of gratitude: to Her Majesty the Queen for graciously permitting me to consult the archives at Windsor Castle, and to reproduce three pictures from the collection there; to Lord Brocket, L. U. Grace, Esq. and to the Trustees of the National Portrait Galleries of

PREFATORY NOTE

England and Scotland for allowing me to reproduce other pictures; to the Countess Mountbatten, the late Lady Desborough, the Marquess of Lansdowne, the Earl of Ilchester, Earl Grey and Lord Hatherton, for allowing me to make use of their private papers.

DAVID CECIL

CONTENTS

		Page
	PRELUDE	1
I	IN OFFICE	17
II	MRS. NORTON	56
III	AFTER REFORM	73
IV	PRIME MINISTER	112
V	THE QUEEN: FIRST PHASE	171
VI	THE QUEEN: SECOND PHASE	246
VII	LAST YEARS	302

ILLUSTRATIONS

LORD MELBOURNE in 1838   *frontispiece*

From a painting by Sir George Hayter in the possession of Lord Brocket.

facing page

THE HON. MRS. NORTON   62

From an engraving after Sir Edwin Landseer.

HENRY, 1ST BARON BROUGHAM AND VAUX   82

From an engraving.

LORD MELBOURNE in 1834   112

From a miniature painted by Sir William Ross in the possession of L. H. Luke.

QUEEN VICTORIA   172

From a watercolour sketch by A. E. Chalon in the National Portrait Gallery of Scotland.

QUEEN VICTORIA AND LORD MELBOURNE riding at Windsor   248

From a painting by Sir Francis Grant at Windsor Castle. *Reproduced by gracious permission of H.M. The Queen.*

xi

ILLUSTRATIONS

QUEEN VICTORIA AND THE PRINCE CONSORT   300

From a painting by Sir Edwin Landseer at
Windsor Castle. *Reproduced by gracious permission of
H.M. The Queen.*

LORD MELBOURNE in 1844   314

From a painting by John Partridge at Windsor
Castle. *Reproduced by gracious permission of H.M.
The Queen.*

CHIEF EVENTS

1827 William Lamb becomes Chief Secretary for Ireland.

1828 Death of the 1st Lord Melbourne.

   Death of Lady Caroline Lamb.

   Melbourne's resignation from the Government.

1830 Melbourne becomes Home Secretary.

   Melbourne meets Mrs. Norton.

1832 Passing of the Reform Bill.

1834 Prime Minister.

   Melbourne's Government dismissed by William IV.

1835 Melbourne becomes Prime Minister for the second time.

1836 Melbourne cited by Norton in his action against Mrs. Norton.

   Death of Augustus Lamb.

1837 Accession of Queen Victoria.

1838 Durham in Canada.

1839 Crisis over the Bedchamber question.

   Queen Victoria engaged to Prince Albert.

1840 Marriage of Queen Victoria.

   Syrian crisis.

1841 Fall of the Melbourne Government.

1842 Melbourne has a stroke.

1848 Death of Melbourne.

WILLIAM LAMB, second son of the first Viscount Melbourne, had arrived at the age of forty-seven without achieving anything of significance in the world. He had been born in 1779 with, it might have seemed, every opportunity for success. Nature had made him handsome, agreeable and intellectually distinguished; fate had placed him in the very centre of the small privileged aristocracy who at that time ruled England; and whilst still in his twenties, he had what the world might consider the additional good fortune to lose his eldest brother. So that he moved among his fellows attended by all the special consequence that adheres to the heir to a rich peerage.

But bad fairies, as well as good, came to his christening: and at first it looked as if their gifts were to prove more potent. His disposition was fundamentally divided against itself. From his mother, a brilliant and unscrupulous woman of fashion, he had inherited a vigorous animal temperament and a hard commonsense intelligence. But

I

there was another strain in him, a vein of dreamy speculation, a power of warm and sensitive feeling. These two were in conflict. Half eighteenth century man of the world, half romantic philosopher, he found his heart stretching out to an idealism which his reason told him was visionary illusion. And unable to decide which side of his nature to follow, he tended from his early years to relapse into a sceptical uncertainty.

The events of his subsequent life did nothing to extricate him from this impasse. He married early and for love. Unluckily his wife, the celebrated Lady Caroline Lamb, was a crazed fantastic egotist who no amount of tenderness and patience on his part could save from degradation and ruin: and the long strain of living with her—she did not die until 1828—only served still further to confirm him in his disillusioned sense of the vanity of things human. He also went into politics. But during the first years of the nineteenth century, the Whig Party to whom he belonged was at the lowest point of its fortunes. Excluded from office by the Tory reaction stirred first by the French Revolution and then by the Napoleonic Wars, it had disintegrated into a welter of quarrelling factions which offered a young man no firm ground on which to build a career. Moreover, William did not agree with the Whigs. He belonged to them from family tradition: but in reality his cautious spirit felt more in sympathy with the middle way policy of that group on the left of the Tory Party which was led by Canning. However, he did not believe in this strongly enough to feel justified in leaving his friends. With the consequence that though he made a name for himself as a young man of ability, he remained, during the twenty-five odd years he was in Parliament, a private member without work and without influence. Indeed, during the last fifteen of them, he had grown so hopeless of his political future that he preferred to spend much of his time away from the House of Commons, reading and meditating in the library of his family's country home at Brocket Hall in Hertfordshire.

Yet his experience, though apparently so frustrating, had not been unprofitable. Compelled to be an onlooker at the spectacle of life, he had made the most of the peculiar advantages afforded by that position. He had learned to observe human nature, as it showed itself in the great world public and private, widely, acutely and impartially. Further, he had made use of his years of enforced leisure to develop his intellectual capacity to the full. He was one of the best read men of his time; in literature, history, philosophy, theology. Nor—and here it was he differed from the usual run of cultivated Whig men of the world—was his mind mainly receptive. Life and books alike started him thinking, questioning, drawing conclusions. Gradually his scattered reflections fused with the inclinations of his temperament to compose themselves into a considered philosophy of life. It was an odd and individual one. So also was the man of which it was the expression. The mature William presented to the world a personality and point of view curiously unlike those of other people. Since their impact on the course of English history is the subject of this book, we may be permitted to pause and examine them in greater detail.

To look at he was extremely prepossessing, "handsome,

verging to portly," said an observer, "with a sweet countenance and an expression of refined, easy, careless good humour. He was too well-bred to seem unpleasantly sensual; but his whole person, expression and manner showed a pleasure-loving nature, indulgent to himself and to others." Indeed, age, while abating little of the sparkle of his youthful good looks, had enriched them with a new mellowness. His well-cut countenance radiated the comfortable glow that comes from years of good living; beneath his thick greying brows the eyes gleamed out, brilliant as ever, but with an added softness of geniality. His demeanour was of a piece with his appearance. Natural talent had united with long experience to make him the perfect man of the world, whose manners, at once unobtrusive and accomplished, could handle the most delicate situation with light-handed mastery, and shed round every conversation an atmosphere of delightful ease. Yet there was nothing studied about him. On the contrary, the first thing that struck most people meeting him was that he was surprisingly, eccentrically natural. Abrupt and casual, he seemed to saunter through life, swearing when he pleased, laughing when he pleased—with an odd infectious explosive "ha, ha!"—sprawling about in chairs, taking his meals with unashamed relish, and jerking out anything apparently that came into his head. It was his frankness that, above all, astonished. On the most dignified occasions, solemn political councils, stiff social gatherings, when everybody else was guarded or stilted, William Lamb talked exactly as if he were at home; came out, in lazy flippant colloquial tones, with

some candid comment that made the whole pompous
pretence immediately ridiculous.

His habits were equally unconventional. He was full of
queer idiosyncrasies of behaviour: gleeful rubbing together of his hands if he were amused, odd ejaculations,
"eh, eh" before he made a remark; and, a curious gesture,
passing a finger to the back of his head while he was talking. His letters were folded and sealed anyhow; the
pockets of his beautifully-cut coats bulged with a confusion of papers and bank notes; he never could be
bothered with a watch, but would just shout to a passing
servant to tell him the time; he went to sleep when and
wherever the mood took him; in a fit of absent-mindedness
he would start talking to himself in the midst of a company
of strangers. Indeed, though they liked him, people found
him perplexing in more ways than one. Here we come
to his third salient characteristic. He was mysterious. It
was partly that, for all his apparent frankness, he was
discreet. Persons coming away from an interview with
him, in which he had seemed to talk with complete
candour, would suddenly realize that he had not given
himself away on any point that really mattered. On the
contrary, they wondered nervously if they had not given
themselves away to him. His air of idle nonchalance lulled
them at first into thinking he noticed little. But then,
looking up at him by chance, they would perceive, dart-
ing out beneath the half-closed lids, a keen glance that
seemed to penetrate to their very hearts.

But most of all his point of view baffled them. His
conversation was fascinating; the fine flower of Whig
agreeability, at once light and learned, civilized and spon-

taneous, but made individual by the play of his whimsical fancy and the gusto of his good spirits—"There was a glee in his mirth," it was remarked, "indescribably charming." But the spirit, the intention behind the discourse—ah, that was elusive. Was William Lamb serious? Certainly he sometimes seemed to be. He would talk ardently on the most solemn subjects, political principle, the doctrines of Christianity. Yet within a few minutes he was conversing with equal animation in a different and less edifying strain. He had the typical eighteenth-century enjoyment of animal humour; "Now," he would say with zest as the dining-room doors shut on the ladies, leaving the gentlemen to their wine, "now we can talk broad." And even on serious subjects his tone was ambiguous. Its salient characteristic was irony, a mischievous, enigmatic irony, that played audaciously over the most sacred topics, leaving its hearer very much in doubt whether William Lamb thought them sacred at all. Paradox, too, was of the fibre of his talk. He loved to defend the indefensible. "What I like about the Order of the Garter," he once remarked, "is that there is no damned merit about it." Much as he appreciated poetry, he professed to welcome the news of a poet's death. "It is a good thing when these authors die," he confided, "for then one gets their works, and is done with them." His paradoxes grew bolder, the more astonishment they created. If he was talking to anyone who struck him as a prig or a humbug, they would pile themselves wickedly one on the other, till his bewildered interlocutor relapsed into shocked silence. Indeed, William's whole personality was a paradox. Racy and refined, sensible and eccentric,

6

cynical and full of sentiment, direct and secretive, each successive impression he made seemed to contradict the last.

Yet each impression was a true one. The outward paradox mirrored accurately the paradox within. He was not at one with himself. On the contrary, maturity had only intensified the discord within him. His intellectual judgment was cynically realistic. All he had seen of the world confirmed him in his view that it was ruled mainly by folly, vanity, and selfishness. And when someone quoted to him an old observation of his own to the effect that man could only learn by experience, "No, no," he returned sadly, "nobody learns anything by experience; everybody does the same thing over and over again."

This last reflects, indirectly, as much on himself as on others. It was the measure of his detachment, that he never excepted himself from his condemnation of human beings in general. His contempt was not arrogant. This makes it more amiable; but it shows how thoroughly disillusioned he was. As for the ideal motives by which people professed to be actuated, he thought them the most fantastic illusions of all; smoke screens raised by men in order to hide from themselves the fact of their own selfishness. If, by any rare chance, idealists were sincere, it could only be because they were too stupid to understand the nature of things. "A doctrinaire," he used to say, "is a fool but an honest man." Or again, "Nobody ever did anything very foolish except from some strong principle."

Yet his heart continued to rebel against the conclusions of his reason. His sensibility was as tremblingly keen as in youth. He did not believe in human virtue:

7

but he recognized goodness when he saw it; and he loved it. Even if public life was in fact a shoddy, self-seeking affair, how heart-stirring a pageant did it contrive to present! A moving tale still brought the tears to William's eyes, an heroic deed still fired him to a glow of generous admiration. The grace of girlhood, the sweetness of friendship, the charm of garden solitude, vain and ephemeral though they might be, set him throbbing with exquisite and poignant emotions. And now and again his spirit was touched by sublimer visitations. Suddenly there would sweep over him a mysterious sense of some august and unearthly power behind the show of things, governing human destiny. "I consider," he once broke out, unexpectedly and with emotion, to an embarrassed Cabinet meeting, "that England has been under the special protection of Divine Providence at certain periods of her history; the Spanish Armada, for instance, and the retirement of the French squadron from Bantry Bay." And on another occasion, "I do not approve," he said, "of the condemnation in Fénelon, of those whom he is pleased to call mystics— to which persuasion I belong." Indeed these curious spiritual intimations of his were in the nature of direct mystical experience. They did not lead him to adopt a thorough-going mystical philosophy; for they came too seldom and too fleetingly for him to feel justified in founding an intellectual structure on them. Besides, he could find no logical ground for believing in their truth. But he was too sincere not to recognize their convincing reality as long as they lasted. And though they did not displace his rationalism, they undermined its security.

8

PRELUDE

Uneasily he hung suspended between two opinions.

No wonder he was paradoxical! What was life but a bundle of contradictions? No wonder he was ironical; faced by the preposterous incongruity of experience, the only thing a reasonable person could do was to shrug his shoulders and smile. His duality of vision appears in his attitude to every sort of subject. No one appreciated better the achievements of culture: but he did not believe they had ever seriously influenced mankind. "Raphael was employed to decorate the Vatican," he said, "not because he was a great painter but because his uncle was architect to the Pope." In politics he united a mystical patriotism and a disinterested wish to do the best for his country, to a scornful disbelief in the sacredness of any human institution, the good sense of any political ideal. Again, though his heart was so abnormally tender that he could hardly bear a tale of suffering without tears, humanitarian schemes raised in him a violent antagonism. "I am not a subscribing sort of fellow," he would reply breezily to earnest persons asking him to contribute to a philanthropic cause. Educational reformers, factory reformers—the only result of their efforts, he alleged, would be to worry the poor. As for the anti-slavery fanatics, he thought them perfectly futile. "I say, Archbishop," he once remarked to Archbishop Whately, "what do you think I would have done about this slavery business if I had my own way? I would have done nothing at all. I would have left it all alone. It is all a pack of nonsense. There always have been slaves in most civilized countries, the Greeks, the Romans. However, they *would* have their own way and we have abolished slavery. But it is all great folly." It was their confidence in their own ability to do good that put him off humanitarians so much. Little did they realize mankind's gigantic propensity to error. "Try to do no good," he asserted trenchantly, "and then you won't get into any scrapes."

But it was in his attitude to religion that his duality of mind appeared most significantly. Many people thought he was an atheist. Certainly he talked flippantly about the most holy topics; he seldom went to church himself, and he did not like other people going often; "No, my Lord," he replied to the disconcerted Archbishop of York, who had invited him to attend the evening service, "once is orthodox, twice is puritanical." And he had a horror of pious emotionalism—"Things are coming to a pretty pass", he exclaimed, after listening to an evangelical sermon on the consequence of sin, "when religion is allowed to invade private life." Roman Catholicism, in his view, was insufficiently calm, and he recommended the Church of England on the ground it was the "least meddlesome". Yet the subject of religion exercised over him a strange compelling fascination. For hours he would sit studying the controversies of the early fathers; every new theological work found its way to his shelves, its margins scrawled with his notes. No doubt this was partly due to historical interest. Religion, he once said, had played so prominent a role in human history, that every educated man should investigate it. Perhaps he also found an ironical amusement in contemplating the extraordinary figments of fancy with which, according to his ideas, human beings had seen fit still further to confuse their already perplexed lives. But there was, all the same, a serious side to his religious preoccupations. He realized the sadness of human life too well not to long for the comfort of religious faith. "Religion sets out with great advantages on its side" he noted ruefully in his common-place book. "To the happy it promises a continued and increasing happiness; to the unhappy a change of circum-stances which for many cannot be for the worse, and for some may well be for the better." Further, the imagina-tive element in him cried out against a purely rationalistic interpretation of the universe. And the mystical strain, stirring always in the hinterland of his consciousness, set him wondering if there was not something in religion after all. Certainly there were things in his experience inexplicable by rationalist theory. If he searched the records of religion long enough, might he not discover an explanation of them—might he not even find grounds for that faith for which, in spite of himself, his spirit yearned? Anyway there was no harm in trying. In a world where all was obscure, the speculations of the theologians had as good a chance of being true as anything else.

For this was the final result of his cogitations. When the evidence of heart and head, of reason and imagination, contradicted each other at every turn, he could put no certain trust in his judgment. And the opinions of others, so far as he had studied them, provided no more satis-factory solution to the riddle. How could one trust the judgment of beings, the essential condition of whose nature it was to be limited and biased and ignorant? "Neither man nor woman," he noted, "can be worth anything until they have discovered that they are fools. This is the first step towards becoming either estimable or agreeable; and until it be taken there is no hope. The sooner the discovery is made the better, as there is more time and power for taking advantage of it. Sometimes the great truth is found out too late to apply to it any effectual remedy. Sometimes it is never found at all; and these form the desperate and inveterate causes of folly, self-conceit and impertinence."

No, life was an insoluble conundrum; and all that a sensible man could do was to try and get through it with as little unpleasantness to himself, and everyone else, as possible; in private to be considerate and detached, in public to do what little he could to guide the world down its uncharted course with the minimum of friction. This generally involved doing very little. It certainly meant refusing to risk an immediate disturbance for the sake of a problematical future good. As for ultimate truth, the nearest an honest man could hope to get to that, was to be vigilantly faithful to the conclusions of his own reason and experience; not to let his candid impressions be distorted by convention or cowardice or the deceptions of his own vanity. Probably, these personal conclusions were as far from the truth as everything else. But they were the only things of which he had first-hand evidence. Anyway only good could come of speaking one's mind, even it if did shock people. "It is a good thing to surprise," he once said. By shaking others out of their complacency one might make them realize how ill-founded human convictions are.

He reaped the reward of his courage. William got

closer to truth, pierced far deeper into the significance of things, than the majority of his hustling contemporaries. All the same his creed was not an inspiriting one. And there was a strong undercurrent of melancholy in him. "To those who think," he was fond of quoting, "life is a comedy, to those who feel, a tragedy." William was far too sensitive not to feel its tragic implications more often than was comfortable for him. Fits of depression overtook him, in which he sat silent and remote, overwhelmed by a sense of the barren fleetingness of existence; and even his brightest moods were shot through by grey streaks of disillusionment. Yet he was not so unhappy as might have been expected. For one thing he was no longer at open war with himself. Though the discordant elements in him were as discordant as ever, he had given up trying to reconcile them. He had imposed an armistice on his inner struggle, he had come to terms with his difficulties. Besides, happiness is an affair of temperament rather than opinions. And William's temperament was all salt and sunshine. The world might be a futile place; but how odd it was, how fascinating, how endlessly full of interest! By now he had acquired the skill of a life-long hedonist in extracting every drop of pleasure from life that it had to offer. "Lord Melbourne looked as if he enjoyed himself," said a surprised observer who had watched him beaming at some tedious city banquet. "There is nothing Lord Melbourne does not enjoy," was the reply. Along with his pleasure in life went a pleasure in his fellow creatures. Most cynics have a fundamental antipathy to their kind; not so William. "The worst of the present day," he once said to a friend, " is that men hate one another so damnably. For my part I love them all!" This was a slight exaggeration. Arrogant people irritated him profoundly, and pretentious ones still more. "There now, that fellow has been trying for half-an-hour to make me believe he knows a great deal of what he knows nothing," he commented after listening to a literary man holding forth at his table, "we won't have him again." But though he did not love everybody, he liked most and hated none. Himself normal in his tastes, he felt at home with the normal run of humanity; sympathized with their aspirations, shared their pleasures, understood their weaknesses. Perhaps human beings were not very dignified; but then, he did not feel dignified himself. Besides, their absurdities and inconsistencies only made them the more entertaining. And if he liked men as a whole, certain individuals among them he loved. Experience had only confirmed the strength of his personal affections. For his sister Emily, for his brother Fred, for his closest friends, he felt an ardent unselfish love that overrode all his deliberately cultivated detachment. Unquenchable beacons of comfort and joy they shone out, radiating a little circle of light in the huge darkness of the universe, warming the shivering heart. Indeed the very paradox of his nature made him a happy man on the whole. A cynic who loved mankind, a sceptic who found life thoroughly worth living, he contrived to face the worthlessness of things, cheerfully enough.

Only there was a chink in the armour of his serenity. It depended too much on keeping in the sun. Since he relied for happiness on the passing joys of pleasure and affection, he must manage his life so that these were always at his disposal. A threat to the amenity of his mode of existence was deeply disturbing to him. As we have seen, he was terrified of revolution. And in private life too, he avoided the disagreeable as much as he could. He had a horror of seeing a corpse, for instance. Even in books, he refused to read anything that dealt with the grim or the sordid. Crabbe, he said, degraded everything he touched; and in later years he put aside *Oliver Twist* after one glance. "It is all among work-houses and pickpockets and coffin-makers," he said, "I do not *like* those things: I wish to avoid them. I do not like them in reality and therefore I do not like to see them represented."

Indeed there was a flaw in his philosophy, a radical defect, implicit in this shrinking from the unpleasant. The happiness that is an expression only of an instinctive mood has no certainty of continuance; William's serenity rested on no reasoned foundation, but only on a precariously-adjusted equilibrium. For the present his sanguine temperament was strong enough to provide a counter-weight to the melancholy of his scepticism. But supposing his mood changed, supposing that, stricken by sorrow or by the failure of vitality, he lost his faculty of enjoyment—at once he would be flung into that slough of despond to which his intellectual convictions might logically seem to consign him. Only as long as he kept his balance was he safe; and in a world of chance and catastrophe, at any moment it might begin to waver.

The truth was that William's mature character, like his youthful, was a compromise. In a sense he had made far

more of a success of it than most people. For he was that
rare phenomenon, a genuinely independent personality.
From the turmoil of warring influences which, from
cradle to middle age, had fought for possession of him, he
had emerged dominated by none, his every opinion the
honest conclusion of his own experience, his every
utterance and habit, down to the way he ate, and folded
his letters, the unqualified expression of his own individuality. But, though he was enslaved to nothing else, he
was not master of himself. Strong enough to reject any
faith that his own reason did not think convincing, he had
not the strength to form a faith of his own. His spiritual
security was at the mercy of circumstances.

And the course of his life too. His philosophy hampered
his power of action. It was not that he was weak, as his
friends were always complaining. On the contrary, no
one could act more vigorously once he was convinced he
was right. The trouble was that he was seldom so convinced. He saw every question from so many sides, most
problems seemed to him so hopeless of solution, that he
was generally for doing nothing at all. Still less could he
direct his various actions to a chosen end: he had never
made up his mind as to whether any end was worth
achieving. If circumstances should happen to push him
into a position of power, he was perfectly ready to take it
on: for men and their affairs inspired him with far too
little respect for him to shrink from assuming responsibility
for them. But, on the other hand, he did not think it
worth while stirring a finger to mould circumstances to
his will. Smiling, indolent, and inscrutable he lay, a
pawn in the hands of fortune.

Chapter I

IN OFFICE

(1)

AT LONG last fortune favoured him. In February
1827 Lord Liverpool, the Prime Minister, had a
stroke. Bereft of his placid and reconciling hand,
the Government split into two opposing sections; the
Ultra-Tories and the Canningite-Tories. Which of the
two was to obtain control depended on the unpredictable
caprice of George IV. After the usual hesitations, he
asked Canning to form a Government. Rather than serve
under him, the Ultras led by the Duke of Wellington,
resigned. Canning therefore, in order to fill the gap left
by their secession, turned to his Whig followers, notably
Palmerston and William Lamb. Even now it seemed as
if William's ironical lazy indifference might lose him his
chance. To his sister Emily's exasperation, he chose to
leave London at the very moment the Government was
forming. However when the list of candidates for office
was placed before the King—"William Lamb!" he
exclaimed, his memory aglow with pleasing recollections
of old Carlton House convivialities. "William Lamb—

17

put *him* anywhere you like!" In May he was appointed Chief Secretary for Ireland. It was the turning point in William's life. At last, at forty-six years of age, his luck had changed: and for good. William stepped on to the public stage, an official ruler of England.

It was a very different England from that of his youth. The lucid leisured eighteenth century was vanished; and in its place, to the thunder of a thousand factory wheels, surged forward the murky and tumultuous era which was its successor. All was movement, the industrial movement, the democratic movement, the Romantic movement, the Irish National movement. All was confusion: religious neo-medievalists jostled progressive rationalists; hard-fisted capitalists clashed with enthusiastic humanitarians: destitution and stupendous wealth dwelled side by side: in England the young Mill hailed the dawn of the age of enlightenment, in Scotland the young Carlyle brooded darkly on the imminent eclipse of human virtue. And the spirit that infused the age was of a piece with its preoccupations; earnest, hopeful, strenuous and foggy—pulsating with energy, aglow with hope, tormented by conscience. The smoke and flame of the factories found their counterpart in the smoke and flame that swirled in the hearts of the people who lived under their shadow.

The new spirit showed itself in the world of politics. Signs were visible on every side that the struggle between the old aristocratic landed régime and the new individualist democratic forces could not be delayed much longer. Till 1815 it had been held up by the Napoleonic Wars, in the disturbed years, which followed, by the fear of revolution. But now Europe seemed settled down into steady peace:

for the time being the country was prosperous. And the restless discontent of those classes who were shut out from political power began to make itself felt; seeping up from the world of revolutionary agitators to infuse itself into the respectable middle and professional classes. Everywhere the cry was reform; law reform, educational reform, fiscal reform of the laws against Nonconformists and Roman Catholics, Parliamentary reform. Parliamentary reform was the crucial issue. For, by destroying the aristocracy's monopoly of seats in the House of Commons, it wrested from it at one stroke the control of government. With it, the men of the new age would be in a position to impose any other change they wanted; without it they could move only by permission of their opponents.

Such were the questions canvassed at reunions of provincial kings of industry, at gatherings of serious thinkers, in working men's clubs. Only in the lordly drawing-rooms of the politicians themselves was the atmosphere less excited. Belonging as they did, Tory and Whig alike, to the old régime, they had no personal interest in a change. However, they could not altogether escape feeling the pressure of the time-spirit. It was becoming clear to them that something new would have to be done; and that, since they alone possessed political power, they would have to do it. Confronted by this new situation, the old party divisions began to lose whatever binding power they still possessed; people began to range themselves into new groups. There were, roughly speaking, three positions that they could take up, that of the Ultra-Tories, that of the Canningite-Tories and that of the large body of opinion who, anticipating the terminology of a later age, we may call the Liberals. The Ultras were against all reform; the Liberals in favour of it in varying degrees; the Canningites stood between them. Strongly against the surrender of aristocratic power, implied in Parliamentary Reform, they yet believed that administration was in need of much modification and improvement; and moreover that by making such practical and executive reform, they would allay the discontent that created the demand for Parliamentary Reform. If, so they contended, people had a better police and poor law and a fairer system of taxation, they would be quite happy to go on being governed by the gentlemen of England.

In 1827 the Canningites got a chance to try their policy. The Ultras, in power for the last thirty odd years, were clearly out of tune with the temper of the times. The Liberals were not yet in a condition to take their place officially. They belonged, most of them, to the Whig Party; and the Whigs were still in confusion. A few like William agreed with Canning; the old orthodox Whigs, led by Lords Grey and Holland, secretly nervous of change and personally distrustful of Canning, shrank from committing themselves in any direction. The professional politicians, led by the brilliant and changeable Brougham still tacked about in a seething turmoil of intrigue, now to the right, now left, according as either seemed likely to bring them office. Anyway, for the time being, the crucial issue of Parliamentary Reform was in abeyance. The reformers quarrelled among themselves, while the public was not yet completely convinced that reform was necessary. Now, if ever, was the time to try the Canningite middle-way.

It came naturally to William to support it. Not that he was much of a reformer, even in the modified Canningite sense. The spirit of the new age left him singularly unimpressed. He did not like earnestness, he did not like energy, he did not like muddle-headedness. And he had the aristocrat's antipathy to the middle-classes. "I don't like the middle-classes," he once observed, "the higher and lower classes, there's some good in them; but the middle-class are all affectation and conceit and pretence and concealment." Further, he thought change always ran the risk of disturbing the security of society; while convinced as he was of the futility of most human effort, he did not believe it ever did the good it intended. On the contrary sensational reforms, like Parliamentary Reform, did positive harm. For by raising hopes that could never be fulfilled they left people more discontented than ever. "I like what is tranquil and stable," he once remarked. This sentence sums up his political creed.

On the other hand, he recognized that the world, unfortunately, was a changing place: and that political institutions, make-shift affairs at best, must change along with it. Tranquillity and stability can only be preserved by a continuous process of adaptation. If a large section of the people were dissatisfied with the existing system, it meant that it was out of date. And, however silly their demands might be, there would be no peace till they were in some degree conceded. Finally since administrative reforms affected their actual lives the most, they were the kind most likely to pacify them. Holding these views, he could follow Canning if not with enthusiasm yet with an honest conviction that it was the best thing to do.

Himself he had only a minor part to play. The Irish Secretaryship carried with it no seat in the Cabinet; though Ireland, as usual, was in a state of furious unrest, there was nothing much for the time being to be done about it. The Irish were agitating for Catholic Emancipation. Canning was in favour of giving it to them: but the King, reverting in a misguided moment to the ideas of his father, refused. All that Canning could do was to send for William and tell him to go over there and try and convince the Irish of the Government's good intentions, until such time as the King's mind might change. In August he arrived in Dublin.

It was a great change from go-ahead England. Under a frail veneer of eighteenth century manners, the country wallowed in bloodstained medieval chaos. The Protestant governing-class divided their time between bullying the natives, wild Hibernian rollickings and killing each other in duels. The mass of the people, savage, superstitious and on the edge of starvation now fawned on their masters in oriental servility, now gathered together in secret societies with fantastic names—Caffees, Bootashees, Whiteboys and Ribbonmen—to plot their overthrow by means of atrocity and assassination. The administration itself was a clotted tangle of corruption and inefficiency. While round the general confusion hovered the Irish nationalist politicians led by the flamboyant O'Connell, seizing every chance to exacerbate the situation. The humane and sophisticated William made an incongruous figure in such a place. But he was not daunted. His commission suited him very well. Catholic Emancipation was one of the few reforms of which he thoroughly approved; both from a deep-seated dislike of religious intolerance and because he thought that discontent in Ireland had grown so widespread as to show, according to his theory of politics, that it was necessary. On the other hand he did not mind its being put off for the moment: temperamentally he was always inclined for inaction. Surveying the scene with calm sardonic detachment he set himself to his task.

The Irish political scene soon began to feel the impact of a new personality. Former Chief-Secretaries, fettered by the conventions of their position, had associated mostly with that Irish Protestant circle who led Dublin Society. Not so William: "The great means by which the Orange gentry have drawn over everyone who has come here," he writes to a colleague, "was by assuming that their set was the only one worth associating with, quite the first company. You, who know Almacks, know that this is one of the strongest, if not the very strongest passions of the human mind." Himself he saw everyone; kept open house to a mixed crowd of every party and creed, and took particular pains to make the acquaintance of seditious opponents. Such behaviour shocked the old officials very much. "Mr. Lamb," lamented one of them, "keeps a lot of bad company!" Indeed William was an unorthodox head of a department in every way. The free and easy habits of the Lamb family, transported into official life produced a surprising spectacle. Every rule of precedent and routine was set aside. Seated in his room with the door open, William would write his letters and interview a deputation at the same time; while around him, a crowd of underlings sauntered through their work amid a hubbub of conversation. If a message was sent in that someone had asked to see him—"Show him in!" he would shout. When the visitor was admitted. "Now," William would begin genially, "don't go too fast, don't ask for impossibilities, and don't do anything damn foolish." Even the Irish were surprised by his methods of conducting business; but, unlike the officials, they liked them. Here at any rate was a change from the formal frigid Englishman they had been accustomed to expect. Nor did William just talk pleasantly to them: he went out of his way to treat Catholics on an equality with Protestants, appointed them in preference to posts open to each; openly proclaimed his disgust at the prejudiced way in which Catholics were treated in the law-courts, set himself against all pro-Protestant agitation and shut the door against informers.

He also threw himself into the study of the Irish problems. It was soon clear that all talk of his laziness was nonsense. Given a job, he worked unusually hard. Every post to England carried with it elaborate memoranda from him; on the Tithe question, the local government question, the land question, the Education question. It must be admitted that these were seldom constructive. The upshot of William's researches was that each problem bristled with difficulties, that most solutions would do more harm than good and that the wisest policy seemed to leave things alone at any rate for the time being. "One is sorry," he observes with caustic melancholy at the end of one of these dispatches, "to trouble anything that is quiet here!" Anyway his own time was fully occupied in keeping Lord Wellesley, the Lord Lieutenant, in a good humour and warding off the never-slackening throng of persons clamouring angrily to have a job done for them. Sometimes their importunities strained William's patience to breaking-point. "I can't give away a place of fifty pounds without making fifty enemies," he exclaimed: and again, "Lord Clare and Mr. Fitzgibbon want a living for a Mr. Westhorpe whose principal merit is that his is the only family in the county of Limerick that will receive Mrs. Fitzgibbon. Tho' I have the greatest toleration and even partiality for ladies of that description, yet I cannot go so far as to say that associating with them in compliance with the wishes of a patron is the best possible recommendation for a clergyman . . . that damned little man milliner Clare!—he knows that I promised him nothing: but, like all Irishmen, if you put one single civil word in your communication with them, they immediately construe it into a promise; and charge you with a breach of faith if they don't get what they have asked."

On the whole, however, he got a good deal of fun out of the spectacle of human infirmity afforded by the Irish scene. One day a little boy, the son of a subordinate, was brought in to be shown his room at the office. "Is there anything you would like here?" William asked him kindly. The child chose a stick of sealing-wax. "That's right, my boy," said William, pressing a bundle of pens as well into his hand, "begin life early. All these things belong to the public; and your business is to get out of the public as much as you can."

He was not to enjoy Ireland long. By the end of January, 1828, political affairs in England were so unsettled as to bring him back for good. Canning had died the previous August. But the King, incensed at what he considered his desertion by the Duke of Wellington, had kept the Canningites in power under the leadership of Lord Goderich, a fussy, timorous politician, henpecked by his wife, terrified of responsibility and often on the verge of tears. Such a man could not long conduct the government of England through a critical period. In January, after an ignominious scene of resignation, in which he was forced to borrow his royal master's pocket handkerchief in order to assuage the effects of his own agitation, Lord Goderich disappeared from the scene.

His departure produced a crisis of the first order. It was clear that no government, not confessedly Whig, could now go on without the help of the Duke of Wellington. Accordingly George IV appointed him Prime Minister; and the declared Whig ministers, led by Lord Lansdowne, then resigned. What should the Canningites do? The Duke, in order to keep them, promised to modify his policy to suit their views. After hours of indecision they decided to remain for fear, they said, lest otherwise Canning's policy might be completely reversed.

William, out of personal loyalty—always his ruling motive—stayed along with his friends. But he thought it a mistake. He was right. Whatever the Duke might say, he differed fundamentally from the Canningites on every important issue: and they found that in practice they could only work with him by constantly acting against their true opinion. This mattered to William less than to most, for few political views were to him a matter of principle. Only once, when he voted against the repeal of the Test Act excluding nonconformists from government posts, did he go against a strong conviction. But no amount of laxity on his part or that of anyone else could keep so divided a ministry going for long. "The Cabinet," said Palmerston, the Canningite Minister for War, "has gone on differing about every question of importance that has come under consideration—meeting to debate and dispute and separating without deciding." Twice in three months the Government came within an inch of splitting. In May the crash came; on the question as to what should be done with the seat left vacant by the disfranchisement of the borough of East Retford. Most of the Canningites, led by Huskisson, were for giving it to a manufacturing town, as a sop to the reformers: the Duke and Peel, fearing this might prove the thin end of the wedge, proposed giving it to a county. After a deplorable exhibition of clumsy vacillation on his own part and unscrupulous strategy on that of the Duke, Huskisson was forced to resign. His followers had to make up their minds whether to go with him. The chief of them were Palmerston, William's old friend Ward, now Lord Dudley and William himself. On the afternoon of Sunday, 25th May, Palmerston, walking along the Horse Guards, saw Ward beckoning him from the balcony of Melbourne House. He went up to find discussion raging. William was for resignation and Palmerston supported him: but Ward, who passionately enjoyed being in office, hung back, "stroked his chin, counted the squares of the carpet three times down and then went off in the agony of doubt and hesitation". That night decision could be delayed no longer. The three went to see Huskisson and then, leaving their cabriolets to follow slowly behind them, strolled back through the balmy stillness of the spring night for a final consultation. Ward walked between the two others. "Well," he began, "now that we are by ourselves in the street and no one but the sentry to hear, let me know right and left what is next to be done—in or out?"

"Out," said Palmerston and William echoed him. Ward was still reluctant. "There is a rumour," he said, "that Huskisson's place is to be filled by a moderate Tory, a young man of promise from a noble Tory family." "I do not know any young man of Tory family who is a man of promise," replied William discouragingly; and then went on to point out with chilling good sense that the fact that Huskisson was to be replaced by an official Tory of any kind meant a change in the character of the Government; and that he himself, unable as he was to state his views in Cabinet, could not feel justified in associating himself with it in its new form. Poor Ward made a last try. "There is something in attaching oneself to so great a man as the Duke," he observed wistfully. "For my part," retorted William, unmoved, "I do not happen to think he is so great a man. But that is a matter of opinion." Next day they were all three out.

It was a little hard on William. For, on the East Retford question, he agreed with the Duke. Still there was no question he had to go. In general he had no confidence in the Duke: and anyway the same loyalty that had kept him in now sent him out. "I have always thought," he once said, "that it is more necessary to stand by my friends when they are in the wrong than when they are in the right."

(2)

Nevertheless it was a depressing time for him. After years of doing nothing he had at last obtained work; and found that he enjoyed it. Now within a few months it was snatched away with no visible prospect of return. However he had long ago learnt not to cry over spilt milk. Soon he was setting to work to distract himself by corresponding with Lady Holland about Greek poetry and writing reviews of theological works for the *Literary Gazette*.

His private life too required attention. Since August it had been at least as eventful as his public. All the old ties were breaking. Lady Caroline had died in January, 1828. Their only child, poor Augustus, still lived, a half-witted youth of twenty-one. But William, though still far too solicitous for his welfare to let him leave home, must by now have given up all hope of his becoming normal. In July of the same year Lord Melbourne's unimpressive life had come to an end at last. It is not to be supposed that this occasioned much sorrow to anyone.

But it was a landmark in William's life. With his father and mother and Caroline gone, the chapter of his youth was completely finished. Moreover he was now head of the family. The Melbourne fortune though still large was somewhat reduced by this time. Melbourne House was sold, as too expensive to keep up; and—taking a new house in South Street, Mayfair—William, or Melbourne as we must now learn to call him, settled down to face the future.

Already, as a matter of fact, his private life was involved in a new disturbance. Feminine society was a necessity to him. And while in Ireland he had made the acquaintance of a certain Lady Branden, the wife of an Irish peer in holy orders. Nothing is known of her, beyond the fact that she was young, lovely, and that she lived apart from her husband. Melbourne spent almost every evening with her when in Dublin: in the following year she settled in London where he continued to visit her. In the summer of 1828, trouble began to raise its head. If scandal was to be believed, the Reverend Lord Branden was not a credit to his cloth. It was rumoured that he had written to Lady Branden, alleging that he had got some compromising evidence about her relations with Melbourne, but that he would overlook the matter, if she would persuade her lover to get him made a bishop. Lady Branden very properly rejected this unseemly proposal. Accordingly in the summer of 1829 Lord Branden brought an action. When it came into court, however, Melbourne turned out to have little to worry about. All the evidence Lord Branden could produce was first, that Lord Melbourne had sent Lady

Branden some grapes and pineapples and, secondly, that a gentleman, alleged to be Melbourne, had been seen leaving her house in Lisson Grove in the early hours of the morning. This was not much: it proved to be even less when the only witness who professed to have seen the gentleman in question, said that he was short, whereas Melbourne was unusually tall. "Pray call someone who will prove something to the purpose," said the judge testily, "you must get him a good deal nearer than this. You have not got him to the lady's house yet": while the Attorney-General remarked facetiously that if there was any suspicion, it attached to the short gentleman. The case was dismissed.

The truth about the matter will never be known for certain. Possibly that Lord Branden had more ground for his suspicions than he was able to justify. It is significant that in his will Melbourne left annuities to two ladies with which his name had been connected; Lady Branden and Mrs. Norton. But whereas he categorically stated that there had been no guilty connection between himself and Mrs. Norton, he made no similar statement about his relations with Lady Branden. Anyway the affair does not seem to have engaged Melbourne's heart deeply. He made Lady Branden an allowance which he arranged to be continued to her after his death: and he kept sufficiently in touch with her to be worried five years later because he had not heard from her for some months. But she had before this ceased to play an important part in his life. With the dismissal of the case, the shadowy figure of Lady Branden vanishes from this history.

LORD M.

Meanwhile in the political world, momentous events were crowding thick on one another. Freed from the incubus of the Canningites, the old régime, under the Duke's leadership, made a last bid to assure and maintain its domination. It failed. The first blow came from Ireland. By 1829 the agitation for Catholic Emancipation had swelled to a pitch of violence which, it seemed, must explode in open rebellion. Rather than face such a disaster, the Duke threw over the principles of a life-time and himself repealed the Anti-Catholic laws. The consequence was that he lost another section of his supporters, the irreconcilable anti-papists of the extreme right. However, weak as his position had now become, the Duke was preparing to carry on, apparently un-perturbed when he was again assailed by a new and even more formidable popular agitation. An industrial depression had made people discontented again: and now that the Canningite middle way had been tried and had failed, they turned to drastic change as the only alter-native to blind reaction. At the beginning of 1830, the movement for Parliamentary Reform flared up with new and extraordinary fury.

At Birmingham, Thomas Attwood organized a huge association for Reform: his example was followed in other great towns: meetings were held all over England: the most celebrated of contemporary agitators, Cobbett, rode round the country on a cob exhorting people to take action. As the year advanced, so did the Cause. George IV's death removed a powerful obstacle to reform: while in Paris, the bloodless revolution of July showed timid reformers that drastic change could be accomplished without catastrophe. By the end of the summer, feeling in the country was stirred to a pitch of excitement unknown since the days of the Long Parliament 190 years before. In the houses of the great and the clubs of St. James, an atmosphere as before a thunderstorm tense with ominous expectancy, hung heavy over the political scene. Everybody felt something tremendous was going to happen, nobody quite knew what. Obsessed by their youthful memories of the French Revolution, people murmured nervously to one another of the ruin and bloodshed that must ensue, unless popular discontent was conciliated. "It was just like France in 1789," said an elderly French visitor.

In August it seemed as if rebellion was already starting. The poverty-stricken labourers of Southern England, roused to frenzy by Cobbett's eloquence, broke out in riot and outrage. Night after night, respectable house-holders looked out of their windows to see the quiet Kentish countryside lurid in the light of blazing ricks: bands of men roamed the lanes, breaking machines and manhandling the agents of the great landlords; placid Mr. Eltons and Mr. Collinses in sequestered rural vicarages found letters thrust under their doors threatening them with assassination unless they remitted tithes; a party of rioters broke into a duke's house and had to be dispersed by force.

Fear increased the strength of the reforming party. Some people who had wavered, turned to it as the one means of avoiding disaster. The question was whether the Duke of Wellington would once more forswear his principles and go with them. In November when

Parliament met, he gave his answer. Our existing constitution, he said, was so perfect that he could never take the responsibility of tampering with it. Within a fortnight his Government had fallen; and a Whig ministry under Lord Grey, pledged to bring in Reform, had taken its place.

It was the crisis of the century. At last that decisive battle between the old order and the new, imminent for the last forty years, was openly joined: and all the varied strains of political opinion, for so long indefinite and fluctuating, rushed to range themselves on one side or the other. The anti-reformers were a solid block of the Tory landed interest and the Established church. The reformers were a more heterogeneous body. There were the radical democrats, the political theorists, the dissenters and the bulk of the manufacturers: all those believed in reform and liked it. There were also a number of people who disliked it, but thought it inevitable. Among these were the Canningites.

Since their resignation their position had been an uncomfortable one. The Tories thought them too Whig; the Whigs thought them too Tory. Now, however, Lord Grey anxious for all the support he could find in his formidable task, pressed them to join his administration. The Canningites hesitated. They had no one to direct them: for their recognized leader, Huskisson, notorious all his life for his physical clumsiness, had recently let himself be run over by a railway train going twelve miles an hour. Further, the Canningites had hitherto opposed reform. It made a great difference to them though that it now appeared the only alternative to revolution and as such the lesser of two evils. After a long consultation, they agreed to join. Melbourne joined with them. Since he had resigned he had taken no prominent part in politics. Once early in 1829 he had spoken against an Irish Coercion Act: he said very sensibly that, until the Irish were conciliated by Catholic Emancipation, coercion would do more harm than good. Later, and more unfortunately he had, out of affection for his brother Frederick, addressed the House of Lords in favour of a more adventurous policy in Portugal. It was against his better judgment, adventurous policies always were: and he made a very bad speech. Otherwise he had kept discreetly quiet. His reputation had grown in consequence. Twice the Duke had tried to inveigle him back into the Government; in 1829 too he was asked to Windsor, where he was amused to note that George IV took particular pains to be attentive to him. On the other hand the Whig leaders felt friendlier to him than they did to most Canningites. He had always kept himself a little detached. When he had joined the Wellington ministry he took care to declare that he did it "purely as an individual", and so could not be accused of compromising the Whig party by his action. Nor did it in fact stop him throughout the next two years from spending as much time as ever at Holland House and Lansdowne House with his old friends. His personality it was that gave him his position. People liked him so much that they wanted him in the Government, whatever his opinions. Further, during his short period of office he had acquired a good name as a colleague. Then as now it was rare to find a minister who got on with everyone and was always in a good humour. So precious indeed did these qualifications appear to a harassed Prime Minister, that on Melbourne's very first entry into a Cabinet, he was given the important post of Home Secretary.

(3)

Those, however, who did not move in Cabinet circles, found the appointment astonishing. By the world in general he was still looked on as an agreeable idle man of fashion—far too inconsiderable for the job, said Greville the Clerk of the Council. He was wide of the mark. Though Melbourne presented a less professional appearance than most of his colleagues, his mind was more penetrating and more original than theirs. And he was only lazy as long as he had nothing to do. All the same it cannot be denied that the world had something to be surprised at. Fortune, to whom Melbourne had resigned the direction of his life, had become infected with his own irony when she made him a Cabinet Minister. Whimsical, speculative and pessimistic, he had never, for all he had been so long mixed up in them, been able to bring himself to take political affairs wholly seriously: and to the end of his life, he remained an alien element in them. He had learnt to play the political game with practised skill; but like a grown-up person playing hide-and-seek with children, he never entered completely into the spirit of the thing. His thought moved from a different centre and on different lines. And he was much too candid not to show it.

36

Ordinary people, bewildered by him at all times, were still more bewildered when he talked politics—when the Home Secretary commented on the policy of his Government with a mischievous and philosophic detachment, as of a spectator himself unconnected with it and out to get as much fun from watching as he could. Still less was Melbourne in place in a reforming Government. Temperamentally an eighteenth century aristocrat and profoundly sceptical as to the value of human activity of any kind, politics most of all, he seemed the last man one would expect to find assisting in the inauguration of a golden age of progressive legislation. As to Parliamentary Reform itself, he was unenthusiastic about it, even for a Canningite. Early in his career he had noted down his reasons for disapproving of it. One of these was unusual. "I anticipate the total destruction of freedom of speech from a reformation of the Parliament, and for this reason. The present House, knowing that there are popular, plausible and prima facie objections to its formation, will endure to hear its conduct arraigned and condemned because it does not wish to stir dangerous questions, but a House of Commons elected according to what is called theory and principle will never bear to hear itself freely and violently censured, though its acts may possibly be such as to deserve the most acrimonious censure." His other objections to Reform were less paradoxical. As an aristocrat, he did not think the country was likely to be well governed by a Parliament of middle-class commercial persons, such as were likely to be elected under a reformed system. As a student of history he had no confidence in the will of the majority. And as a man of prudence, he feared Reform might lead to disaster. For since it would inevitably fail to produce all the benefits hoped from it, its disappointed supporters would insist on more and more drastic changes, till the whole constitution collapsed in ruins; to be succeeded, as the recent history of France indicated, by a Napoleonic despotism, in which the liberty and tolerance which Melbourne valued more than anything else in the world, would be extinguished. However, it was one of his fundamental principles not to stand out against a widespread popular movement. And as early as 1821 we find him saying that Reform might turn out to be unavoidable. Now in 1830 he was sure it was. His realistic commonsense also told him that unless reform was fairly extreme, it would not satisfy people enough to be worth while. "I am for a low figure," he said at a preliminary Cabinet held on the subject, "unless we have a large basis to work on, we shall do nothing." All the same at heart he still disliked it thoroughly.

In fact he was not called upon to play much part in passing the Bill. The Home Secretary's role was rather to keep the country calm and orderly, while it was going through. This was a heavy enough task for one man. The accession of the Whigs had not eased the tension of the last few months. In the South the ricks still burst into flames nightly: and hordes of marauders marched about carrying banners ominously inscribed "Bread or Blood". Moreover unrest had now spread to the North: the hungry workers of the industrial towns were, it was reported, forming themselves into sinister communal organizations called Trades Unions, who spent their nights secretly drilling and who had the purpose of ousting employers from the rightful command of their labour. Strikes and riots broke out in which one employer was actually murdered. What made the situation especially alarming was that outside London there was as yet no regular police force, and that the army which alone filled its place was a mere handful of men. To the propertied classes it seemed as if the very foundations of civilized life were crumbling beneath their feet. A wave of panic swept over them. Every day Melbourne's post bag at the Home Office arrived heavy with fantastic alarmist tales; that the disturbances were part of a deep-laid Jesuit plot, that they had been worked up by the French preparatory to invasion, that the ricks were set alight by fireballs, projected from a great distance by guns cunningly disguised as umbrellas. Melbourne preserved his calm in face of these dreadful suggestions: but he threw himself into his task with unexpected energy. For once he felt no hesitation. To preserve order had always, in his view, been the first function of government. And he acted with a vigour and decision that left his critics gasping. Within a month people were heard saying that Lord Melbourne was the one strong man in the Government.

The trouble in the South was the most urgent. Melbourne posted in soldiers in the most disturbed areas: gingered up the magistrates to act firmly: and in order to enforce the law more quickly appointed a special commission of judges to go down and immediately try such persons as had been arrested. The effect of these measures was instantaneous. Order was restored in three months.

At a cost though: the tale of the repression of the labourers' revolt of 1830 is dark and terrible; a stark Hardy-like tragedy of elemental blood and anguish and man's inhumanity to helpless man, all the more shocking to the imagination when we find it occurring in the cheerful, urbane England of Brooks's Club and Holland House. The law, which the judges were called upon to enforce, was so appallingly harsh for one thing. A man could be hanged for setting fire to a rick or for demanding food with menaces: he could be transported for life for writing a threatening letter, and for seven years for breaking up a piece of agricultural machinery. And the cruelty of this code seems intensified when we consider who were some of its victims; ignorant, illiterate rustics, struggling to support ten children on six shillings a week, misled by crude agitators and their own despair, into striking out blindly at those whom they were told were the authors of their misery and starvation. In fact the law was not carried out in its full rigour; of several hundred men condemned to death only a handful were actually executed. But what happened was sufficiently dreadful. The reader's blood runs cold at the reports of the scenes outside the Court rooms at Salisbury and Winchester; the ragged, wailing wives and mothers watching boys of nineteen dragged to the gallows, fathers of young families, manacled and hustled into the carts that were to take them to the grim hulks in which they were to be transported to a lifetime of slavery in the convict settlements of Australia.

It is painful and disturbing to think of the tender-hearted Melbourne as involved in such events at all, let alone as responsible for setting them in motion. But in fact his conduct in the matter is not so uncharacteristic or so unjustifiable as might at first be supposed. After all it was not he who had made the laws. Or who tried the cases; that was the judges' affair. And he had no reason to suppose that the judges did not carry out their duties correctly and conscientiously. Melbourne's concern was with general policy. That policy was in harmony with his whole political outlook. He had always thought civil disorder the worst of all evils. "To force," he said, "nothing but force can be successfully opposed. It is evident that all legislation is impotent and ridiculous, unless the public peace can be preserved and the liberty and property of individuals saved from outrage and invasion." If this were true at any time, it was especially true in 1830. Melbourne, in common with most responsible people in England, was sure the country was tottering on the edge of bloodstained chaos. Not unnaturally, when they woke every morning to hear of mobs burning down houses and robbing harmless citizens, without anyone being able, apparently, to stop them! What made these events more ominous was that the men who composed the mobs were no worse off than they had often been during recent years; yet never before had they broken out in this sinister fashion. It looked as if these disturbances must be deliberately provoked by some revolutionary plot. Now if ever, Melbourne felt, was the time for a Government to act strongly. Above all, a reforming Government! He

41

thought reform a risky business at best: the risk was only justified if the country was kept under iron control while it was going through. The surest, and ultimately the most humane way to do this, was to stamp hard and at once on the first stirrings of rebellion. People needed a fright. Even when he did not intend that a prisoner should be executed, Melbourne approved of sentencing him to death. "The death sentence," he remarked, "is an example more strict."

In all this he showed thorough good sense. Only too often have Governments of moderate change brought catastrophe on a nation by a weak, timid inability to control the disruptive forces which they themselves have let loose. Melbourne deserves some of the credit for the fact that England, alone of European countries in the nineteenth century, succeeded in getting rid of the old régime without a revolution. Nor indeed, by the standards of his age, was he unusually severe. On the contrary, many people thought he was not nearly severe enough. William IV in particular was always writing him endless agitated letters urging him to forbid trades unions, to increase the legal penalties for rioting, to call out the military. And many persons more intelligent than William IV said the same things. To their excited urgings, Melbourne remained blandly impervious. The existing law, he said with truth, was quite severe enough if it was properly enforced. Trades unions were no doubt undesirable institutions; but to suppress them was illegal and a dangerous blow at liberty. Calling out the soldiers was an hysterical, tyrannous proposal. And when one of his colleagues suggested employing spies and agent provocateurs in order to discover the ringleaders of revolt, Melbourne sent him away with a polite flea in his ear. "I am sure you must feel," he wrote, "that in our anxiety to discover the perpetrators of these most dangerous and atrocious acts we should run as little risk as possible of involving innocent persons in accusations, and still less of adopting measures which may encourage the seduction of persons now innocent, into the commission of crime." Firmly and unsentimentally, he chose as usual to follow a rational and middle way.

All the same, it is disconcerting to find him so very unhesitating and unruffled about it all. Surely so kind a man should have had more qualms about applying, however moderately, a criminal code of this ferocity. There are moments when an air of philosophic detachment is out of place. Here we come up against the limitations alike of Melbourne's circumstances and his outlook. A man born in 1779 was all too used to people being hanged and transported for small offences: if, in addition, his life moved on the Olympian heights of Melbourne House and Brooks's Club, he was unlikely to enter imaginatively into the sufferings of agricultural labourers, unless he made a considerable effort. Melbourne did not make the effort. No doubt this was partly due to his good sense. He knew that all statesmen had to do disagreeable things sometimes; having decided a disagreeable thing was necessary, why make it worse by fruitless worrying? But his apparent imperturbability was also, paradoxically, the defect of his very soft-heartedness. Just because he hated the painful so much, he tended to shut his eyes to it. He shrank from imagining the

43

labourers' feelings for the same reasons that he was later to shrink from reading *Oliver Twist*. And of course his sympathies were further frozen by secret fear: that stab of uncontrollable fear which always attacked him at a serious threat to the tranquillity and stability which he valued more than anything else in the world.

Anyway, if he had felt a qualm, it might well have been stifled by the chorus of congratulations with which his policy was greeted. Everyone whose opinion he could possibly be expected to value, thought he had done admirably. The Tories were profoundly relieved to discover that a Whig Minister could be as firm against revolution as they were: Liberals were delighted the country should realize that reform could be carried through without disorder. Macaulay, the typical man of the new progressive middle-class, asserted that the sins of reactionary landlords were no excuse for Jacobin outrage. Even Miss Harriet Martineau, stern pioneer of feminism and popular economics—though in general she disapproved of Melbourne as a reprehensible example of aristocratic frivolity—felt bound to praise him for the mingled firmness and moderation with which, in her view, he had dealt with the disturbances of 1830. His colleagues backed him to a man. And when the Radical Hunt proposed a general pardon for offenders in the House of Commons, his motion was rejected by a huge majority. Melbourne's reputation as a statesman was growing steadily higher.

Besides putting down disorders, he also took steps to see they should not break out. Highly characteristic steps; into the Home Office in London he imported the free and easy methods of conducting business which surprised the officials of Dublin. He was ready to see people at the most unconventional times and places— notably in his dressing-room when he was getting up in the morning. His eyes concentrated on his shaving glass and his chin white with soap, he would listen inscrutably to what his visitor had to say. From time to time he jerked out a brusque, acute question. After he had found out what he wanted to know, genially he brought the interview to a close. People were disconcerted too by the men he employed. What were they to think, for instance, of his secretary Tom Young, a sharp vulgarian of dubious connections and breezy over-familiar manners, whom Melbourne had somehow managed to pick up when he, Young, was acting as Purser on the Duke of Devonshire's yacht. Melbourne, however, was too sure of his own dignity to mind his familiarities; while Young's doubtful connections he found a positive advantage. "He's my weather gauge," Melbourne remarked, "through him I am able to look down below; which is for me more important than all I can learn from the fine gentlemen clerks about me."

He had special need of information from below at this period. The revolutionary movement was not confined to the countryside. Beneath a smooth and orderly surface, London was seething with unrest, murmurous with discontent. Every evening that autumn when dusk had fallen on the great city, groups radical and revolutionary, would meet in shops and obscure upper rooms, to discuss schemes, sometimes legal, sometimes illegal, by which the defeat of the anti-reformers might be

45

assured. Melbourne wanted some first-hand information about these people; to find out what they were really plotting and, if possible, to influence them towards lawful courses. As at Dublin, he saw that it was hopeless to try and do this through official channels and by means of decorous civil servants. What he wanted was a man like Tom Young, accustomed to knocking about in all sorts of queer company and who did not take no for an answer.

Conspicuous among these radical groups was one which gathered at a sort of combined bookshop and political club called the Charing Cross Library and was dominated by Francis Place, a maker of leather breeches who has left his name in history as a pioneer of democratic radicalism. A dour-faced, bristle-haired person, capable, aggressive, self-educated and self-satisfied, he represented that important middle section of his party which combined a bitter hostility to lords and landowners with an equally bitter contempt for unpractical extremists on his own side. In the days of his festive youth, Melbourne had bought his breeches from him; in fact Place had once dunned him for an unpaid bill. This inauspicious circumstance, however, did not now stop Melbourne from picking him out to be the means by which he might get into contact with the working-class movement. Accordingly in November he sent his brother George Lamb to ask Place to appeal publicly to the agricultural labourers to stop rioting; he also set up regular communications with him through the medium of Tom Young. Place received these overtures with shrewdness and suspicion; he refused to have anything to do with George Lamb's proposals and was not taken in by Young's false joviality; "A cleverish sort of fellow who has a vulgar air of frankness which may put some people off their guard," he noted caustically. On his side, Melbourne did not put much confidence in Place. That type of man in his experience was always, in fact, ready to break the law, whatever he may say to the contrary beforehand. He also noted that Place's information always seemed to support the policy Place wanted the Government to adopt. However, each felt he had something to gain from the other. On a healthy basis of mutual distrust, the connection established itself.

Meanwhile, the battle for reform thundered on. After passing its Second Reading in the House of Commons by one vote, it was beaten in Committee. Clearly the Whigs would never get it through without a larger Parliamentary representation. Prompted by Lord Grey, William IV therefore hurried down to Westminster and cramming his crown hastily on to one side of his head, entered the Chamber and dissolved Parliament. A stormy general election followed in which the Whigs got their increased majority. Once again, the Bill was brought in: this time it passed the Commons and proceeded to the House of Lords. Its first appearance there was the occasion of a memorable full-dress debate. The outstanding speakers were Lord Grey, who revived for the wonder and delight of a new generation the stately splendours of eighteenth century oratory; and Lord Chancellor Brougham, a master of the more trenchant modern style. His speech culminated in a peroration in which, falling on his knees and with outstretched hands, he implored the peers not to throw out the Bill. Unluckily, in order to stimulate his eloquence, he had during his speech drunk a whole bottle of mulled port, with the result that once on his knees he found he was unable to get up until assisted to do so by his embarrassed colleagues.

Melbourne did not emulate the rhetorical feats of his leaders. But he supported the Bill in a characteristic speech, full of detachment and digression and apt quotations from Livy and Lord Bacon; and in which he frankly explained the reasons for his changed attitude to reform. He did not believe in it any more than before, he said, certainly its results were likely to disappoint its more enthusiastic advocates. But the popular demand for it had become so widespread that, according to his theory of statesmanship, there was less danger in passing it than in turning it down.

These cool and prudent reflections did not succeed in converting their Tory-minded lordships. On the morning of 9th October, the pro-reform papers announced, in an edition specially printed on black-edged paper, the House of Lords had thrown the Reform Bill out. The effect of this news on the country seemed to justify Melbourne's reading of the public mind; and his belief in the danger of revolution as well. Riot and outrage broke out even more violently than the year before; and this was not only in the country, but also in the great centres of population. Towns blazed as well as ricks. In Derby the jail was broken into and several people killed; Nottingham Castle was destroyed; Bristol was a scene of spectacular destruction, with the red-coated soldiers firing on the crowd and the Bishop's palace in flames against the dim November dawn.

More alarming to those in power, because more generally formidable, were the signs of organized revolution which were beginning to show themselves. The Political Unions for instance; they protested that their only function was to maintain law and order while Reform was going through. But they were disciplined, they had the advantage of efficient middle-class leadership, and their moving spirit, Attwood, was as bitter a radical as Place himself. What purpose might not he turn them to, if he began to think that the cause of Reform was in danger! Moreover, in the North working-men's unions had sprung up, whose aims were openly revolutionary. There were the usual sinister rumours of secret drilling and arms practice after dark. Civil War looked close. In the polite circles of London feeling reached a new height of tension. Ladies in drawing-rooms repeated to each other horrific reports of respect-able squires' wives torn brutally from their beds by savage mobs, who broke up their furniture and made merry in their cellars; in clubs gentlemen had it on good authority that a rebellious army was at that very instance marching on the capital. The King's letters to his ministers grew more and more frantic. Even Lord Grey wondered if the Government had taken the trades union movement seriously enough. Indeed almost alone among Ministers Melbourne appeared his ordinary smiling self. People were even more struck by his coolness than they had been the year before.

This was the more remarkable because the times were

49

more anxious. Once more it was his responsibility to repress disorder. Once more he rose to the occasion. London was the chief danger spot; the seat of government must at all costs not be allowed to get out of hand. Nonchalantly, unconventionally, effectively Melbourne took his steps. Troops and private negotiations were his means. He posted soldiers at strategic points, forbade public meetings and sent Young off to see Place. Within a week or two all danger of disturbances in London had passed. In the country with equally successful results, he got into touch with Attwood and dispatched military detachments to especially unruly districts. For the rest, his time was taken up with soothing down the King and his colleagues and with dealing with his official correspondence. Panic had started a new flood of letters to the Home Office, passionately adjuring the Minister to do something drastic and to do it at once. Melbourne noticed they seldom said what. He was not impressed. "When in doubt what should be done," he reflected, "do nothing."

But he was not as calm as he looked. How should he be, when the strife and chaos he dreaded loomed apparently ever nearer! Underneath his indolent surface, throbbed a growing nervous tension. Once for an instant it betrayed itself. There was in September a debate in the House of Lords about the spring-guns which some landowners had set up in their fields to keep off rick burners. Melbourne defended them in a speech marked by a strange and uncharacteristic note of hysteria. "Rick burning", he cried, "seems to have no object or motive; but to arise from a pure unmixed and diabolical feeling of senseless malignity." His heightened state of emotion also showed itself in a change of attitude towards the Reform Bill. What with the House of Lords on the one side and the Political Unions on the other, it was clear that it was not going through as easily as the Government had once hoped. A crisis was approaching in which Ministers would have to decide whether to pacify the Lords by modifying the Bill or satisfy the reformers by creating enough peers to force it through. They began to divide themselves into two groups according as to how far at heart they really wanted to reform. Melbourne inevitably inclined to that group which did not want it. Indeed the effect of his anxiety was to bring out all his latent prejudice against it. What nonsense it all was! What a nuisance that anyone should ever have raised the question! Secretly he would not have been sorry to see the Government go out and the whole issue drop. He found himself feeling suddenly exacerbated by those of his colleagues who clamoured that the Bill be put through at all costs. The excitable Lord Durham in particular, shouting abuse at Lord Grey in Cabinet for what he considered his weakness in hesitating to create peers at once—"If I'd been Lord Grey," said Melbourne, "I'd have knocked him down." And again when Durham fulminated against any proposals to alter the Bill in order to conciliate its opponents. "I doubt if he knows what the alterations are," commented Melbourne tartly, "as he will not let anyone tell him."

On the other hand Melbourne's emotions were not so out of control as to silence the voice of that good sense which had previously brought him round to agree to reform. In some ways it had been reinforced by the disturbances in the autumn. Melbourne had been quite right in thinking that the popular demand for reform was now so strong as to make it risky to refuse it. More risky than before as their hopes had now been raised! "It is a very dangerous way of dealing to retract what you have once offered to concede," he said.

In the end these considerations triumphed; good sense generally did with Melbourne. The proposals for modifying the Bill came from a group of moderate Tory peers—the Waverers, they were nicknamed. These wanted the recall of Parliament put off in order to give time for their plans to be thoroughly considered. Melbourne was against this: a delay would rouse public suspicion. Riots and rick burning would begin again, and he would have to put them down. Besides, though he sympathized with the Waverers' intentions, he did not think their policy likely to do any good. Rather would it lead to the break up of the Government, he told Palmerston, and to a general exacerbation of feeling. The Ministers' chief aim should be to keep things together until people had a chance to cool down. Besides, it would be letting down Lord Grey to assist in breaking up his Government. As often before in Melbourne's history, he felt strongly about personal obligations because he was so uncertain about any others.

Doubtfully, reluctantly, resignedly he reverted to his old acceptance of reform. The complex contradiction of his sentiments on the subject showed in his demeanour. The tone of his talk became even more bewildering than usual to simple-minded persons. By turns flippant and pessimistic, frank and enigmatic he seemed wholely detached from the Government of which he was a member. Of course reform was folly, he would say. Yet, when anyone suggested resisting it, he would burst out laughing, rub his hands and turn the subject. One observer was especially mystified by him. Charles Greville, the Clerk of the Council, had constituted himself an unofficial intermediary between the Waverers and the Ministers. He was always buttonholing Melbourne, in the Park, in South Street, at the Home Office, in order to extract from him some statement of his views. Greville was ingratiating, persistent and conceited—"The most conceited man I ever met," said Disraeli, "though I have read Cicero and known Bulwer Lytton"—the very type Melbourne most enjoyed teasing. Sometimes he set out to shock Greville by openly mocking the whole idea of reform, sometimes he tantalized his curiosity with half confidences about his colleagues, sometimes he lounged back "in his lazy, listening, silent humour, disposed to hear everything and to say very little". Never though, did he quite commit himself. Greville found these interviews extremely unsatisfactory. What a pity it was, he reflected, that at this important moment in English history, one of His Majesty's chief Ministers should be no better than a frivolous cynic; and a dissipated spendthrift into the bargain. Leaving South Street one morning he noticed with a pleasurable sense of moral disapproval, a Jew waiting in the hall and a valet de chambre sweeping away a bonnet and shawl.

With the new year events began to move towards their

culmination. It became obvious that the Whigs would not get the Bill through without at any rate pledging themselves to make peers. Were they prepared to do this? Many hated the idea, Melbourne most of all. What a dangerous precedent would it provide for forcing all sorts of other odious reforms through Parliament in the future! For a moment he was moved from his attitude of detached resignation; and protested so strongly that in January it was thought he might resign. In the end, however, common sense and loyalty once more prevailed. When the final crisis came in May, Melbourne in Cabinet voted for demanding from the King the power to make peers. But up to the last he was in a queer uncertain mood. Greville met him in April at a ball at the French Embassy. Melbourne suddenly said to him, "I don't believe there is a strong feeling in the country for the measure . . . might it not be thrown out?" "Do your colleagues agree?" asked the astonished Greville. "No," said Melbourne. Greville said that he ought to persuade them. "What difficulty can they have in swallowing the rest?" replied Melbourne, "After they have given up the rotten boroughs . . . I don't see how the Government is to be carried on without them. Some means may be found; a remedy may possibly present itself but I am not aware of any." No doubt he was still teasing Greville by a display of cynicism. But he was also giving voice to his secret convictions. When it came, the glorious triumph of the reform cause left Melbourne noticeably unexhilarated. Reluctantly he had supported it as the only means of pacifying popular discontent. Now he began to wonder if it would produce the desired effect.

After all they had been led to hope, the people would certainly be disappointed by the results of reform; with the consequence that they would get more angrily discontented than ever. One day soon after the Bill had passed, he met Attwood. "If the people don't get their belly-full after this," Attwood said, "I shall be torn in pieces." "And so much the better, you deserve it," retorted Melbourne with unwonted bitterness. Moreover, even if by a stroke of luck, the people did stay quiet, the new Parliament would not. Gloomily Melbourne envisaged the prospect of a House of Commons full of earnest, strenuous middle-class persons insatiably clamouring for more and more reforms; and with the power to get them. One thing he was sure of: they were not easily going to persuade him to help them again. "There is no knowing to what one may be led by circumstance," he wrote to his brother Fred, "but at present I am determined to make my stand here and not to advance any further."

However, it was not in him to give way to depression. Perhaps things were not as bad as he feared; anyway it was never any use worrying. Ruefully and philosophically he shrugged his shoulders at the future and went off to dine at Holland House.

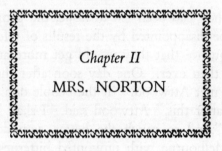

Chapter II

MRS. NORTON

FOR LUCKILY he had other resources to fall back upon, when affairs looked melancholy. He was able to take things philosophically because he was detached; and he was detached partly because politics were never to him the be all and the end all of existence. Though he had thrown himself with such surprising energy into his work, his character was not so far changed as to make him forgo his old enjoyments. He still read enormously. At the height of the disturbances of 1831 he contrived to find time to study the subject of the Druids and to explore the obscurer bypaths of Elizabethan dramatic literature—Heywood's *Apology for Actors* and Rumbold's *Collection of Stage Plays*.

He re-read old favourites, too, notably *As You Like It*. "It is the prettiest play in the world," he once said. Moreover he liked it because he seems to have felt an affinity with the character of the melancholy Jacques. Into his commonplace book he copied Jacques' remark after hearing Touchstone talk of Ovid,

56

MRS. NORTON

"Oh knowledge ill inhabited, worse than Jove in a thatched house!"

"A man," comments Melbourne, "may be master of the ancient and modern languages, and yet his mind and his manners shall not be in the least degree softened or harmonized by discipline and by force and beauty of example. The elegance, grace and feeling which he is continually contemplating, cannot mix with his thoughts or insinuate itself into their expression: but he remains as coarse, as rude and as awkward, and often more so than the illiterate and the ill-instructed."

Such a passage illustrates typically Melbourne's attitude to literature. Books appealed to him primarily not for their learning or as a source of artistic pleasure but for the light they threw on experience. Always he relates what he reads to what he himself has observed. For—and here he is unlike most men of affairs—he never lost his interest and his curiosity as to life in general. His mind did not grow so tired and pre-occupied as to stop him questioning and reflecting. Seated in Cabinet, gossiping at a dinner party, he continued to notice and draw his characteristic conclusions. When he was back in his library at South Street he pulled out his commonplace book and jotted these conclusions down. They were varied, according to what aspect of life had stimulated them. Sometimes they arose from his political experience.

"People complain of the instability of human affairs, but in fact the state of man, if fixed and certain, would not be endured."

LORD M.

Sometimes they are the results of his classical reading.

"Greek and Latin literature is thought so good because so much of it is lost."

Social life was for him a great stimulus to reflection.

"A well-looking man should dress himself more carefully because his appearance attracts attention to his attire, and if the latter sits ill or be ungraceful it points out and strengthens the contrast: whereas an ill-looking fellow and an ill-made suit appear both of a piece."

"Wit of all things suffers most by time."

"Nothing hurts the character or degrades the understanding so much as suffering wit and humour to dominate and hold the first place in discussion . . . the ludicrous is an admirable auxiliary but it should not be depended upon as a principle."

"Labour is so necessary to the health and vigour of the body, and consequently of the mind, that those who by their wealth are exempted from it as a means of subsistence are yet compelled to seek it as a diversion."

"Persons who are foolish enough to do that which requires admonition are rarely wise enough to refrain from the practice for which they are admonished."

His own character was another favourite object of his curious contemplations. He viewed it with an impartial detachment.

"I am very good-tempered if I have my own way; and that is not saying little for myself. For many are just as ill-tempered when their wishes are complied with as when they are thwarted."

Such modified self-approval, however, as is implied in this saying is rare. The melancholy and sceptical view which Melbourne took of human life in general extended to himself; all the more as with advancing years he grew aware of the incurable nature of his own weaknesses and of the failure of his youthful hopes.

"Misfortunes are often accidents, yet the calamities inflicted on us by the hand of God are very few in proportion to those which come from our own errors."

"The advantages of youth are those which we prize least and employ most when we possess them: and regret most when we lose them. There is no man who, at an advanced period of his life were he able to choose, would not at once ask for the restoration of the strength and health of his early years."

"In youth we are anxious to affect the gravity and experience of age, and in age, still more vainly, the spirit and gaiety of youth."

LORD M.

The best of these entries in Melbourne's commonplace book are interesting as showing how his circumstances frustrated the full development of his talents. Why, with a mind so penetrating and individual, was he not one of the great aphorists, an English La Rochefoucauld, a nineteenth century Halifax? The answer is surely that he did not write well enough: his mode of expression is as a rule improvised and diffuse. This was not because he lacked a gift for words. The phrases he tossed off in conversation are unforgettably pithy and racy. But he never took trouble to acquire that sustained art which is needed to turn good conversation into good literature. His literary energy had been weakened and dispersed by too much politics and too many parties.

For he kept up his social life too: dined out, went to the club, above all took trouble to satisfy his need for feminine society. The bonnet and shawl, which Greville noticed with such interest in the hall of South Street, indicates that he sometimes took the opportunity to gratify his more agreeable passions. But passion in itself never meant very much to Melbourne. What he required from women was companionship of mind and sentiment; and these he could only find in his own civilized world. During the reform years two new female characters make their appearance in his story. One was not his usual type. Miss Emily Eden, the thirty-five-year-old sister of Lord Auckland, was an aristocratic example of the kind of English lady whose most distinguished representative is Jane Austen; a clever, sensible, delightful spinster, combining a rational belief in orthodox, solid virtue with a zestful worldly-wise interest in her fellows

and a sparkling satirical humour. Melbourne used to
meet her staying with his sister Lady Cowper at
Panshanger, he found her charming company; and she,
though she could not bring herself wholly to approve
of him, was peculiarly qualified to appreciate his oddness
and his wit. Soon they were close friends, meeting often
and writing to each other about politics, theological
points and the foibles of their acquaintances. Naturally
enough, Lady Cowper and others soon began to talk of
their marrying. Miss Eden would obviously be better off
with a husband and what an excellent wife she would be
to Melbourne! At once intelligent, pleasant and good,
was she not exactly the woman he had all his life been
in need of? Perhaps she was! Perhaps she and Melbourne
would both have been happier if they had had the wisdom
to marry each other! Alas, love is not the child of
wisdom; and neither of them wanted to. Miss Eden was
of a cool prudent temperament and had long ago
decided that she much preferred staying at home and
looking after her brother to running the risks of matri-
mony. Certainly not with Melbourne: "He bewilders
me and frightens me and swears too much," she said
laughingly when she heard of the suggestion. Anyway,
she was sure that she was not the sort of woman he could
ever feel romantic about. "I stand very low on the list
of his loves," she remarked, "and as for his thinking well
of my principles, it would be rather hard if he did not,
considering the society he lives in." These comments
show her shrewdness. Cool and rational himself, Melbourne did not look for these qualities in his wife: his
heart could only be set on fire by a personality that

glowed with the passion and enthusiasm he lacked.

His other new woman friend was not deficient in this respect. In December, 1830, he got a letter from a Mrs. Norton, the grand-daughter of the great Sheridan, asking him, on the strength of his old acquaintance with her family, if he could find a job for her husband. Since he had heard she was an attractive woman, he resolved to answer her letter in person. And one evening he called on her at her house in Storey's Gate, Westminster. He was ushered up into a minute drawing-room, bright with flowers and muslin curtains and almost filled by a large blue sofa, from which rose to greet him a young woman of glittering beauty—all opulent shoulder and raven's wing hair, who bending forward a little, looked up at him meltingly from under sweeping lashes and whose blood, as she spoke, mantled delicately under a clear olive skin.

Her conversation was as vivid as her appearance. Her countenance alive with changing and dramatic expressions, and speaking in a softly modulated contralto, she poured forth a flood of words in which ardent opinions and flights of high-flown sentiment were interspersed by flattering attentive pauses and lightened by a free-spoken rollicking Irish humour. Melbourne found her society agreeable enough to make him want very much to see her again. Accordingly he set about getting Mr. Norton made a police court magistrate. Soon all London was gossiping about this Home Secretary's new entanglement. Every morning, it was said, Mrs. Norton could be seen waving to Lord Melbourne from her balcony as he walked by to his office; and every evening on his way home, he called in to see her.

Caroline Eliz^{th} S Norton

THE HON. MRS. NORTON

MRS. NORTON

She cannot much have minded the gossip. Caroline Norton was a natural *prima donna*, born it would seem to move through life under a spotlight of publicity. She had in a high degree the characteristics of her type; was vital, warm-hearted, impulsive, temperamental, egotistic and not quite a lady. It would have been a wonder if she had been, considering her history. At twenty-two years old she had already seen a remarkable amount of the seamy side of human existence. The Sheridan family hovered on the fringes of society, showy and impoverished, and surrounded always by a faint aura of scandal. For three generations they had set the world talking of their brilliance, their debts and their elopements. Mrs. Sheridan, worried to death about the future of her penurious daughters—there were three of them all beautiful—had married them off as quickly as she could. At the age of nineteen Caroline became the wife of George Norton, the younger brother of Lord Grantley. From the first, the marriage had been a failure. It was not Caroline's fault. Even her enemies—and she was to have many—have not a word to say for George Norton; a coarse, shifty cad, pathologically mean about money, subject to fits of brutal ill-temper and always talking about the state of his stomach. Within a few weeks of the honeymoon, he had thrown an ink bottle at his wife's head. He followed this up later by kicking her, setting fire to her writing-table and scalding her with a tea kettle. Caroline was not the woman to take such treatment lying down. On the contrary, she now and again vented her outraged feelings by doing whatever she thought might most annoy him. With some skill; on one occasion, when they had returned squabbling very late from a ball and George Norton flung himself dog-tired into bed, she kept him awake by refusing to join him and instead standing at the window apparently in exalted contemplation of the dawn. For once we can hardly blame him for leaping up and throwing her heavily to the ground. She also retaliated on him by insulting his Scotch family pride, mocking at the dowdy dullness of the Nortons and pointing out their ludicrous inferiority to the radiant Sheridans.

However, she was neither sensitive nor spiritless enough to let her matrimonial troubles obsess her. If for once in a way Norton was in a friendlier humour, she was always ready to respond. For the rest, she turned her mind to other things. This was not difficult for her. Passionately she thirsted for pleasure, achievement, admiration. She also wanted money. George Norton had no fortune to compensate for his lack of other attractions. And since he was incapable of earning much himself, Caroline soon decided that, if they were to live in anything like the style she liked, she it was who must provide the means. Settling in London, she opened her campaign. Her chosen weapon was her pen. With some of her grandfather's literary gift, she had inherited all his professional facility; that ability to master the tricks of the trade which later enabled her to turn out a well-made lively novel or pour out her feelings in fluent Byronic verse with a competent effectiveness which put her work from the first in quite a different category from that of the lady amateur. Already by 1830, she had with some success published two books of poems and had a play produced at Covent Garden. She also added to her income by

writing articles and editing a fashionable magazine.
But writing, though it filled her pocket, did not satisfy
her dreams. It was as a woman, a queen of fashion and the
salons, that she aspired to shine. What with her looks and
her wit, she found it easy. By the time Melbourne got to
know her, we find her name in every social record of the
day; at dinners, at balls, notably at a masquerade where
she dazzled all beholders in the costume of a Greek slave.
In fact, her position in society was not as good as it looked
to an outsider. Most of the great ladies who were its
rulers thought her altogether too flashy and theatrical—
Miss Eden, we note with interest, did not take to her—
and they never admitted her into the inner circle of their
acquaintance. The gentlemen, however, were less particular. "A superb lump of flesh," said one of them,
"looking as if made of precious stones, diamonds,
emeralds, rubies, sapphires." When they discovered that
her talk was as scintillating as her beauty, they gathered
round her.

They also went to her house. The little drawing-room
in Storey's Gate—so conveniently close to the Houses of
Parliament—became a centre where the cream of mascu-
line London, statesmen and authors, artists and journalists,
distinguished old gentlemen and rising young ones, met to
relax and converse and sparkle. Caroline was well able to
hold her own with them. Indeed she was not a woman
to be trifled with. If interrupted while telling a story, or
if anyone dared to raise a laugh at her expense, she was
liable to lose her temper. But more often she sat on her
sofa making animated contributions to a political or
literary discussion: and when discussion lapsed, she would

rise to entertain the company with an improvisation on the piano or a humorous song in the Irish brogue.

It was a delightful place for Melbourne to spend his evenings. There, forgetful for a blessed moment of blood-thirsty trade unionists and irascible Cabinet Ministers, he sat observing with amused curiosity the clever young men. Now and again his hostess would bring one up to be introduced and he would say a friendly word to him. "Well now, tell me—what do you want to be?" he asked the youthful Disraeli, flamboyant in satin trousers and ornate black ringlets. "I want to be Prime Minister," replied Disraeli gravely. Melbourne was taken aback; odd as he realized that the new England was likely to be, he could not conceive of it being so odd as to make such an eventuality at all possible. Genially he tried to warn the queer entertaining young man not to place his ambitions quite so high.

Often there were no young men; and he saw Caroline *tête à tête*. She also visited him alone at South Street. Soon the relationship was a feature of importance in both their lives. It was natural. Intelligent, ambitious, at sea in a difficult world, Caroline was the sort of woman who always feels drawn to clever and older men. She delighted to learn from Melbourne's knowledge and civilized wisdom; and she turned to his experience for advice. Soon he had heard the whole story of George Norton's misdemeanours. These had not ceased with the improvement of his fortunes. He seems to have been one of those men who think that the best way to accept favours without incurring loss of self-respect, is to receive them with a bad grace. He did not cut much of a figure at his wife's

parties: when he did speak, he was truculent and uneasy.
In the Spring of 1831 he caused a new trouble by insisting
on having his sister to stay for a few months. Miss
Augusta Norton was an unpleasing person of eccentric
manners who wore her hair cropped short, and dressed in
bloomers. Poor Caroline felt her social position too in-
secure for her to be able to face appearing in public with
so unpresentable a companion. She refused to take Miss
Norton about with her. Thereupon her brother said that
she too must stay at home; otherwise, he declared, he
would cut the traces of her carriage. The house rang with
rows of ever-growing intensity, until the time came for
Miss Norton and her bloomers to take their departure.

Politics too were a source of dispute between husband
and wife. Caroline was a Whig; temperament and
family tradition alike disposed her to take the progressive
adventurous side. So also did the fact that the Norton
family was Tory. She threw herself actively into the
campaign for reform, talking, writing and canvassing
Members of Parliament. Norton stormed at her for
publicly acting against his opinions. All these troubles
were poured out to Melbourne, who was amused and
sympathetic and counselled patience.

Caroline felt the more warmly towards him because
she was sorry for him. Lonely, burdened with responsibilities and with no home life of his own, he was not, she
soon perceived, as happy as he looked. There was a
strongly maternal streak in her emotional nature and she
particularly sympathized with his anxieties about Augustus.
The doctors had ordered that he should never be left alone
for long and Melbourne was never sure whether his

attendants obeyed this command when he himself was not there. In the middle of a conversation with her at South Street, he would suddenly become silent and inattentive; she realized he was listening tensely to hear if there was any ominous sound from Augustus's room. Her impulsive heart welled out in pity.

She also entered into his other difficulties; listened if he was worried about what was happening to Lady Branden and took an interest in his political future. Since with her interest meant action, she also did what she could to help him. She brought him into contact with people who might be useful to him and tried to pick up information he might want to hear; so efficiently that he began to make use of her as a go-between when he wanted to get into unofficial communication with a member of the opposition. She also gave him advice herself. "Don't dine with Ellice,[1] and drink and say Damn Politics!" she writes on one occasion. "It hurts your Government and your reputation." These were wise words. When her judgment was not clouded by her egotism Caroline Norton was both sharp-eyed and clear-sighted. It did not take her long to grasp the main facts about Melbourne's character and the English political scene. Indeed she was unusually suited to satisfy his imperative need for a woman in his life. The difference of age did not matter. He had always enjoyed the role of mentor to the young; now more than ever when he was growing older and could drink in from his pupil some of the invigorating freshness of her youth. Caroline also knew just how to amuse him. How entertaining it

[1] Edward Ellice was a Government Whip in the Grey Administration.

was when she was away on a visit at a country house to open a letter from her describing gay evenings when "Mrs. Heneage was never out of Lord Edward Thynne's arms and Lady Augusta Baring never off Mr. Heneage's knee", and Lord Edward said something to Caroline at which George Norton took offence so that everyone thought they were going to fight a duel on the spot; or giving a racy account of young Lord Ossulston bursting into her own bedroom in the middle of the night "with his large blue eyes opening and shutting like the wings of a Cashmere butterfly", and so aflame with dishonourable intentions that it took her some time and all her tact to get rid of him without anybody hearing. In these lively communications Melbourne breathed once more the scandalous delightful atmosphere of that Regency world in which he had grown up.

But there was a more intimate reason why he was drawn to her. She possessed the one quality common to all the women he cared for most in his life; the zestful positiveness of nature, blending spontaneous joy in living with an inability to doubt or hesitate about anything, which was the antidote to his own sad questioning scepticism. It was this partly he had loved in that other Caroline who was his wife. Indeed the two women were not unlike. Caroline Norton was, in every sense of the word, a less uncommon phenomenon. She was not exquisite or elfin or mad. But she also loved the limelight; she also was dynamic and restless; she also was an incurable self-dramatist in the high romantic style. And in her, as in her namesake, these qualities exhilarated Melbourne and made him laugh and touched him.

Did they do more? Did he love her? Not certainly as he had loved Caroline Lamb. He was not young enough for one thing. And moreover with so much that appealed to him, Caroline Norton lacked the untarnished child-like quality that was needed to kindle his heart and his imagination into full flame. And the refinement. "All the Sheridans are a little vulgar," he said to Queen Victoria some years later, in an unguarded moment. We remember that the Sheridan he knew best was Caroline Norton.

He grew very fond of her though, and there was something of the lover in his feeling. He was too much a man for it to be otherwise. The relationship between them was pitched in a slightly raised emotional key: it had its flirtatious gaiety, its moments of tender sweetness, and its spasms of jealousy. "You, I suppose, will be happy at Panshanger with the virtuous Stanhope and the virgin Eden," she writes tartly to him. He equally could not help complaining a little when Caroline seemed to be enjoying herself wholeheartedly, away from him. She hastened to reassure him.

"My dear Lord,

Do not be angry with me if I say that it is selfish to be discontented with me for being amused here—you talk of my romping and flirting—and forgetting everything else. I have not forgotten anything. I am sure your name is always on my lips and there is hardly anything they can say or do that does not bring back some of your opinions or expressions. If I could be always with you, if you were with me in any country house you would find that you would seem the one person to talk to. But I cannot be with you always and therefore I amuse myself as I can—or rather I amuse others—for they come and coax me out of my room if I attempt to write there or sit by myself and they will do nothing without me . . . I can assure you I should much rather sit by your sofa in South Street than be Queen of the Revels here. You won't believe me and yet it is true. God bless you.

Your affectionate,
Caroline."

The tone of this letter, though light, is not that of a mere sensible sexless friendship.

Yet their relationship remained platonic.[1] Nor, in the circumstances, was this so curious as a censorious world may suppose. Caroline had always professed a strict regard for virtue. "Adultery is a crime not a recreation" —thus she had firmly repulsed the attentions of the blue-eyed Lord Ossulston. Moreover she always maintained that it was friendship, not love, she wanted from men. "The saddest moment for me," she confided to a

---

[1] Cynical persons have questioned this—not unnaturally in view of the character of the parties concerned. But for once cynicism appears unjustified. Mrs. Norton in a self-justifying pamphlet on English Laws for Women, published in 1854, quotes a letter from Melbourne, written in April, 1836, when her husband's action against her was pending, in which he tells her she need have no fear since she is innocent. As the context shows this to be a private informal letter in which Melbourne has no need to disguise the truth, this would seem to settle the question. This conclusion is further confirmed by the fact, alluded to on page 31, that at his death Melbourne left a note asking his brother to continue the allowances he made to Lady Branden and Mrs. Norton, and reasserting his innocence in regard to Mrs. Norton.

friend, "is when a man seems uneasy at being left alone with me, when his voice lowers and he draws his chair nearer; I know then that I am about to lose a friend I love and to get a lover I don't want."

This remark does not ring absolutely true. In it, Caroline shows herself a little too obviously anxious to appear superior to the petty vanity of commonplace women and also to prove that she was not so fast as the malicious world liked to make out. But there is something in what she said. For all her temperament, she was not the amorous type. *Prima donnas* dream first of influence and admiration, not of love.

If she was unwilling, Melbourne on his side, was not the man to compel her inclinations. Thirty years older than her and scrupulously honourable and considerate in personal relations, he might well hesitate before involving her in the possibility of a scandal which, with a husband and a reputation like hers, would have meant her certain ruin. There was a streak too of the paternal in his sentiment for one young enough to be his daughter, inconsistent with violent passion: and after all, sympathy of spirit, not sensual satisfaction had always been what he wanted most from the other sex. Now in the cooler calm of his middle age, he was contented to ask no more of fate than pleasant evenings alone with beautiful Caroline in her drawing-room; evenings of lively talk, of easy laughter, of warm confidential intimacy; and caressed deliciously at moments by a light breath of romance.

H E HAD NEED of consolation during the next few years. For the political scene was not such as to cheer his foreboding spirit. To anyone, but especially to any member of the governing class, the atmosphere of England after the passing of the Reform Bill was tense, dark and uneasy. It was obscurely realized that the Bill marked the beginning of a completely new epoch; but what that epoch was going to be like, no one could tell. In consequence, those who had anything to lose felt all the time jumpy and apprehensive. The pessimists among them, like the Duke of Wellington, even took the view that they were in for a period of violent revolution, that now, with the citadel of aristocratic power surrendered, it would only be a few years before King, peers and private property were swept away in a storm of bloodshed. Certainly, as Melbourne had expected, extreme parties were already showing themselves angrily disappointed by the results of reform. The Home Office still got reports of secret plots to overthrow the Constitution: from time to time there were still outbreaks of riots and violence. Now loud, now soft, the murmur of popular discontent was ominously audible.

Whether or not it could be quieted depended on Parliament. But Parliament, in its new reformed state, had itself become an unknown quantity. Not only was it largely made up of what Melbourne called "the blackguardly interest"—manufacturers, Nonconformists and other dingy and unpredictable persons—but they and their fellow members were susceptible, as never before, to the pressure of their constituents, who could threaten to turn them out if they did not approve of their actions. Could they be relied on to stand firm, if firmness was likely to be unpopular? Besides, every day that passed revealed the Reform party, which formed the majority of members, as very divided. Reform had been passed by a combination of people who wanted it for widely different reasons. The Radicals looked on it as the first necessary step in a general reform; reform of the Church, reform of local government, reform in Ireland, reform of the House of Lords, reform of the Corn Laws. The old-fashioned Whigs and the Canningites, on the other hand, hoped that by granting Parliamentary Reform, they would pacify discontent sufficiently to stop the demand for any other reforms. In between these two extremes hovered a crowd of people, willing for more reform than the Canningites, though not for so much as the Radicals, but who could not agree as to what particular reforms they each desired. All these different groups had united together to fight for Parliamentary Reform.

Now that they had got it, however, their differences began to show. It looked as if these might become so sharp as to break up the party and bring down the Government. And who was to succeed them? Not the Tories; for the time being they were a beaten, punch-drunk rout with no confidence in themselves and no hope of getting a majority in the country. The result might well be that, for want of an alternative, the Radicals would sweep in and effect by constitutional means changes almost as extreme as those proposed by the agitators for revolution. To avoid this, strong and skilful leadership was needed. It did not look as if this was going to be obtained from the existing Government.

Indeed, they were an odd set of men to be guiding England along the path of progress at this crucial moment. A scratch team of aristocrats gathered hastily together to pass the Reform Bill, they were, for the most part, them-selves men of the past; who, whatever their theoretical opinions, were unqualified alike by tradition and experi-ence to envisage the new bourgeois and industrial epoch which it was their fate to inaugurate. Moreover, as much as their followers, they were divided as to what they wanted to happen. They, too, had supported reform for diverse reasons: and now they, too, reacted differently to the prospect of the future. Every shade of opinion except that of the extreme left was represented in their ranks.

So variously-minded a body could only have worked together easily if its individual members had been them-selves conciliatory persons. This, however, was far from being the case. Some of them, like Melbourne himself or Lord Holland, were reasonable enough. But there were others who would have been troublesome members of a team at any period. To be born and bred a ruler does not encourage a man to be accommodating; and the high-nosed, be-chokered countenances that gazed down at one so arrogantly from the portraits of the Reform ministers exhibit them as possessed of all the wilful and idiosyncratic independence of their Whig blue blood.

The two most influential members in deciding the course of policy were Lord Grey, the Prime Minister, and Lord Althorp, the Chancellor of the Exchequer. Grey was a shy, reserved, formidable *grand seigneur* of un-bending principles and distinguished manners, who had become celebrated in his younger days as a pioneer of reform. Since he would never join an administration not specifically Whig he had kept out of politics for many years. Now, brought back to lend the authority of his name and his character to the Reform Government, he found himself, like Rip Van Winkle, in a world utterly unlike that of his youth. He did not like it. The age of enlightenment and progress, for which he had once fought so ardently, turned out, now it had arrived, to be a vulgar, restless affair. Not a day passed that Grey did not yearn to be back in the quiet and freedom of his country home at Howick Hall, Northumberland, with his books and his grandchildren and his sporting guns: and, though a stern sense of duty kept him at his post, the strain of living in so uncongenial an atmosphere kept him permanently irrit-able and ill at ease. At the slightest extra friction—and this occurred almost monthly—Grey threatened to resign.

Lord Althorp, though easier-tempered than his chief, was also liable to proffer his resignation on small excuse.

He was a curious and lovable character of a peculiarly English type. With his heavy figure and plain red weatherbeaten face, he looked like a farmer; and in fact there was a lot of the farmer about him. Country pursuits were the only things he enjoyed; even during the crisis of the Reform Bill, he always opened letters from his bailiff before looking at the rest of his post. Yet beneath this John Bull exterior lurked a quixotic strain of enthusiastic idealism which led him far from the path Nature would seem to have marked out for him. He had loved his wife with so romantic a passion that when she died he gave up fox hunting, which he enjoyed more than anything else in life, for ever; no less a sacrifice could, he felt, express his utter desolation at her loss. He also threw himself into the cause of Reform against all his natural instincts as a landowner, simply because he thought Reform was the cause of justice. The same motive kept him still in office afterwards, though he had no ambition and was as miserable in London as a sporting dog. Not that he could feel that he did much good there. "I am nothing in Cabinet," he remarked with humorous humility, "I have no great talent nor ill temper, so nobody cares for me." It was not true. Althorp's influence with his colleagues was considerable. With the House of Commons it was more. Who could resist so endearing a mixture of honesty and modesty and homeliness? The fact that he was a poor, halting speaker somehow only made members like him more. He could do anything he liked with them. Once when an opponent had raised a point against the Government, Althorp replied that he had some facts with which he was sure he could answer it, but for the moment he had mislaid them.

Both sides of the House at once accepted his answer as perfectly satisfactory. Indeed, so far as the management of Parliament was concerned, Althorp was the most important member of the Government. "He is the tortoise," said Melbourne, "on whose back the world reposes."

Four other personalities stand out especially in the history of those years; the Hon. Edward Stanley, Secretary for Ireland; Lord John Russell, the Privy Seal; Lord Durham, the Paymaster General, and Lord Chancellor Brougham. Stanley represented the extreme right wing. Only family tradition put him on the Whig side. By temperament a despotic oligarch, he has been a leading Waverer over Reform; and now ruled Ireland by a policy of ruthless coercion in the interests of the Protestant Ascendancy. For the rest, he was youthful, brilliant and combative with an extraordinary gift for aggressive, effective debating, and off-hand patrician manners which induced a disagreeable sense of social inferiority among the more bourgeois members of his party. They were mystified by the race-course metaphors with which he sprinkled his discourses, and resented his habit of lounging back on the Treasury bench with his feet propped up on the table in front of him, for all the world as if he were taking his ease at Brooks's Club.

Lord John Russell also lacked the common touch. A small, prim young man, with a large head and a precise, old-fashioned mode of speech, he often failed to recognize a follower of ten years' standing and conversed in a strain of cold, flat candour that was the reverse of winning. On one occasion he described to a friend how at a party

he had left the Duchess of Inverness to talk to the Duchess
of Sutherland because she was sitting farther from the fire
and he felt too hot. "I hope you told the Duchess of
Inverness why you left her," said the friend. "No," said
John Russell after a pause. "But I did tell the Duchess of
Sutherland." All the same, if John Russell was not loved
he was, unlike Stanley, deeply and growingly trusted by
his party. This is a little surprising because, in addition to
his lack of social charm, there was something depressingly
commonplace about John Russell's mind. Perhaps,
though, this was an advantage to him. Intellectual origin-
ality does not make for popularity in English politics.
What the average member likes is ordinary ideas supported
by brains and character stronger than the ordinary. This
was just what John Russell possessed. His outlook was
the orthodox Whig outlook of the new generation, who
believed in adapting old institutions to a new situation by
a process of cautious reform. But John Russell did not
hold this in a vague, instinctive, amateurish fashion.
Intellectual and highly educated, he never rested till he
had clarified and ordered his opinions in relation to a
system of defined and rigid political principles. He was a
doctrinaire of the middle way. With a doctrinaire's
certainty, too; here we come to the final cause of his
influence. A strong, narrow character, fortified by the
unhesitating self-confidence which was the inheritance of
every member of the august house of Russell, he never
doubted that he was always in the right about everything.
"There is not a better man in England than Lord John
Russell," said Sidney Smith, "but he is utterly ignorant of
moral fear: there is nothing he would not undertake. I

believe he would perform the operation for the stone—build St. Peter's—or assume, with or without ten minutes' notice, the command of the Channel Fleet: and no-one would discover by his manner that the patient had died, the church tumbled down and the Channel Fleet been knocked to atoms." Self-confidence on this scale, though irritating to his acquaintance, was a great help to John Russell in imposing his will on more hesitant persons.

Black-browed, "Radical Jack" Durham, the champion of left-wing ideas in the Government, was equally sure he was right. But he was less successful at persuading others to share his belief. The rich Radical seldom carries conviction, especially if he is as fantastically rich as Durham. Justly or not, it is hard to accept, as spokesman of the poor, a man who is reported to have spent £900,000 on doing up his house. Besides, Durham's character was even more paradoxical than his political position. Independent, courageous, and with fitful gleams of political vision, he was also a theatrical, unbalanced egotist whose infirmities of temper had been developed to the highest pitch by bad health, bad nerves and too much money. Accustomed to indulge every changing mood, and follow every impulse, his character was a bundle of inconsistencies. He was an autocrat at home and a democrat abroad, spoiled his children and cuffed his servants, was delightful to his friends one moment and insulted them the next, gave magnificent dinner parties through which he himself sat in sullen silence, risked his reputation to serve the cause of liberty and equality at the same time as he was pulling every string he could lay hands on to get himself made an earl—"shall the richest commoner in England be no more than the last of her barons?" he demanded furiously. As a member of a Cabinet Durham was impossible. Not only did he deliberately provoke his less progressive colleagues by the revolutionary violence of his proposals, but he advocated them with a lack of self-control that made discussion with him impossible. He stormed, he sulked, he made scenes, he burst into tears, he flung out of the room, he squabbled incessantly with Stanley; and he bullied Lord Grey—who, incidentally, was his father-in-law—so unmercifully that the poor gentleman, losing all his patrician poise, cowered in a corner, while kindly Althorp sat with his face buried in his hands out of sheer embarrassment. Outside the Cabinet Durham intrigued with disaffected members of his party against his own leaders and made public speeches of extreme indiscretion. In the autumn of 1832, to the general relief it was arranged he should go on a mission to Russia. Russia sounded comfortably far off. But before many months were over he was back, and the scenes were raging away as intolerably as ever. By 1834 there were few of his colleagues with whom Lord Durham had not personally quarrelled.

All the same it is doubtful if he was quite such a nuisance as Lord Brougham. Durham's views kept fairly steady, even if his temper did not. Not so Brougham's. He was the one important Minister who was not an aristocrat; a middle-class Scottish lawyer who, from the time he had entered political life twenty odd years before had, by the sheer brilliance of his personal gifts, established himself in the forefront of the Whig Party. During its long period of eclipse he had done more than any other one man to modernize its appeal and keep up its fighting spirit. By 1830 he was generally considered the most dynamic single force in politics and possibly the cleverest man alive. Certainly Brougham was a phenomenon; as flamboyantly eccentric as a character of Dickens—and as preternaturally vital. The queer, lanky figure with the baleful, restless eyes and twitching, inquisitive nose was never still for an instant. Across the page of history he strides, fidgeting, posturing, scratching his head, picking his nose and incessantly pouring forth a flood of talk in which ideas and scurrility, jokes and voluminous learning were strangely and sparklingly blended. No one could help listening to Brougham when he really got going. "Lord Brougham," writes a fashionable lady, "kept us spellbound at breakfast talking about the habits of bees, as charming as a fairy tale." In serious conclave with his colleagues, he was equally riveting: the one member of the Government with expert knowledge of the special problems of the new age—educational problems, legal problems, economic problems—and with projects for solving them all. "This morning," remarked the sardonic Rogers about him, "Solon, Lycurgus, Demosthenes, Archimedes, Sir Isaac Newton, Lord Chesterfield and a good many others went away in one post-chaise!"

But what lay behind this astonishing display? Not profound thought. Examined today and unassisted by the magnetic light of Brougham's personal presence, his learning shows up as superficial and his ideas as no more than commonplace. Morally he was even less impressive—undignified, boastful, drunken, and directed

HENRY BROUGHAM ESQ.ᴿ M.P.
The Queen's Attorney General

HENRY, 1ST BARON BROUGHAM AND VAUX

by no consistent principles whatsoever. His days passed in
a turmoil of plot and counter-plot, trickery and double-
dealing in which he tacked about so often and so quick
from section to section of his Party, according as to which
seemed most likely to further his career of self-
advancement, that it was impossible to be sure at any one
moment which side he was on. To complete the confusion he created, there was a streak in him of sheer
irresponsibility. Out of jealousy or temper, or just from
an impish delight in stirring up trouble, he was always
liable to do or say something which set everyone by the
ears. Indeed, the more Brougham is studied, the more
surprising it becomes that he should have succeeded in
getting where he did. For there was nothing constant in
him, but an unsleeping egotism and a wonderful skill
in showing off. Upwards rushed the rocket, deafening
the ears with its roar and lighting up the whole sky with
a shower of stars. But when they had faded, all that
remained was a bit of charred stick and a faint ominous
whiff of sulphur.

His contemporaries were dazzled by the stars, but they
smelt the sulphur all right. "Beelzebub", "the Arch-
Fiend", "old Wickedshifts"—such were his nicknames.
None of the Whig leaders trusted him enough to want him
in the Government; but they feared he might be more
dangerous outside it. So Grey made him Lord Chancellor. He soon regretted it. Perhaps in an unusually
disciplined and united Ministry Brougham's energy and
brains might have been subdued to serve some useful
purpose; but not in the Whig Ministry of 1831! The
Arch-Fiend used his great position only as a platform

from which to make his personality felt by his own characteristic methods, which included meddling in other Ministers' business behind their backs, and conducting his own without any reference to the lines of policy laid down by his leaders. Like an elderly and malignant Puck, incongruously clothed in Lord Chancellor's robes and wig, Brougham flitted about leaving a trail of bad faith and bad blood wherever he went.

With such a team to drive it is no wonder that poor Grey longed to be back at Howick Hall. He himself did not feel inclined for further reforms; only as much of them as would keep the Radicals quiet without annoying the old Whigs so much that they withdrew their support from him. Helped by Althorp and in a less degree by John Russell, he managed to pursue this middle course more successfully than might have been expected. Some substantial measures were passed in those years, notably those dealing with banking, legal, factory and poor law reform. But the Government was too divided to settle down into any kind of stability. Hardly two months went by without someone threatening to resign; Durham and Brougham from temper, Stanley and John Russell from principle, Althorp and Grey from the simple desire for a quiet life. The Cabinet lurched on from dangerous crisis to dangerous crisis; and, though for a time catastrophe was averted by a succession of hastily patched-up compromises, yet each crisis left the Government weaker in itself and more discredited in the eyes of the world. At last the left and right extremes broke off. Durham went in the spring of 1833; Stanley followed him in May, 1834. It was clear that one

more rumpus, and the whole thing would fall to pieces.
From his customary position of detachment Melbourne
surveyed its decline and approaching fall. Himself he was
in favour of Grey's middle-way policy. It was not that he
liked reforms any better than he had done: or that he was
less apprehensive about the future. So far as he could
judge from the reports that came into the Home Office,
popular feeling was still very disturbed. He was appalled,
so he told Greville, driving up with him to London from
a country house visit in the autumn of 1832, by the
desire for change and general restlessness which prevailed,
and he judged violent revolution to be likely enough to
insist on the Commander-in-Chief being a non-party
appointment. If it came to fighting he thought, it was
essential that the forces of order should have the confidence of all respectable people behind them. Melbourne's
very fear of disorder, however, modified his instinctive
conservatism. Better concession than civil war, he would
agree after some grumbling. It might pacify people for a
bit at any rate; and it would help to keep the Government
united. As much as ever he felt its unity to be more
important than anything else; and did all he could to
promote it. "I was always exhorting different sections
of Lord Grey's Government to shuffle over differences,"
he related later. Personally he always took care to avoid
rows and tried to get on with everyone: so successfully
that he was the only Minister whom all the others liked.
This did not mean that he liked them. Coolly and
silently, he observed his colleagues and drew conclusions
about their characters for future use. As politicians, he
esteemed them only in so far as their conduct encouraged

what was tranquil and stable. By this test Grey and Althorp, along with some old friends like Lord Holland, came out not too badly—though Melbourne mocked at Grey's reluctance to make the best of anything. "Lord Grey," he said, "in or out, successful or unsuccessful, was never satisfied with anything, least of all with himself." Melbourne got on also with John Russell well enough. Of course John Russell worried too much about his principles, but his views were moderate, his word was to be trusted; and anyway Melbourne had known him all his life. The others were not so satisfactory. Stanley was the best of them. Melbourne sympathized with his dislike of reform and was enthusiastic about his oratory. "He rose like a young eagle above them all," he cried, after listening to one of his star performances in the House of Commons. But Stanley could not be described as a tranquillizer. "He has about him both the faults of great spirit, haste and rashness, and those of being discontented and disgusted," Melbourne told Fred. So also had Brougham and Durham without any of Stanley's compensating virtues. Durham was everything that irritated Melbourne most—idealistic, vain and rude. Besides, it was impossible to believe a word he said. All that fuss about his ill health for instance!—Melbourne noticed that he was only ill when he wanted to get out of doing something. He could not bear Durham. About Brougham, he was not able to bring himself to feel so strongly. Melbourne always had a soft spot for amusing ruffians, and all the more if they were eccentric. He even went so far as to say that Brougham had a good heart lurking about him somewhere. This did not mean that he liked having him in the Government. As early as the autumn of 1832 he had made up his mind that he was an untrustworthy nuisance. Three years later he declared, "Brougham is mad and will one day, by sacrificing everything to his personal whim, end by sacrificing himself." Melbourne thought that the sooner this happened the better.

Altogether the spectacle of cabinet life served to confirm him in his general sense of the infirmity of human beings and their institutions. "A Cabinet is a delicate and fragile machine," he writes tartly in the summer of 1834, "this is still more the case when it has recently been shaken and broken, and repaired with new materials. Those who remain are anxious not to have to concede anything to their new allies: those who join are equally desirous of obtaining as much concession as possible, in order to justify themselves for having accepted office. . . . Such a body is not to be approached without the utmost care and even alarm!" For the rest, his colleagues provided abundant food for his sense of comedy. He was especially entertained by the way they—like Ministers in all periods—insisted on believing themselves to be both indispensable and popular. "They think themselves fixtures," he exclaimed in comic wonderment, "I cannot think why!" Yet, he reflected, his irony taking another turn, they might be right. When did unpopularity ever bring a Government down? Perhaps, on the contrary, it kept it in! "Now we are as unpopular as the Tories," he remarked after the passing of the Bank Bill, "we may stay in as long as they did." Certainly he got a lot of fun out of being a Minister, in spite of his gloomy views. By a characteristic paradox, he was at once the most pessimistic and the most cheerful member of the Government. During the next three years every glimpse we get of his figure reveals him in some joyous attitude; writing to Miss Eden "in tearing spirits", lounging back with a look of arch amusement at a Guildhall banquet, swilling wine joyfully with John Russell, giving jocose infectious grunts of pleasure as he browses in the Holland House library, genially relaxing with his feet up on Lady Holland's elegant drawing-room chairs; and everywhere loudly laughing. "Lord Melbourne," said Tom Moore, "laughs more and at less than ever."

We get a more extended view of him in those moments of relaxation through the eyes of Benjamin Haydon, diarist and painter. Haydon, naive, acute, egotistic, idealistic and preposterous, made Melbourne's acquaintance in the autumn of 1832. After a lifetime's unsuccessful struggle to persuade the public and the Royal Academy that he was a great artist, his luck had turned. He was commissioned to paint a picture of the official banquet to celebrate the triumph of reform. The Ministers came down to his studio to sit for their likenesses. Their patrician grace of manner appealed alike to Haydon's snobbishness and his aesthetic sense. He was enchanted by them all, but especially by Melbourne. "A fine head," he noted, "a delightfully frank, easy unaffected man of fashion. There is nothing like them when they add intelligence to breeding."

Melbourne, on his side, was very much entertained by Haydon—here was a new type to be added to his collection of human oddities—and he encouraged him to display his eccentricities to the full. He asked him questions about himself and his queer friends, Keats, Shelley, Hazlitt and so on; and in his turn regaled Haydon with anecdotes about Charles Fox and Sir Joshua Reynolds. "Reynolds was a hard working old dog," he said. "He worked too hard to be happy." The two also had long discussions on politics, art and religion, in which Melbourne listened with apparent gravity to Haydon's exalted rhapsodizings. Now and again he pulled him up by a shrewd well informed comment; but never in such a way as to make him ill at ease. On the contrary—"I am always brilliant with him," Haydon noted complacently. Indeed, he found Melbourne so sympathetic that he was soon trying to enlist his help in what was the most cherished object of his heart, namely to persuade the State to become an active patron of historical paintings and more especially of the historical painting of Benjamin Haydon. Alas, he had mistaken his man! Melbourne was against the State taking on any task that was not a necessity; he did not look on historical painting as a necessity. Moreover, it is likely that he realized that Haydon was far from being the great artist he fancied himself. Accordingly, when Haydon mentioned the subject of State patronage, Melbourne gazed at him with a mischievous look and answered evasively. A dreadful doubt began to steal into Haydon's mind. Could it be that Lord Melbourne did not take him seriously? "His manner suggested that I was a disappointed enthusiast," he noted, "whom he found it amusing to listen to, however absurd it might be to adopt my plans."

This was pretty near the truth. But Haydon had never been one to let truth get in the way of his dreams, without a struggle. In 1834 he returned to the charge and called on Melbourne at his house. Melbourne, just out of bed, appeared delighted to see him. But the upshot of this, and of subsequent interviews, was to confirm Haydon in his disillusionment. Not that he ceased to respond to Melbourne's charm. How graceful his gestures were, he noticed, how infectious his laugh, how like an antique statue's was his neck revealed by the open collar of his grey dressing-gown! All the same, his attitude to Historical Art was, so far as Haydon could see, nothing short of lamentable. "God help the Minister that meddles with art!" he had remarked shockingly. Indeed, he seemed to take a positive pleasure in bantering and tantalizing Haydon on the subject. One day he would be maintaining perversely that State patronage was harmful to painters; on another that the Government was against paintings in public buildings because they wanted to emulate "the simplicity of the ancients". Sometimes he did not even bother to answer Haydon's eloquent adjurations; but merely rubbed his hands, burst out laughing, and turning to the looking glass, began to brush his hair.

Haydon's patience was finally exhausted when the question of decorating the new House of Lords came up; and Melbourne, simply to tease, suggested employing the academician Callcott, a noted enemy of Haydon's. A man who could make such a proposal even as a joke, reflected Haydon, was, it was clear, hopelessly frivolous. Sadly he decided that talking to Melbourne, seductive though it might be, was a waste of time. This did not prevent him from writing to Melbourne a year later to ask for some money. Melbourne sent a cheque for seventy pounds at once, adding, kindly but firmly, that Haydon must not expect any more. After this, we notice, communication between them seems to have ceased.

Laughing at Holland House and listening to Haydon, however, only occupied Melbourne's leisure hours. These were more limited than he liked. He still had plenty of work. His main duties were two-fold; answering for the Government in the House of Lords and performing his functions as Home Secretary. In the House of Lords he was only moderately effective. Since he was shrewd and tactful he could be trusted not to let the Government down; but no amount of practice could make him an orator. The last thing he felt inclined to do was to cajole other people into adopting his opinions, let alone those of his party. All too well he realized how doubtfully right these were. Moreover he never learned to concentrate his thoughts in a purposive flow. Now and again, provoked by some unusually foolish or unjust remark from the other side, he would gather his wits together to make a sharp-edged effective reply; but for the most part he let himself wander along, now and again touching on the practical point at issue, but soon drifting off to pursue some curious train of generalizing thought, the upshot of which was always that since no one really knew anything about the matter, it was better to take no action on it, beyond allowing people to do what they liked. The only measures he enthusiastically approved were those for removing restrictions. Certainly let the Jews be relieved from their civil disabilities—"all disabilities are injurious," he declared, "and most are ineffectual." He was also against stopping Trades Unions from holding meetings on Sundays, and poured scorn on the idea that you could make people more law-abiding by controlling the sale of drink. Indeed, all new-fangled schemes for checking crime struck him as futile. Perhaps some good might be done by insisting that convicts should keep themselves clean—they would be sure to dislike that. But do not try to educate them. "Recollect that crime has existed in all ages," he remarked, "all attempts at eradication have hitherto proved useless. Education will not help, for education is knowledge . . . which can be good or bad." Indeed he once suggested that the criminal law involved issues so obscure and deep as to be a subject for the philosopher rather than the statesman. It was part of the science of man; and "the science of man, if it is a science," he said, "is one of the most unsettling and at the same time most curious lines presented for our investigation". Such speculations led the peers of England into mental regions in which they were not at home. Melbourne's speeches left them more bewildered than impressed.

As Home Secretary he was also bewildering. Strangers continued to be startled by Tom Young's manners, and disconcerted to find themselves being interviewed by Melbourne shaving in his dressing-room at midday. Even when he did get down to the Office he carried his own atmosphere of eccentric informality with him. This was especially startling to deputations—those deputations of public-spirited persons keen to advocate some cause, which were a new and characteristic phenomenon of the age of reform. What were they to make of a Minister who received them lounging back nursing a sofa cushion; who, while they ponderously delivered their carefully prepared recitals of cogent argument and authenticated fact, pulled a feather out of the cushion and began blowing it about the room; and who after they had finished, answered briefly and with a bland smile that he was afraid he could not help them as he knew nothing about the matter in question. Was the Home Secretary an irresponsible ignoramus, they wondered?

Of course Melbourne was nothing of the kind. Anyone who worked for him could have told the deputation that most likely he had sat up half the night before, reading up the subject of their discourse. But he had no intention of letting them know this. This was partly out of mischief. Earnest well-informed persons with liberal ideals and nonconformist consciences are always powerful stimulants to the comic spirit. Melbourne could not resist the temptation to tease them. But there were more sober motives for his behaviour. Often he did not wish to commit the Government; to pretend ignorance was an easy way of doing this. There was generally a method in Melbourne's madness. Queer and haphazard though his way of doing things might seem, his work got finished and his ends achieved. If efficiency is the art of getting what one wants, Melbourne was an efficient man.

As far as the Home Office was concerned his efficiency was limited by his political views. These were not constructive; for them to be so would have involved his taking an interest in social reform. Social reform bored Melbourne and he did not think it did any good. During his long period of leisure he had read some economics. His reading had converted him to the new doctrine of *laissez-faire*. It seemed to him proved beyond doubt that the problems of poverty could only be solved by allowing the forces of supply and demand to take their course. He realized that this process involved considerable suffering for the poor: and since even the study of economics could not transform Melbourne into a hard-hearted man, this disposed him more than ever to avert his mind from the subject. Here was yet another painful aspect of existence which he preferred not to think about.

His point of view appears vividly in an account of some conversations a few years earlier. In November, 1830, Lord Suffield, an enthusiastic peer of humane ideals, approached the Government with a scheme for relieving distressed agricultural labourers by settling them on waste lands as smallholders. In vain: to the orthodox opinion of the period all such schemes were cranky nonsense. So they were to Melbourne. He told Suffield he could have nothing to do with his plans. "I fear you have not devoted much attention to the subject," said Suffield. "I understand it perfectly," replied Melbourne crisply, "and that is my reason for saying nothing about it." "How is this to be explained?" asked Suffield. "Because I consider it hopeless," retorted Melbourne. Suffield said hotly that he supposed Melbourne agreed with Malthus that vice and misery were the only cure for the evils of poverty. Melbourne shrank from accepting so harsh and bald a version of his opinions.

"No," he said, "the evil is in numbers and the competition that ensues, etc." "Well then," said Suffield, "I have means to propose to meet that difficulty." "Of that I know nothing," said Melbourne, and changed the subject. Suffield could get nothing more out of him.

The same mixed uneasy state of feeling showed itself in his attitude towards the new reform measures. The Poor Law for instance; in so far as it was grounded on sound economic theory, he was in its favour. But both as a conservative and a man of heart he disliked it. The fact that it put power into the hand of commissioners to act without the permission of the Secretary of State, struck him as a dangerous bureaucratic innovation; and he was repelled by the idea of dragooning the poor into thrift and industry by stopping the old easy-going system of outdoor relief. The consequence was that he defended it in a lukewarm speech, and was heard swearing in a loud, angry undertone as he gave his vote for it. His mind was similarly divided over the Factory Acts for the protection of working children. He felt sorry enough for the children to sponsor the Bill in the House of Lords. On the other hand, in his view any legislation of this kind meant interfering with the action of economic laws; and as such was futile. The result was he could not throw himself into the fight for it with the enthusiasm which is born of faith. One afternoon, a member called Denison stopped him, just as he was getting on his horse outside the Home Office about to start home, and proposed some improvements in the Bill. Irritably Melbourne told him to go and see his brother George Lamb, who was working out the details for him. "I have been with him half-an-hour," said Denison, "but I could get no way with him; he damned me, damned the clauses and damned the Bill." "Well, damn it all," said the exasperated Melbourne, "what more could he say?" Then an impulse of compunction swept over him. "But I will see what I can do about it," he added. No doubt he did; he was a man of his word. But the story shows that he was not at heart a believer in social reform. On the contrary. "The whole duty of government," he said, "is to prevent crime and to preserve contracts."

In consequence his activities as Home Secretary were confined to the same object as in 1830: namely to maintaining order without infringing existing traditional liberties. This meant that he had to fight on two fronts. On the one hand he must see that the law was in fact properly enforced: on the other he had to resist proposals to introduce new and tyrannical legislation which was still urged on him by a large number of people, including the King and the Duke of Wellington. Of these the King was the most tiresome. Since the passage of the Reform Bill he had become yet another source of bother to an already harassed Government. William IV was a classic example of a man not up to his job. As a prince he had been merely harmless and comical; a bustling, chattering old buffoon of a sailor, with a head shaped like a pineapple, and a large troop of illegitimate children. As a King he made a more disturbing impression. On the throne of England a buffoon is no laughing matter. The glory of his position is likely to turn his head; it also gives him greater scope for displaying his folly unchecked. So it was with William IV. The mere prospect of becoming King began to throw him off his balance. When he heard George IV was dying and the crown within his grasp, he took to wearing overshoes and gargling every morning in front of an open window, for fear he might be carried off by a sudden chill before the splendid prize was actually his. Once King, he took steps to make his personality felt. At first he set up as a democratic monarch suitable to the new democratic age; and dismayed his subjects by spitting in a plebeian manner out of the window of the State Coach, and by walking about the streets unattended and followed by a crowd who jostled and pushed him with unseemly familiarity. His democratic sympathies, however, were not deeply grounded enough to survive the disturbances of the Reform Bill period. These left him so frightened that he turned into a panicky reactionary who smelt bloody revolution in every breath of popular feeling. His nerves were further irritated by a justified suspicion that his Ministers did not take him very seriously. Altogether he found that being King was not the pleasure he had hoped it was going to be: with the result that the jolly old buffoon became a surly, touchy, bewildered old buffoon who sought to compensate for a sense of impotence by bombarding his Ministers with reams of futile complainings and inept advice. Since his chief worry was popular unrest, the brunt of his agitation fell on the Home Secretary. Melbourne dealt dexterously with him. To his communications he replied with a judicious blend of respectfulness, firmness and good humour. Now and again he allowed himself a note of irony, too discreetly worded to penetrate the intelligence of his royal correspondent. When William clamoured for legislation to stop workmen combining, Melbourne replied by sending him a list of thirty-six Acts beginning in Edward I's time that had been passed for this very purpose—all of which, he added gravely, had been since repealed as ineffective. "Upon the whole," he concluded, "Viscount Melbourne humbly trusts that Your Majesty will rest assured that the subject will be considered by His Majesty's servants with that circumspection which is suggested by its evident difficulty, and at the same time with the firmness and determination which are required by its dangerous and formidable character." Such replies did not stop the King from writing. Nor did they make him like Melbourne very much. He had grown incurably suspicious of all Whigs by this time. Moreover, Melbourne's mind was too subtle, and his personality too aristocratically confident and stylish, for the silly, homely old sailor King to feel really at home in his company. Melbourne said of him, "He hasn't the feelings of a gentleman; he knows what they are, but he hasn't them." However, the King found Melbourne more genial than most of his other ministers; and he was quite incapable of standing up to his diplomatic skill. Melbourne was always able to manage him in the end: he was also able to manage the Duke of Wellington and other complaining correspondents. With them his tone was different. He was not so respectful, he let himself go a little more. But his terse, caustic notes generally succeeded in quietening them.

The most important topic of these different correspondences was the rise of the Trades Union Movement. As Melbourne had expected, the working-class found themselves no better off as the result of the Reform Bill. In order to improve their conditions, therefore, they turned to industrial agitation. Trades Unions were the means by which they hoped to achieve their ends. Unions of the workers in individual trades were already in existence, when the Reform Government came in. After 1832 they increased by leaps and bounds. Towards the end of 1833 Robert Owen started a scheme for still further strengthening their bargaining power by uniting them into one organization entitled the Grand National Consolidated Trade Union. The aims of this body were political as well as economic. Not only was it to be concerned with practical day-to-day questions of wages and hours, but it declared itself out to establish "a different order of things, in which the really useful and intelligent part of society only shall have the direction of its affairs; in which industry and virtue shall meet their just distinction and reward, and vicious idleness its merited contempt and destruction." The Grand National Consolidated Trade Union caught on even more quickly than had the individual Trades Unions. Within a few months an enormous number of town labourers belonged to it. Early in 1834 it began to gain adherents in the country districts as well.

The middle and upper classes viewed these events with growing alarm. The name Trades Union, we must remember, did not suggest to them the established and respectable bodies that it does to us, but rather dangerous and sinister secret societies of a kind happily unknown

H   99

LORD M.

in England before, round which hovered a murky atmosphere of violence and conspiracy. Admission to them, it was reported, was accompanied by all sorts of melodramatic initiation ceremonies involving skulls and oaths of silence and names signed in human blood. Nor did the middle classes in the least sympathize with their aims. In so far as the Trades Unions tried to modify labour conditions they were interfering with what was thought by the best opinion to be the natural and healthy working of economic law, while their political professions had an ominous whiff of revolution about them. It was enough to make the prosperous citizens' flesh creep to think of "a different order of things", in which property was apparently to be redistributed in accordance with what the more discontented members of the working-class happened to think morally just.

Melbourne shared the general disapproval of Trades Unions. How could he do otherwise considering his fear of disorder and his belief in *laissez-faire?* So far from benefiting the oppressed poor, he thought they would only make their lot worse. Trades Unions, he told a manufacturer in 1833, were "inconsistent, impossible and contrary to the law of nature". From the time he took office he had been sufficiently worried about them to appoint a commission under Nassau Senior, the Professor of Economics at Oxford, to investigate their activities. However, his anxieties were not strong enough to modify his natural bias towards liberty and inertia. And, when the commission came out with a report recommending drastic legislation to put the Trades Unions down, Melbourne opposed it. Apart from the fact that he was sure the House of Commons would never be persuaded to pass such a measure, he himself thought it unnecessary. He had already remarked to an anxious correspondent on the subject, "I recommend above all not being above measure disturbed by new evils and dangers, to which human society is always liable." Trying to tamper with the inevitable working of economic law was so futile, he said, that it could not be long before even the stupidest working man would realize it; and then the Trades Union movement would collapse of itself.

When, however, it showed signs of spreading to rural England Melbourne's mood began to change. His fear of revolution grew stronger, and his dislike of doing anything weakened. Men of his age could never forget that the French Revolution had started in the country. Though he was still against new legislation he began to wonder if everything possible was being done within the existing law to put the Unions down; and he consulted the crown lawyers on the subject. After foraging about, they discovered an Act passed at the time of the Nore Mutiny in 1799, but since pretty well forgotten, making it an offence to administer secret oaths. Trades Union Societies often took secret oaths: here was a new weapon against them. Melbourne instructed magistrates to take every opportunity to use it. "Perhaps you will be able to make an example by such means," he wrote.

The result of his words was an episode which was to become famous in history. In March, 1834, it was discovered that a new Trades Union at Tolpuddle in Dorset had administered secret oaths, as part of its ceremony of admission. Accordingly several of its members were arrested. A Commission was sent down to try them, and they were condemned to the maximum penalty of seven years transportation. Before confirming the sentence, Melbourne asked the local magistrates what sort of men the prisoners were. They told him that they were thoroughly bad characters. Relieved that he could carry out his policy of making an example without doing any injustice to individuals, Melbourne confirmed the sentence. Meanwhile he told the local authorities not to penalise the prisoners' families in any way; nor, he said, should employers take advantage of the sentence to dismiss workmen just because they belong to a Trades Union. Trades Unions remained perfectly legal if they did not administer secret oaths. Finally he warned farmers against trying to reduce wages below their just economic level.

In spite of these conciliatory gestures, however, the trial of the Dorset labourers produced a storm. Seven years transportation did seem a very severe punishment for breaking a law of which many people had forgotten the very existence. The whole working-class movement broke out in furious protest; it was supported by the radical intelligentsia and by an important section of the Press. Melbourne paid no attention. He would have been disinclined to do so, even if he had felt himself in the wrong; for he thought it in the last degree contemptible to yield to popular clamour. In fact he had never felt more in the right. It was the plain duty of any Government to discourage Trades Unions so far as it could do so legally. From all over the country he got letters telling him that agricultural workers were waiting to see what penalty was inflicted in Dorset before deciding whether or not to join a Union. Clearly it was a crucial moment. Now or never was the time to make an example. Melbourne's firmness did not at first stop the protests. A petition demanding pardon for the labourers was signed by a quarter of a million people. On 21st April a crowd, thirty thousand strong, headed by a clergyman in full canonicals, marched down with it to Whitehall. Melbourne, smiling and unperturbed, watched them from the window of the Home Office. When the leaders asked leave to present the petition to him he refused to see them. If it were brougnt by a reasonable number of persons, he said, he would be willing to read it; but he was going to do nothing that might give the impression that he was overawed by a display of force. The procession dispersed and soon the violence of the agitation began to die down. More important, the Trades Union Movement received a check from which it took years to recover. Melbourne's policy had proved triumphantly right. The existing law as it manifested itself in the trial of the Dorset labourers, turned out to be strong enough to make any further legislation unnecessary. Once again, as after the disturbances of 1830, the large majority of educated Englishmen united to congratulate the Home Secretary on the quiet effectiveness with which he had maintained the cause of order.

Once again posterity has not shared that satisfaction. As in 1830, one finds oneself brought up with a jarring shock against the contradictions of the period, the discrepancy between the civilized humanity of upper class private life, and the blood and iron harshness which was accepted as a necessary feature of the criminal law. What makes the story of the Dorset labourers especially distressing is that the victims themselves seem to have been undeserving of their fate. Prejudice or panic had led the local authorities to mislead Melbourne about their characters. So far from being criminals and revolutionaries, they were sober, respectable men enough, driven into lawless courses largely by ignorance and hunger and by the struggle to bring up their families on wages lately reduced to seven shillings a week. Melbourne was not to blame for not realizing their true characters. He was not there, and he had to trust to the reports of his subordinates. Moreover, all along he had done his best to follow his usual course of combining firmness with moderation. But it is true that the affair, like so many of his dealings with working class agitation, does curiously reveal his limitations. For all his superior breadth of vision, he did not see further into the lives of the poor than the average intelligent man of his circle, especially when his fear of revolution was aroused. The same fear united with his dislike of unnecessary trouble to move him from his characteristic attitude of impartial detachment. His letters show him a little over-ready impatiently to brush aside anything that might be urged on the labourers' behalf. Further, his moral scepticism led him to adopt too exclusively a deterrent view of punishment. For some obscure reason retributive punishment is often looked upon as likely to be crueller than deterrent. The reverse is the truth. According to the retributive theory a man can only be punished as much as he deserves; which, unless he is accused of some unusually heinous crime, does not mean anything unbearably severe. The exponent of deterrent punishment, on the other hand, regards himself as justified in going to any lengths required to deter effectively: and in fact the most notorious persecutors ancient and modern have sought to justify their actions on deterrent grounds. Poor Melbourne was far from being a persecutor. All the same he did look on himself as the guardian of order rather than the instrument of ideal justice; and was too dominated by the determination to get the law obeyed at all costs to consider sufficiently whether he was in fact being morally just to the labourers.

However, it was not a matter about which he felt strongly, as subsequent events showed. For the story of the Dorset labourers did not end with the procession of April, 1834. As time passed and tempers cooled, more and more people began to doubt the justice of the sentence. A year later John Russell wrote to Melbourne asking him to pardon the labourers. Melbourne's first impulse was to resist. He was sure the labourers deserved all they got, he said. Anyway, the matter was settled; why, oh why bring it up again? John Russell, however, his conscientiously held principles now vigorously in operation, returned to the attack. Melbourne began to think that resistance would involve more trouble than concession. Immediately he gave in. "I myself do not care what is done about the labourers," he remarked with cheerful impatience.

As a matter of fact the affair occupied his mind very

little. To him it was at worst a disagreeable episode in
the ordinary routine of his Home Office work. Besides
he had other and to him more important things to think
about. The Reform Government tottering for so long,
was now on the point of final collapse. It was the Irish
question that finished it. Ever since 1830 it had threatened
to do so. There had been a hope that Catholic Emancipation would pacify the Irish. And it is just possible that
it might have done so, had it been followed by a policy
of bold conciliation designed to satisfy the national and
religious aspirations of the Irish people. But the Government were too frightened and too prejudiced to risk
such a policy. Protestants, not Catholics, were still given
the important jobs in Ireland; and they used them to
maintain their ascendancy. The Irish, therefore, as
discontented as ever, entered under the guidance of
O'Connell on a fresh campaign; this time for the repeal
of the Act of Union. They were able to do this the more
effectively because they were now represented in the
English Parliament; and were thus in a position to make
difficulties for any Government there, if they were not
given their way.

Meanwhile in Ireland O'Connell encouraged a new
outbreak of violence and disorder. The Irish began
burning, pillaging and rioting as merrily as in the days
before Emancipation. Clearly any English Government
must make up its mind to do something about Ireland.
Either it must subdue her by force or try to win her over
by concession. Here was yet another issue for the
ministers to quarrel about. Quarrel they did—and far
more bitterly than over home affairs! For Ireland raised,

as home affairs did not, questions of religion and patriotism; two topics about which mankind has always been peculiarly unreasonable. Stanley and Grey both thought that the dignity of England would be fatally outraged if concessions were made, before law and order was restored. To Althorp and Durham, on the other hand, coercion unaccompanied by concession seemed an act of indefensible tyranny. The question of appropriating Church endowments raised another issue of principle. Since the Irish were overwhelmingly Roman Catholic, John Russell considered that they ought not to be made to pay high taxes, for keeping up the Protestant Church: some of the money should surely be appropriated for secular purposes. Stanley, an ardent Protestant, looked on such a proposal as a direct attack on the cause of true religion. With ministers thus divided and angry it was clear that the Irish question was a perpetual danger to the stability of the Government. At first Grey tried to tide things over by never mentioning it himself, and changing the subject if anybody else did. His efforts were vain. Inevitably Ireland cropped up. Whenever this happened, someone felt it their duty to make a conscientious stand on one side or the other. The result was a major political crisis. It was over Ireland that first Durham and then Stanley had in turn resigned.

Now in the spring of 1834, a new crisis loomed up. Stanley's Coercion Act had run its course. Since Ireland was still unsettled, Wellesley the Lord Lieutenant wrote to Grey pressing that it should be re-enacted *in toto*, including some clauses forbidding public meetings, which were especially hated by the Irish. At this Brougham made

one of his fatal interventions. The Arch-Fiend had begun
to notice that he was unpopular. He fancied he might
win some of the progressive Whigs to him, by setting
up as a friend of Irish freedom. He therefore embarked
on a secret intrigue with the new Irish Secretary
Littleton, by which Wellesley was persuaded to write
a second letter to Grey asking that the obnoxious clauses
should be, after all, omitted from the Coercion Act.
Brougham also arranged that O'Connell should be told
of his services to the Irish in this matter; and by con-
cocting some false version of the negotiations, tricked
Althorp into giving his approval of his part in them.
He had reckoned without Grey, who flatly refused to
have the clauses touched. The Act was therefore introduced unchanged into the House of Commons. O'Connell
rose and publicly accused Brougham, Littleton and
Althorp of cheating him. The upright Althorp sat
listening to this attack on his honour. "The pig is killed,"
he said to John Russell; and he resigned. Overjoyed at
last to find a decent excuse for retiring to Howick, Grey
said he could not carry on the Government without him,
and resigned too.

Though Irish affairs in those days were under the
Home Office, Melbourne had taken little part in all
these manoeuvres. His mind was even more divided
over Ireland than over most things. His belief in tolerance
had united with his own experience as Chief Secretary
to make him for once genuinely in favour of a reform
policy. But the results of Catholic Emancipation, though
they had not exactly reversed his views, had cooled his
enthusiasm. In spite of the fact that the Irish had been

given what they asked for, there did not seem much prospect of tranquillity and stability in Ireland. "What all the wise promised has not happened," he said, "and what all the damned fools said would happen has come to pass." He found this thought more depressing than surprising. Only too well did it harmonize with his general sense of the baffling irony of human affairs. Perhaps giving men what they wanted was the best way to make them discontented! If the men were Irishmen, he was pretty sure this was so. In dispassionate mood he meditated on the root causes of Irish discontent. "The dependencies and provinces of great monarchies," he concluded, "have always been apt to grow too great and too strong to be governed by the mother state; and that, perhaps, exactly in proportion to the degree in which their true interest has been consulted and their prosperity has been allowed to develop itself." This reflection reveals a far more searching vision into the nature of the forces governing political affairs than is vouchsafed to many professional statesmen. But it was a vision that left Melbourne—so far as Ireland was concerned—passive and fatalistic.

Over the immediate crisis preceding the collapse of the Government, Melbourne with occasional hesitations, backed Grey. After the troubles of the Reform Bill years, he was all against seditious persons being allowed to hold public meetings. Besides, he was very much annoyed with Brougham and Wellesley for trying to manage Irish affairs behind the Home Secretary's back. He was not, however, so upset by the affair to be moved from his customary detachment. On the day the

Government fell, an observer noticed that Lord Melbourne, going off to join a party of ladies on the river, wore an air of philosophical calm.

All the same, it turned out to be one of the most important days of his life. The departure of Grey did not mean the departure of the Whigs. For the Tories, though gaining in power, were not yet strong enough in the country to take on the Government. Much against his will, therefore, William IV had to find another Whig Prime Minister. Clearly, it had to be someone sufficiently on good terms with the differing sections of the party to have some hope of holding it together. This excluded Brougham and John Russell. Althorp would have done, or a great Whig magnate like Lord Lansdowne. But Lansdowne refused, and the King distrusted Althorp as too radical for his taste. Melbourne, on the other hand, was known to be on the right of the party: and the King, though he did not like him much, liked him better than he did his rivals. Accordingly on the following morning, when the Cabinet met to take formal leave of one another, Grey handed Melbourne a sealed letter. In it was a letter from the King asking him to come and see him to discuss the formation of a government under his leadership. True to form in this, the supreme decision of his career, Melbourne hesitated. He thought himself unlikely to enjoy being Prime Minister. It meant more work and responsibility and committees and deputations; it meant humouring the King and keeping Brougham in order; it meant less time than ever to read the early Christian Fathers and flirt with Mrs. Norton. And to what end? Melbourne had long ago given up the idea

that governments could do much good. On the other
hand he did not like to let down his friends and his party
by refusing. Wavering and doubtful, he spoke his
thoughts aloud to Tom Young. "I think it's a damned
bore," he said. "I am in many minds as to what to do."
"Why, damn it all," answered Young, "such a position
was never held by any Greek or Roman: and if it only
lasts three months, it will be worth while to have been
Prime Minister of England." There are moments when
a hair will turn the balance; "By God, that's true,"
exclaimed Melbourne. "I'll go!"[1]

Thus casually, unexpectedly, through a transient
combination of circumstances—a chance turn of the
political wheel, a whim of William IV, an unconsidered
remark of Tom Young, and without effort or inclination
on his part—Melbourne at the age of fifty-five became
ruler of England. The year before he had copied, into
his commonplace book, a couplet of Voltaire's.

"Mais Henri s'avançait à sa grandeur suprême
Par des chemins cachés, inconnus à lui-même!"

"The case with every great man," Melbourne commented,
"much of what is attributed to design is accident; the
unknown cause leading to the unknown end." As he
wrote the words, was he peering into the dark mirror
of the future to discern his own destiny?

[1] We have this story second-hand from Greville. Hayward, who
claimed to know Melbourne well, does not believe it. But it is in
character.

Chapter IV

PRIME MINISTER

(1)

"EVERYBODY WONDERS what Melbourne will do. He is certainly a queer fellow to be Prime Minister." So wrote Greville in June, 1834: so thought a lot of people. In spite of his success as Home Secretary, Melbourne's reputation, outside the circle of his immediate colleagues, was not of the sort that befits a Prime Minister. Queen Adelaide found his views on religion lax and his conversation disagreeably paradoxical. Many of her subjects agreed with her. To their solemn sensitive nineteenth century nostrils there was a disquieting whiff of the Regency about him. However, they could comfort themselves with the thought that his Government could not possibly last for long.

Melbourne drew comfort from this too. The weak Whig Government was weaker than ever now. Not only was it bereft of some of its most distinguished members, but it looked as though the time for an emergency Government of this kind was over. If the people wanted

112

LORD MELBOURNE in 1834

reform, they wanted it more radical than the old Whigs offered. If—and this seemed more like the truth—they were reacting against reform, they inclined to the Tories. Melbourne himself did not mind this. Privately, he said that he hoped the Tories would come in. The King agreed with him: so much so, that he suggested Melbourne should try to form a Tory-Whig coalition. The feelings of the Whig Party, however, put this out of the question. All Melbourne could do was, for the time being, to try and carry on as before. With the help of Althorp, who reluctantly agreed to rejoin the Government, he patched up a new administration out of the remnants of the old: and unhopefully set himself to his task.

It proved as thankless as he could possibly have feared. All the same questions began making trouble again; and all the same people. William IV, now convinced that England was on the slippery slope to an atheistic republic, wanted Melbourne to pledge himself first never to give a Radical office; and secondly not in any way to suggest altering the existing constitution of the Irish Protestant Church. Melbourne managed to parry both these attacks, but only after many letters and some painful interviews, each of which lasted several hours. Hardly less trying than the King, were his colleagues. There was Lord Lansdowne, nearly resigning in a pet because two protégés of his had not been given jobs; and there was John Russell who chose this of all moments to suggest that O'Connell should be given office in order to drive a wedge between him and his Irish supporters. Apart from the fact that the very idea of such an appoint-

ment was certain to throw both the King and the more
cautious Whigs into a panic, Melbourne thought it
would obviously fail of its object. "Taking office
would not shake O'Connell's influence with the people
of Ireland one jot," he wrote sharply. "The people of
Ireland are not such damn fools as the people of England.
When they place confidence, they don't withdraw it the
next instant." A new stormy petrel too had appeared on
Melbourne's horizon in the shape of Lord Palmerston,
the Foreign Secretary. Personally, Melbourne got on
with him well enough. For Palmerston—jaunty, plain-
spoken and unchaste—was also a survival from the
Regency. But he was a vulgar version of the Regency
type, marked, as Melbourne was not, by its characteristic
blemishes of arrogance and insensitiveness. Melbourne
learnt with dismay that he seemed likely to antagonize
every foreign diplomat in London by the casual bluntness
of his words and manners. Palmerston's manners were
not his only defect; Melbourne was also suspicious of his
policy. Europe during this period was divided by what,
for want of a more agreeable phrase, must be called an
ideological split. On one side lay the autocratic Eastern
powers, Russia, Austria, Prussia, who wished to suppress
within their own and other people's countries that
Liberal Movement which was the child of the French
Revolution. On the other there were the Western
powers, France and England, who were its supporters,
so long at any rate as it showed no signs of growing
dangerously revolutionary. Palmerston vigorously
espoused the Liberal cause. His steady aim, pursued
sometimes in action and always in words, was to make

England its active leader. This came partly from the fact that he was a man of adventurous and domineering temperament whose instinct it was to intervene in other people's disputes and partly because he thought that Liberalism, and those middle classes, who everywhere were its chief supporters, was far more likely than despotism to produce governments stable, pacific, and friendly to England and English trade. This was not a point of view to commend itself to Melbourne. His attitude to foreign affairs was of a piece with his attitude to home affairs. As at home, tranquillity was his first object; and, as at home, his sense of reality taught him that Liberalism was now so strong a force that refusal to meet its claims in some degree could only end in disturbance. On the other hand he never could like Liberal progressives of any nationality, nor did he see any reason to suppose that they would be more friendly to England than the autocrats were. "All these chambers and free presses in other countries are very fine things," he said, "but depend upon it they are still as hostile to England as the old governments." Let not Palmerston think that they would be grateful to him for intervening on their behalf. "The case with all foreign powers," he remarked crisply to him, "is that they never take our advice on any of their previous steps; they treat us with the utmost contempt; they take every measure hostile to our interests; they are anxious to prove that we have not the least influence on them. And then when by their misconduct they have got themselves into an inextricable difficulty, they throw themselves upon our mercy and say, 'For God's sake re-establish us . . . that we may run again the same course of domestic error and hostility to England'." Melbourne, too, did not share Palmerston's belief in the middle classes as a bulwark against revolution. "The bourgeois are timid always," he said, "I should have some fear, if difficult times were to arrive, of our own boasted middle classes." Finally, his temperamental dislike of adventurous courses in general was as strong as Palmerston's liking for them. The world was quite full enough of trouble as it was; why stir up more? As Melbourne watched Palmerston bombarding foreign powers with scoldings and unasked-for advice he felt sceptical, irritable, anxious.

But, as might have been expected, the greatest nuisance among his colleagues was Brougham. Rage that he had not been made Prime Minister swept away any vestige of self-control that may have remained with him. To soothe his vanity he gave out that Melbourne was his creature, who, for some mysterious reason of his own, he had chosen to put in office: he introduced a highly controversial Bill about a judicial matter in the House of Lords without mentioning a word about it to his colleagues: and he besieged the King—who detested him—with impertinent and unasked-for letters of advice. His most sensational performance, however, took place during the August Recess when he embarked on a sort of public progress round Scotland, making speeches in which he openly attacked his colleagues, and infuriated the King still further by representing himself as his only confidential friend among his ministers. In his intervals of relaxation he created scandal by playing Hunt the Thimble with the Great Seal in an Edinburgh lady's drawing-room, and arriving at the local races dressed in the full regalia of Lord Chancellor's wig and gown and roaring drunk.

To outward appearance Melbourne was unperturbed by all these disturbing events. He still ate enormously, saw a great deal of Miss Eden and Mrs. Norton, and found time to spend pleasant evenings at Holland House; where he awed the unwilling Greville by the breadth of his learning—he seemed equally conversant with Greek history, etymology, and the details of the texts of Shakespeare's plays—and dazzled him by the lively boldness of his views. "Henry VIII was the greatest man that ever lived," he asserted with a cheerful oath. "Melbourne loves dashing opinions," noted Greville.

But beneath his smiling exterior, Melbourne during these months, was apprehensive and despondent. He did not see how he was to keep the Government going. He was also depressed by the general mental atmosphere of the age. On the night of 16th October, the Houses of Parliament were burnt down. Melbourne watched the huge conflagration as it reflected itself in the dark waters of the Thames. He looked cool and jocose, but in reality his heart was filled with strange and mournful emotions. The spectacle was symbolic. Thus also was the England he had always known being destroyed before his eyes. And no one seemed to mind: even *The Times* shocked him by the practical and utilitarian tone in which it spoke of the event. It seemed nothing to the men of today that the time-hallowed scene of so much of England's past and England's glory, the place where in

the hopeful ardour of his youth—now alas so irrevocably
distant—his heart had thrilled to the eloquence of Pitt
and of Fox, should be a heap of ashes. In so alien a
world, he felt little spirit to proceed with his anxious and
thankless task, even had he thought that there was much
prospect of his making a success of it.

Now an event took place which rendered success
more unlikely than ever. On the 10th November Lord
Spencer died. This meant that his heir, Althorp, was
translated to the House of Lords; and the Whig Party
lost its leader and most influential member in the
Commons. Melbourne did not want to carry on in
these reduced circumstances; he pretty well told
William IV so in a letter. But he felt that he owed it to
his party to agree to stay if required, and went down
to Brighton where the King was at that time residing, to
talk the matter over with him. After a lengthy dinner,
in which William IV regaled his Prime Minister with
naval anecdotes and did not mention politics at all, he
suddenly said: "By the way, Lord Spencer is dead I hear.
So is the Government, of course: where the head is dead,
the body cannot go on at all. Therefore there is no help
for it, you must all resign. Here, my Lord, is a letter I
have written to the Duke of Wellington, directing him
to form a Government. Be sure you give it to him
directly you arrive in town." Melbourne suggested
John Russell as a possible successor to Althorp. The
King repudiated the proposal violently. "That young
man"—it was in this disparaging phrase that he always
referred to John Russell—was associated in his mind
with those alterations in the Irish Church which had

become to him a symbol of all that it was his royal duty
to resist. Indeed it was his feeling about the Irish Church,
coupled with his dislike of Brougham, which had just
decided him to get rid of the Whigs. After more
fruitless and interminable conversations both that night
and the next day, Melbourne arrived in London late in
the evening. Just before he went to bed, Brougham
burst in asking for news. Melbourne told him what had
happened: but asked him not to say anything about it
till he had had time to inform the rest of the Ministers.
Brougham promised: but on leaving the house hurried
off as fast as he could to give the news to *The Times*.
Most of the Ministers woke up to learn of their dismissal
from the morning paper.

They were extremely indignant at the King's behaviour; and surprised that Melbourne was not more so.
They could hardly believe their ears when they heard
that he had been seen at the theatre the very next night
laughing heartily at a farce about the dismissal of a
minister. As a matter of fact, though he was a little
nettled by William IV's brusqueness and high-handed-
ness, Melbourne was relieved to be out. He had
conducted the whole negotiation in a detached, take-it-
or-leave-it tone, which was not calculated to persuade
the King to change his mind. But he did not choose to
risk undermining his party's confidence in his loyalty
to their cause by admitting his true feelings even to his
intimate friends. Rather let them think that his calm was
the expression of a proper pride that scorned to parade
its injuries in public. "I have always considered complaints of ill usage contemptible," he told Miss Eden,

"whether from a seduced, disappointed girl or a turned-out Prime Minister." Once more we note that Melbourne was a good deal more discreet than he appeared.[1]

He needed all his discretion during the months that followed. The left wing of his party—in order to revive that reforming enthusiasm in the nation which had swept them to victory four years before—wanted the Whigs to come out at once with a provocative programme of bold drastic reform. Melbourne was against this. Apart from the fact that he thoroughly disliked drastic reforms, he thought, with reason, that they were the last thing to appeal to an electorate obviously swinging to the right. On the other hand he had to avoid revealing himself as so unsympathetic with his party's aspirations as to shake their faith in him. Accordingly he made a couple of vague, moderate-sounding, reassuring public speeches, and then, retiring to the country where no one could get at him, refused to make any definite statement about future policy at all. In January there was a general election. The Tories under Peel returned considerably stronger, but not in sufficient numbers to have a majority over the combined votes of Whigs, Radicals and Irish. After a month or two of minority government Peel was beaten on the crucial question of what was to be done with the revenues of the Irish Church. In March the Whigs

[1] There are various conflicting accounts of the Government's actual dismissal. Croker says that Melbourne resigned voluntarily. The account in Lord Holland's unpublished diary shows that if this was so, he concealed the truth, not only from the world but from his closest colleagues. This is not in keeping with his character. Besides they must have found out: and would have lost all confidence in him in consequence.

were in office again. Melbourne was not surprised: he
had doubted whether the pendulum had swung far
enough yet to bring the Tories back. But he was far
from pleased. He had resisted any proposal to turn the
Government out till a question of fundamental principle
like that of the Irish Church had arisen. And even then
he did his best to avoid taking on the full responsibility
of the Government himself. First he made some secret
enquiries, using Mrs. Norton as go-between to find out
if there was any possibility of arranging a coalition with
some of the more moderate Tories. Then he tried to persuade Grey to take his place once more as leader of the Whig
Party. It was only after both these attempts had failed,
that Melbourne reluctantly resigned himself to taking up
his burden again.

(2)

One can understand why he was unwilling. The
prospect facing the Prime Minister in the second
Melbourne Government was not an inviting one. The
party's position could hardly have seemed worse. It was
virtually in a minority. The King and the House of
Lords were solidly against it. In the House of Commons
it held its majority largely by favour of the Irish: this was
a very uncertain quantity. Further, the Whig Party
itself was more acrimoniously divided than ever. Its
right wing had been weakened by the loss of Grey and
Stanley, with the result that the Radicals had become
more confident, more unmanageable, and more unwilling than ever to submit to what they considered the

reactionary tendencies of their official leaders. All this meant that the life of the Government was perpetually in danger from three sides. If the Radicals or the Irish felt they were not getting what they wanted, they could either of them vote it out of office: if, on the other hand, the Tories considered that the Government was giving in too much to the Irish and the Radicals, they were able, with the help of the House of Lords, to make themselves so obstructive as to render the Government's continued existence impossible. Melbourne's only hope of carrying on, therefore, lay in a balancing, trimming, procrastinating policy, yielding a little to the left here and to the right there, according to which happened at the moment to be the greatest threat to him: and also in creating a generally relaxed and reassuring personal atmosphere in which differences of opinion lost their sharpness.

Luckily such a policy had more chance of success than might have appeared on the surface. For one thing none of the three potential sources of danger really wanted the Government to fall. The Radicals and Irish both knew that the alternative to the Whigs was the Tories, under whom they would fare far worse. Peel, for his part, did not want to come in until such time as he could be sure of having a solid majority of the country on his side. Moreover, Melbourne was admirably equipped for his particular task. It is paradoxical that the most suitable head for a supposedly progressive Government should have been a man who disbelieved in progress. But in fact Melbourne's scepticism was a help to him. For it meant that his conscience was not upset if he had to make concessions to the Tories. As a matter of fact he often agreed with Peel more than with most of his own colleagues. Yet scepticism equally prevented him from being too dogmatically unprogressive. He was quite willing to agree to a reform if it seemed likely to stop a row and was thus the lesser of two evils. On the other hand, just because he feared unrest so much, he was not at all sceptical as to the importance of keeping the Government together. And he knew just how to do it. Friendly and easy-going, he easily liked people and easily made them like him. Yet no one could dominate him and no one could take him in. With negligent mastery he maintained his detachment amid the clamouring crowd of idealists, careerists and wire-pullers by whom he was surrounded. And, if he felt it necessary, he could put his foot down unhesitatingly and very hard.

This appears in his choice of his Cabinet. Four years of keen observation and harsh experience had taught him that this was a matter of critical importance. Never again, if he could help it, was he going to make a hard task harder by saddling himself with troublesome colleagues. What he wanted from them first of all was loyalty; he must be able to depend on them to back him up. "I will support you as long as you are in the right," said a politician to him on one occasion. "That is no use at all," replied Melbourne, "what I want is men who will support me when I am in the wrong." A whole team of such self-sacrificing persons was, he realized, too much to hope for in an imperfect world. But certainly he was determined to have ministers who could be trusted not to work actively against him, or without consulting his aims and feelings. He would not have any avowed Radicals. Most of them were doctrinaire Benthamites, and, said Melbourne, "Benthamites are all fools." No—let Radicals join deputations and sit on Royal Commissions if they wished: deputations and Royal Commissions, thank God, seldom accomplished anything. But there must be no Radical ministers. There were certain individuals also whom Melbourne meant to keep out if he could. He did not want to have Durham, or Wellesley, or Brougham—at any rate, not in positions of influence. And he wanted to keep Palmerston out of the Foreign Office. These were bold decisions, for, if they were offended, all these men could give a great deal of trouble. Lords Grey, Holland and Spencer agitatedly implored him not to take the risk of antagonizing them. Smiling and immovable, Melbourne disregarded their warnings. Over Palmerston he was beaten. Palmerston said if he could not be Foreign Secretary he would not join the Government at all: and Melbourne thought him too important to be prepared to lose him. Back to the Foreign Office, therefore, stepped Palmerston, jaunty as ever. But Melbourne got his way about all the others. Durham was packed off to Russia again; Wellesley was fobbed off with a Court appointment; and Brougham was not offered a job at all. The last two protested violently. Wellesley even talked of challenging Melbourne to a duel. Melbourne went to see him. "His language," related the outraged Wellesley afterwards, "was rough, vulgar and such as has never been employed from a person in his station to one in mine." However, in spite of this, there was no more talk of a duel; nor was Lord Wellesley promoted. Brougham was a harder nut to crack. The trouble with him had started soon after Melbourne left office. Brougham had heard that his late colleagues were talking against him; he wrote angrily to Melbourne to ask why. He got a plain answer. "It is a very disagreeable task," Melbourne said, "to have to say to a statesman that his character is injured in the public estimation: it is still more unpleasant to have to add that you consider this to be his own fault; and it is idle to expect to be able to convince almost any man, and more particularly a man of very superior abilities, and with unbounded confidence in these abilities, that this is true. I must, however, state plainly that your conduct was one of the principal causes of the dismissal of the late ministry; and that it forms the most popular justification of that step." Brougham demanded details. Not without zest, Melbourne provided them. "You ask for specific charges. Allow me to observe that there may be a course and series of very objectionable conduct, there may be a succession of acts which destroy confidence and add offence to offence, and yet it would be difficult to point to any marked delinquency. I will, however, tell you fairly, that, in my opinion, you domineered too much, you interfered too much with other departments, you encroached upon the provinces of the Prime Minister, you worked, as I believe, with the Press in a manner unbecoming to the dignity of your station, and you formed political views of your own and pursued them by means which were unfair towards your colleagues. . . . Nobody knows and appreciates your natural vigour better than I do. I know also that those who are weak for good are strong for mischief. You are strong for both, and I should both dread and lament to see those gigantic powers which should be directed to the support of the State exerted in the contrary and opposite direction." To soften the blow, he ended his letter on a friendlier note. "I can only add that whatever may be your determination, no political difference will make any change in the friendship and affection which I have always felt and will continue to feel for you." However, he had already decided not to take Brougham back. "If left out he would be dangerous," he said, "but if taken in, he would be simply destructive." Brougham was so obsessedly vain that despite all Melbourne's home-truths, he was dumbfounded when he actually heard he was not going to get a place. His nose twitching more violently than ever, he strode round to Melbourne's house, fulminating wrath and demanding redress. "Do you think I am mad?" he kept on shouting furiously, "do you think I am mad?" "God damn you," said Melbourne, "you won't get the Great Seal, and that's the end of it." Brougham left the house routed.

It was for ever, too. He never got office again; and he proved too crazy and too distrusted to be much danger to the Government in opposition. At last the Arch-Fiend's bluff had been called. And it had been the easy-going Melbourne who had done it. Here was more evidence that he avoided rows, not because they frightened him, but because he thought them useless. No one could make a row with more thundering effect, when he judged a row was needed.

(3)

The result of his firmness was that the first months of
the new Government were the calmest for a long time.
And if the calm did not last, the Government did.
Though apparently always on the verge of sinking, the
leaky, rickety vessel under the command of its flippant
and indolent-seeming Captain, kept afloat for six years.
It had, it must be admitted, an uncomfortable thwarted
voyage. Events followed a recurrent pattern. The
Whigs brought in first one and then another measure
of reform—the most important were those concerned
with Church Finance, Irish tithe, and the reformation
of the Municipal Corporations of England and Ireland.
Each Bill passed the House of Commons and proceeded
to the House of Lords, who either held it up or threw it
out. Then followed an interim period in which Melbourne and Peel strove to persuade the extreme members
of their respective parties to agree to some compromise.
This interim period was marked by crises, sometimes of
sufficient intensity to threaten the very existence of the
Government. In the end most of the bills were passed,
but often in so modified a form as to defeat the intention
of their original promoters.

It was not a satisfactory state of things for people who
believed in the measures. John Russell in particular was
in a continual state of exasperation. Could not they create
Peers he said, in order to force the bills through the House
of Lords? If this was impossible, then better go out;
even opposition was preferable to staying in checked at
every turn. Melbourne soothed him. What would be

the good of going out, if the other side could not form a Government? Back the Whigs would have to come again. "It is no use popping in and out like a rabbit!" he observed sensibly. Himself, he saw no reason for resigning. In his heart of hearts he was pleased rather than otherwise when a reform was stopped: and he still feared that resignation might lead to a situation in which neither of the great parties could form a Government. "Perhaps it is a chimerical fear," he told John Russell, "and one which vanity and self-opinion very much minister to, and therefore should not be entertained. But I—being somewhat of an alarmist on this side, not having quite the confidence in the stability of popular and constitutional forms of government which others have, and thinking them very likely to break up of themselves and from the exaggeration of their own principles—cannot feel quite free from it." Do what he might, the spectre of possible civil war and revolution still hovered, dimly menacing, in the hinterland of his mind.

These various considerations conditioned his outlook on political affairs during these years. In general, he was for standing still. "I am for holding the ground already taken, but not for occupying new ground rashly," he announced to his colleagues. He set himself to act as a brake in the machinery of government. The words "delay", "put off", "postpone", echo through his letters and speeches like a series of Wagnerian leit-motifs. Of course, if the Radicals got dangerously restive, it was right to pacify them by some concessions: in practice, Melbourne showed himself surprisingly ready to do this. But he did not like doing it; and always felt bound to justify himself on the ground that it was the only means of keeping things quiet. He even grew irritated with John Russell for mentioning the Reform Bill without saying it was a necessary measure. "If it was not absolutely necessary," he remarked sharply, "it was the foolishest thing ever done." As for encouraging people to bring forward new reforms, it was simply laying up trouble for the future. They would get the habit of asking for more and more; in the end they would have to be stopped; by which time it would be an almost impossible task. "My esoteric doctrine," he proclaimed, "is that if you entertain any doubt, it is safest to take the unpopular side in the first instance. Transit from the unpopular, is easy . . . but from the popular to the unpopular the ascent is so steep and rugged that it is impossible to maintain it." So far as specific measures were concerned he approved of them only in so far as they seemed likely to make things calm. He was against the secret ballot, for example, because he suspected that it would encourage subversive persons to express their preferences more boldly than before. He was against admitting nonconformists to the University as he thought it would put Anglicans in a bad temper. He was against schemes for popular education because they seemed likely to create a new class of semi-educated discontented people. "You may fill a person's head with nonsense which may be impossible ever to get out again," he said. He also thought such schemes were futile in themselves. For one thing, no one could ever agree what form they should take. "All are agreed about the benefits of education, but are unable to agree as to the means of carrying them into effect," he

told the House of Lords, "I am afraid this will afford
those satirists, who disparage human nature, some matter
on which to plume themselves." Besides, only the intelligent in Melbourne's view, were susceptible to real education, and surely the intelligent always educated themselves.
Anyway, he sometimes wondered if education was really
of any use, so far as success in life was concerned. The
careers of his acquaintance seemed to indicate the reverse.
"I do not know why there is all this fuss about education,"
he once remarked to Queen Victoria, "none of the Paget
family can read or write and they do very well."

On the other hand, he was not against the act that proposed reforming the municipal councils. For one thing,
he thought there was a strong feeling in the country in
favour of it: and he considered, as he had over the Reform
Bill, that a wise statesman defers to such a feeling even if
he does not happen to share it, in order to keep things
peaceful. Secondly, the Bill seemed likely to give more
local influence to the middle classes. Melbourne rightly
judged that the middle classes, whether or not they called
themselves liberal, were a conservative-minded body who
would dislike dangerous changes. Even so, he did not
feel enthusiastic about the measure; and was not upset
when the House of Lords threw it out the first time it was
introduced there. "What does it matter?" he said. "We
have got on tolerably well with the councils for five
hundred years. We may contrive to go on with them for
another few years or so." And when at last it did go
through, "It is a great *bouleversement*, a great experi-
ment," he remarked doubtfully, "we must see how it
works!" Certainly he did not feel sure that the Whigs

were especially efficient at running local affairs. The Tories in the House of Lords made an attack on some magistrates who had recently been appointed by the Home Secretary. Out of loyalty to a colleague, Melbourne defended these appointments. But after the debate was at an end, he strolled over to the other side of the House to speak to an opponent. "Have we really been so bad in our appointments?" he unexpectedly asked him.

His attitude to Irish affairs was of a piece with his attitude to English. The Irish question was not so troublesome as usual, for John Russell, with Melbourne's tacit connivance, had negotiated an unwritten pact with O'Connell by which the Repeal campaign in Ireland was to be called off in return for promises to administer Ireland in a more pro-Catholic spirit than before.[1] Melbourne did not object to doing this. He had always thoroughly disliked the Irish Protestants. His tolerant spirit was especially irritated by their bland assumption that, because they owned most of the property in the country, their church had a right to be supported by money wrung from the pockets of a poverty-stricken peasantry who thought them heretics. "Religious establishment," he said with unusual bitterness, "is for population not property. Its existence is for the poor and needy, not for the opulent who have the means to provide spiritual instruction for themselves." All the same, the moment that pro-Catholic action showed signs of seriously annoying people in England, Melbourne hung

[1] Melbourne, who both as an Englishman and a gentleman disliked O'Connell, professed to know nothing of this compact. But he certainly took advantage of it as indeed was necessary for the success of his own Irish policy.

back from it. John Russell, as before, proposed a bill to reform the Protestant Church in Ireland and to strip it of some of its revenues. Uncertain and unwilling, Melbourne agreed. "I am afraid the question of the Irish Church," he said, "can neither be avoided nor postponed. It must therefore be attempted to be solved." However, when the House of Lords threw out this bill, he wanted to drop it. He was the more reluctant to proceed in the matter because growingly he doubted that it, or any other bill, could do much to solve the Irish question. The more he saw of the Irish the more he was confirmed in his conviction that their discontent arose from something born in them. "I never thought," he said, "that their crimes and outrages had much to do with former misgovernment and present politics. I believe them to arise from the natural disposition of the people and the natural state of society, which would have been much the same under any dispensation."

As a matter of fact Melbourne did not play much part either in planning or initiating the positive legislation activities of his Government. He left such work to John Russell. Not only did his conservatism of spirit make him dislike new legislation, but it was mostly concerned with administration; and he was still as bored by administration as ever. It needed more than four years as a Minister of the Crown to turn Melbourne into a man of action. The old Melbourne, like the young Melbourne, was interested less in getting things done than in studying why they happened. In so far as active politics did provide a field for his talents, it was on their personal side; in the opportunity they offered him to use his gift for managing individuals. This opportunity involved quite as much work as Melbourne liked. He found his hands full keeping his colleagues together and the King in a good humour. Even over this he was careful to expend his energy economically. He prudently refused to remove from South Street to the Prime Minister's official residence in Downing Street. The last thing he wanted was to be in the thick of things, with his colleagues bursting in at any moment of the day or night, asking awkward questions and urging quick decisions. Nor did he think it the Prime Minister's business to take a hand in the detailed running of every department in his administration. Canning, he noted, always maintained that a Government worked best in which each Minister was allowed to do his own job independently, and where the Prime Minister only intervened if any specially critical situation arose. Melbourne was pleased to find that his opinions and his inclinations alike led him to agree with Canning. "The companion rather than the guide of his ministers", so he was described; and he kept just sufficient eye on their activities to notice if they seemed likely to do anything unusually foolish. This, however, with a team like his and the situation so precarious, entailed the exercise of an incessant and vigilant diplomacy. He conducted it in his customary unofficial, undress sort of way —by means of a casual word dropped in the card room of Brooks's Club or over the port wine at a dinner party; and also by letters. Every day a stream of notes proceeded from South Street; pithy, racy, conversational notes counselling moderation and good sense, couched in a tone that artfully combined subtle tact with an air of friendly frankness. Now and again a glint of his

paradoxical humour showed itself; and also his love of
bold generalization. "Political dinners are very good things
when you can be sure of apparent unanimity," he will
say, "when great differences are found, they are dangerous." Or, "People are very fond of stating others to be
dead or in a hopeless state and are very much disappointed
to find them alive or not so bad as they gave them out to
be." Sometimes such sentences disconcerted his correspondents; so much so as to undo the effect of his tact.
He realized this. "I observe," he confessed sadly, "that
these speculative letters, especially if they are written in an
impartial or conciliatory tone, give the greatest offence."
The English party system has much to be said for it: but it
does not provide a natural home for the detached thinker.

For the rest, Melbourne's working day was occupied
with routine activities; leading the House of Lords and
dispensing patronage. He was still only moderately
successful in the House of Lords. It was not in him to
assume that stately and formidable public personality by
which a born Leader of the House like Grey awes his
opponents and rallies his noble supporters. Melbourne's
was incurably a private face. Because the debates bored
him he tended to leave the management of many bills to
his deputy, Lord Duncannon; when he did it himself he
was often listless and perfunctory.

His individuality showed itself more happily in the
dispensing of patronage. The letters he wrote on the
subject are some of the most entertaining in his correspondence. Nowhere do the diverse strains in his nature
exhibit themselves more curiously. His judgment was
extremely detached. The fact that a man had attacked

him did not in the least bias him against giving him an honour. And he had an acute eye to perceive genuine merit. On the other hand, he thought it foolish as a rule to waste an honour on a man who could do nothing to help the Whig cause. This disinclined him to reward literary achievement. "Literary men are seldom good for anything," he said. He also had an aristocratic distaste for rewarding successful business men. "Never mind the clamour of the magnates in the city," he told Lord Holland, "they grunt like pigs unless everything is done to suit their convenience." This did not stop Lord Holland pressing for an honour to be given to a Mr. Goldsmith whom, he assured Melbourne, was not a vulgar commercial type of man. Melbourne replied, "I wish you would not press Goldsmith upon me. I hate refined Solomons. God knows I hate doing something for these Stock Exchange people; there are as many refined Christians as Goldsmith; and, after all, there is not so much merit in being a Jew as to cause him on that account to be selected in a manner which must provoke much clamour and discontent." The Holland family were a great nuisance to Melbourne where honours were concerned. Lady Holland was so importunate as to come in for an incisive rebuke on the subject. "You seem to have one fixed principle," Melbourne told her, "and that is to choose the man with the worst character in the list of candidates." Certainly none of his friends and colleagues were considerate of him when they wanted a job done for a friend. John Russell himself forgot to be conscientious if there was a chance of promoting the advance of a member of his own family. "The Duke of Bedford and

John Russell," Melbourne exclaims on one occasion,
"plague me for William Russell, a snuffling Methodist
and a foolish fellow. No one has the least sense where
their own connections are concerned, and a large family
is a greater impediment than riches to a man's entry into
the Kingdom of Heaven." And the obscure were just as
clamorous as the great. "Turn round," Melbourne
whispered hurriedly to a companion when they were
riding in Rotten Row, "is not that Dacres coming?
There is no bore so great to a Prime Minister as a country
gentleman." All the same—and in spite of the bother
that it involved him in—Melbourne got a great deal of
amusement out of his job as patron. It was so delightfully
revealing of human absurdity and vanity. Who, for
instance, could have known that so many men wanted
to be baronets? "I did not know that anyone cared any
longer for these sort of things," he said. "Now I have a
hold on the fellows!" He was also entertained by the
self-confident tenacity with which the Scotch nobility
claimed honours for themselves. "Give him the Thistle!"
he remarked about a notably half-witted Scottish Peer,
"Why, he'd eat it!" Not that the English Peerage were
much better. An Earl came to him demanding to be made
a Marquess. "My dear sir," replied Melbourne, "how can
you be such a damn fool!"—and about an insatiable
applicant, "Confound it! Does he want a Garter for his
other leg?" Sometimes it seemed to him as if people
demanded rewards precisely in proportion as they were
undeserving of them. "The list of applications which I
have," he writes to John Russell about candidates for the
Civil List pensions, "comprises Mrs. James, widow

of the writer of *The Naval History*; Leigh Hunt, distinguished writer of seditious and treasonable libels; Colonel Napier, historian of the war in Spain, conceited and democratic Radical and grandson of a duke; Mr. Cary, translator of Dante, madman; Sheridan Knowles, man of great genius but not old nor poor enough for a pension. Say what would you think ought to be done." It is to be noted that several of the names on this list did in fact get their pensions. Melbourne's lack of illusions served, if anything, to increase his ironical tolerance. It also had the advantage of making him impervious himself to the temptations to which he perceived so many of his countrymen were susceptible. William IV urged him to accept the Garter; but, said Melbourne, "a Garter may attract to us somebody of consequence which nothing else can reach. But what is the good of my taking it? I cannot bribe myself!"

His most onerous work as patron was that concerned with ecclesiastical appointments. The Church of England was entering upon one of the most strenuous and turmoiled phases of its history. Like other traditional English institutions, it had woken from the placid summer afternoon slumber of the eighteenth century to find itself in a strange and disturbing world. The rise of liberalism, political and intellectual, appeared to be threatening its very existence: on every side the air re-echoed with the menacing cries of atheist radicals, now demanding its disestablishment, now questioning the very foundations of the Christian faith. However, the Church herself was susceptible to the spirit of the new age; romantic mysticism and the moral earnestness of the nineteenth century middle class flowed together into her veins to re-invigorate her with a fresh vitality; and she energetically rallied all her forces to resist her enemies. Unluckily, these forces could not agree as to how best this was to be done. There was the Liberal school who wanted to bring religion up to date; to strip its creed of what it considered its Medieval anachronisms and re-edit it on progressive "rational" lines. The new High Church party, the Pusey-ites of Oxford, on the contrary, were out to make the Church much more Medieval; surely she was strongest when she was mysterious and supernatural and authoritarian, as she had been in the great Age of Faith! Meanwhile, the Evangelical party, longer established than its rivals, stuck to its old prescription of philanthropy, puritan morals, and strict adherence to the literal words of the Scripture. All three parties regarded each other with righteous abhorrence. When an important position in the Church fell vacant, each loudly clamoured for it to be given to a candidate of its own persuasion. The unfortunate Prime Minister, in whose gift lay most important church appointments, had to decide between the claims of these vociferous and intolerant clerics.

Melbourne cut an odd figure in such a role. In one sense, he was better equipped for it than many statesmen; for theology had always been a hobby of his. But this very fact brought out in sharper relief how unlike his attitude to the subject was to that of the people with whom he was dealing. What were Dr. Pusey and the rest of them to think of a man who treated the most awful and momentous preoccupations of the human soul as matter for a hobby—and a whimsical hobby at that? These stiff, grave, conscience-ridden divines were disconcerted indeed to find themselves being tackled as to their views on the Virgin Birth or the Apostolic Succession in the cheerful man-of-the-world accents of a dinner party at Holland House. In 1840, for instance, we find Melbourne interviewing Dr. Thirlwall, a candidate for a bishopric, who had rendered himself a little suspect at Cambridge because he had translated from the German a doubtfully orthodox book on St. Luke's Gospel. Dr. Thirlwall found Melbourne in bed surrounded by heaps of patristic folios. "Very glad to see you," said Melbourne. "Sit down, sit down; hope you are come to say you accept. I only wish you to understand that I don't intend if I know it to make a heterodox bishop. I don't like heterodox bishops. As men they may be very good anywhere else, but I think they have no business on the Bench. I take great interest in theological questions, and I have read a good deal of those old fellows"—pointing to the folio editions of the Fathers—"They are excellent reading and very amusing; sometime or other we must have a talk about them. I sent your edition of Schleiermacher to Lambeth, and asked the Primate to tell me candidly what he thought of it; and look, here are his notes in the margin; pretty copious, you see. He does not concur in all your opinions; but he says there is nothing heterodox in your book."

Dr. Thirlwall was a liberal theologian. Melbourne tended to favour these most. The evangelicals, he thought, were a set of bigoted, uneducated spoil-sports; and as often as not, hypocrites as well. "One good thing," he writes to John Russell after reading Wilberforce's life, "is that it shows the great philanthropist

Thomas Clarkson to be a sad fellow." The Puseyites were less objectionable—there was an agreeable odour of antique learning about them—but their mode of thought was so remote from his as to be unintelligible. "I hardly make out what Puseyism is," he told Lord Holland. "Either I am dull or its apostles are very obscure. I have got one of their chief Newman's publications with an appendix of four hundred and forty-four pages. I have read fifty-seven and cannot say I understand a sentence, or any idea whatever." Melbourne certainly had survived into an age remote from that of his youth. It is comically incongruous to think of him in his armchair at South Street, puzzling over the sublime hair-splittings of Newman.

He found the thoughts of the liberal theologians easier to follow. Learned, sensible persons of a kind he expected to meet in academic circles, they were at least commendably open-minded about the mysterious subjects of their cogitations. He was also disposed in their favour by the fact that they were generally on the Whig side politically. This was a fact that the Prime Minister had to consider: the Government's position was so precarious, and bishops had votes in the House of Lords. Indeed, in these days, most important Church appointments carried political implications with them. The realistic Melbourne was the last man to forget this. "I feel myself bound to recommend for promotion clergymen whose general views on political matters coincide with my own," he told the Archbishop of Canterbury firmly. He added, however, that he did not want to advance any man whose views were heterodox, or who, for whatever reason, was unpopular with the main body of the clergy. Peace and quiet, as always, were the things he cared most about; and any sympathy he might personally feel with a man or with his opinions was kept strictly in check by his overriding determination to avoid a fuss. For this reason, he refused to make either Sidney Smith or Dr. Arnold a bishop. In delightful Sidney's case, this was with regret and a certain feeling of guilt. "We shall not be forgiven for not having made Sidney Smith a bishop," he exclaimed in his old age. No such qualms troubled him about Arnold. Humourless, busy and progressive, Arnold represented those aspects of the new age which Melbourne found most uncongenial. Besides, Arnold's manner of preaching struck him as unpleasantly vehement, and he thought that he had very crotchety ideas about education. Alas, all Melbourne's care did not save him from sometimes causing a storm by his ecclesiastical appointments. "I have always had much sympathy with Saul," he once remarked. "He was bullied by the prophets just as I have been by the bishops who would, if they could, have tied me to the horns of the altar and slain me incontinently."[1] Such being his experience, it is not odd that he flinched at the prospect of adding to their number. "Damn it! Another bishop dead!" he would sigh, "I believe they die to vex me."

In point of fact, the biggest row he got into over a matter of this kind was not concerned with a bishopric.

[1] It must be admitted that Melbourne on his side had no great opinion of the Bishops. "What a good, simple-hearted old man the Archbishop of Canterbury is!" said a colleague to him one day. "He is the damnedest fool alive!" replied Melbourne.

LORD M.

In 1836, the Regius Professorship of Divinity at Oxford fell vacant. After much consideration, Melbourne offered it to Dr. Hampden, a man eminent for his learning, and a Whig. Unluckily, he had also acquired distinction by delivering a course of lectures in which he had betrayed himself as a little dubious about the doctrine of the Holy Trinity. In consequence, his appointment roused a storm of protest. William IV, the Archbishop of Canterbury, and Dr. Pusey himself, all wrote agitatedly remonstrating with Melbourne; and some pious peers made angry speeches on the matter in the House of Lords. Dr. Hampden, whose temperament seems to have been less bold than his theological speculations, offered nervously to retire from the field. Melbourne, however, was not the man to let himself be bullied once he had made up his mind. Besides, he was determined to do nothing which looked like a surrender to the spirit of intolerance. Genially he soothed Dr. Hampden's anxieties. "Be easy," he said laying a hand on his arm. "I like an easy man." Himself, he used his usual pacifying tactics with King and Archbishop and wrote a letter to Dr. Pusey suavely putting him in his place. "I entirely concur with you in the necessity of agreement," he said, "if it can be created consistently with other more important objects, upon the greater points between those who fill the theological chairs in the same university. It is hardly necessary to go to Germany to learn so plain and so obvious a truth; and the theological colloquy and religious belief which prevails in the universities of that country is, if it be such as it is popularly represented, no very favourable testimony to the results of those institutions and to the manner in which they are conducted. Uniformity of opinion, however desirable, may be purchased at too high a price. We must not sacrifice everything to it; soundness of opinion, reasonableness of opinion, extent of knowledge, powers, intellectual and physical, must also be taken into account. . . . I do not myself dread bold enquiry and speculation. I have seen too many new theories spring up and die away to feel much alarm upon such a subject. If they are founded on truth, they establish themselves and become part of the established belief. If they are erroneous, they decay and perish. . . . I return you my thanks for calling my attention to the general state of religious feeling in the country, and to the deep interest which is taken in religious questions and ecclesiastical appointments. Be assured that I am neither unaware of its extent nor of its fervour, and that I have not been a careless observer of its progress. I doubt not that it is working for good, but the best and most holy aspirations are liable to be affected by the weakness of our nature and to be corrupted by our spirit of ill will, hatred and malice, of intolerance and persecution, which in its own warmth and sincerity it is apt to engender; a spirit to which, in whatever form or place it may show itself, I have a decided antipathy, and will oppose at all hazards all the resistance in my power."

The House of Lords had less claim to be treated respectfully in these matters. Melbourne made this clear in a speech. "Very few of your Lordships," he said bluntly, "have the means of forming any sound opinion on such extremely difficult and abstruse points as these. . . . I know very little of the subject and yet I believe I know more than those who have opposed the Doctor's nomination."

Melbourne's dealings with ecclesiastical affairs were not confined to the question of patronage. The spirit of reform was out to make itself felt in every established institution. A great many of these institutions were connected in some way or other with the National Church. Accordingly, during the period of Melbourne's Government, progressive reformers were always coming forward with schemes that affected it; schemes for reforming tithe and church-rate and the constitution of cathedral churches; for legalizing civil marriage and abolishing religious tests at universities. In order to please his colleagues, Melbourne reluctantly agreed to support some of these projects. But he disliked them all. He was a liberal only in matters of thought: so far as practical Church reforms were concerned, he was as conservative as Dr. Pusey himself. He was against schemes for equalizing clerical incomes; "I am all for inequality and rich clergy," he remarked gaily to a committee of the House of Lords. And how could anyone be so sure of anything, he would wonder, as to have conscientious scruples against being married in church, as their fathers and grandfathers had been before them? The same conservatism appeared in his dealings with the Church of Scotland. In 1835, it was proposed that the Government grant to the Scottish Church should be increased. Scottish divines were divided as to whether this would be a good thing. Some held that the cause of religion required financial support: others, that to accept State aid of any kind, was sinful and erastian. After listening to their arguments, Melbourne made his comment in a letter to the celebrated Dr. Chalmers. "The one party looks to nothing less than a general change in the state of human nature and human society by means of increased pastoral exertion; and the other is dreaming upon the pure and prosperous state of the Christian Church in the first centuries, and the evil and degradation which it has incurred ever since the unfortunate conversion of the Emperor Constantine. You will excuse the plainness of my phrase, but to persons so influenced by heat and enthusiasm, to use no stronger terms, it is vain to expect that any arrangement can be satisfactory." He was opposed, he concluded, to any alteration in the financial arrangements of the Church of Scotland.

So far as established Churches were concerned, Melbourne's method did not work badly. Established institutions need, first of all, to be kept running smoothly. Melbourne's spirit of civilized moderation helped him to do this. It was not so appropriate when he came into contact with independent and extreme religious bodies. One day a deputation of Dissenters came to see him. "Now, sir," he said after listening to one of them, "you talk like a man of sense. It's these damned Anabaptists who do all the mischief." Another member of the deputation felt impelled to testify to his faith. "I am an Anabaptist," he announced gravely. "The devil you are!" replied Melbourne, laughing and rubbing his hands, "well you've all done a great deal of mischief—and I should like to hear whether you are wiser than the rest!"

Towards the Church of Rome his manner was more

respectful. No doubt it was superstitious and tyrannical, and Melbourne was extremely glad that England was not under its sway. Moreover, he did not like Roman ritual which struck his gentlemanly and English eye as too theatrical to be consistent with a true spirit of devotion. But the Church of Rome was an ancient and venerable institution that appealed to his historic sense and with which he thought it wise the English Government should be on good terms. Melbourne thought that the Whigs had always underrated the importance of the Church of Rome as a factor influence in public opinion. He regretted that Protestant bigotry made it impossible for him to send an ambassador to the Vatican. As it was, he made efforts to get into good unofficial relations there. These were not very successful as far as practical results were concerned. His tone was not quite right. "The present Pope was very rude to me," Melbourne complained on one occasion. "I wrote to him asking him to give a Cardinal's Hat to an Irish bishop who had been of great use to us on the management of the country. But he took no notice of my request." It would have been odd if he had. The Vicar of Christ should not be addressed as if he was a political colleague to be breezily cajoled into doing a job for a harassed Prime Minister.

Indeed, Melbourne's attitude to religion in its corporate manifestations was incorrigibly secular. Not in its personal ones though; here he remained paradoxically ambiguous as ever. He could not be called a believer. Yet he felt himself instinctively opposed to all professional unbelievers. He took a mischievous pleasure,

when he found himself staying at Holland House with
the atheistic Bentham, in beguiling him into attending
Divine service at the local church. This was partly due,
no doubt, to a dislike for dogmatic prigs of any kind.
But not altogether: Melbourne had a positive feeling
for religion that no amount of intellectual scepticism
could dispel. He might have been expected to sympathize with Henry IV of France for becoming a Roman
Catholic in order to keep his country at peace. On the
contrary; "I would have died rather than do it!" he
exclaimed to Queen Victoria; and he was seriously concerned lest the dying William IV should not see a
clergyman. Moreover, Melbourne's interest in theology,
apparently so whimsical, was connected with the
deepest movements of his nature. Amid all the distractions of office, his perplexed spirit continued to brood
intermittently over the riddle of man's relation to the
universe. One day Haydon called to find him reading
the Greek Testament. "Is not the world," Haydon
asked him, "evidence of a perpetual struggle to remedy a
defect?" "Certainly!" mused Melbourne. "If as Milton
says," went on Haydon, "we were sufficient to have
stood, why then did we fall?" At these words, Melbourne
suddenly sat bolt upright. "Ah! That is touching on all
our apprehensions," he exclaimed.

This remark betrays a troubled spirit. Indeed, these
were not happy years for Melbourne. His forebodings
before becoming Prime Minister had proved justified.
For all his growing reputation, for all that he was
succeeding better than anyone had expected in staving off
his Government's defeat, he was usually harassed and

often depressed. After all, though his policy might be the wisest in the circumstances, it was not a glorious one. It is not satisfying to be continually compromising and conceding, especially when the best that can be hoped from them is to put off the inevitable coming of some more or less evil day. Even on a short view, their success was precarious: any violent turn of events and the whole careful structure of his diplomatic skill would fall to pieces. Besides, to maintain it was wearing. It meant being constantly watchful, and tactful, and patient and good-tempered. Against considerable temptations to the contrary, too: so many people made themselves a nuisance to him so often. "Damn it! Why can't they be quiet?" he would sigh to himself. As always, the King was the greatest trial. Soured by his failure to keep the Whigs out, William IV's temper had become more uncertain than ever. During the first months of the new Government, he refused to speak to his Ministers at all, except on business. "I would rather have the devil than a Whig in the house," he exclaimed, and sat sulking evening after evening, alone with a bottle of sherry. John Russell and Lord Glenelg, the Colonial Secretary, were his particular aversions. He insulted Glenelg so often and so publicly that Melbourne had to remonstrate with him. With good effect; indeed, Melbourne was admirable in dealing with the King who, under the influence of his mingled tact and firmness, did begin to grow friendlier. But his good humour did not last long. By the following summer, he was once more violently hostile—"Crazier than ever!" said Melbourne gloomily. Every week, he received some long, rambling, grumbling complaint from the Palace; about the Navy, or the Militia or the shocking behaviour of the Duchess of Kent —of whom, as the mother of the heir to the throne, William IV was furiously suspicious.

The King's rudeness annoyed the Ministers. Melbourne then had to soothe them. "It is best not to quarrel with him," he would remark. "He is evidently in a state of great excitement." But so, often, were they! Even without Brougham and Durham, they had turned out a difficult team to drive. Palmerston was rash and unmanageable, Glenelg feeble and languid; even John Russell, whom Melbourne looked on as the strong central pillar of his administration, was liable to what the cautious Melbourne considered fits of extreme indiscretion. Without a word of warning, in the Cabinet or, still worse, in public, he might come out with some dogmatic statement about his own opinions that was bound to cause a row. The chance that this might happen made Melbourne nervous. "I hope you have said nothing damn foolish," he writes to him on one occasion. "I thought you were teeming with some imprudence yesterday." Besides, if John Russell found himself unable to speak his mind as his principles directed, he was inclined to throw up the sponge. Three times at least, during these years, he threatened to resign: and had to be cajoled by his chief into staying in office. This irritated Melbourne. His irritation grew sharper when John Russell took upon himself to tell him that he ate too much and did not take enough exercise.

The King and his colleagues were not the only people to give Melbourne trouble. There was the Radical wing of his party exploding in righteous wrath every time he made a concession to the Tories: there was the Opposition in the House of Lords, always on their toes to trip the Government up, factious, carping, asking awkward questions and exulting in ugly pleasure over any Whig slip. It was true that Peel, for his own good reasons, did his best to keep them in check. But Melbourne could not feel that this was done in a spirit of sporting goodwill. Peel, in his view, was a cold, ungenerous, ungenial type of man—"Not a horse into whose stable you should go unadvisedly and without speaking to him before!" he warned John Russell; and again "he is cross and sarcastic which I take to be the nature of the man: it is only prudence and calculation which make him otherwise."

Altogether, being Prime Minister was fully as troublesome as he had feared. Gradually the strain began to tell on his nerves. He slept very badly, and suffered from rheumatic attacks that kept him in bed for days at a time. Every month brought some new abortive crisis: every crisis left the Government a little more discredited. The nadir was reached in the late summer of 1836 after the Government had suffered a series of defeats in the House of Lords and every one—King, Irish, Radicals—seemed in a thoroughly bad temper. "It would try the patience of an ass," Melbourne broke out one day. For the first time he began to wonder whether it might not be wiser to resign.

Dissatisfaction with his immediate situation merged into a more general sense of sadness and disillusionment. He felt the fleetingness of things mortal more acutely than ever; saw himself more than ever as an alien in the new age. Especially down in the country at Brocket, where he had time to reflect and the atmosphere was soaked in memories of his happy childhood and brilliant youth, regret swept over him like a wave. The golden September sunlight bathing the stretches of turfy park-land seemed only to mock by contrast the sunless autumn of his own prevailing mood.

"Thou bringest the light of pleasure fled,
And hopes long dead."

So he would be heard murmuring to himself as he gazed out of the window.

(4)

The events of his private life contributed to his depression. He had lost Miss Eden for the time being. In 1835, Miss Eden's brother, Lord Auckland, was made Governor-General of India; and she went away with him. No longer could Melbourne look forward to calling on her each week, for an entertaining talk on the foibles of his colleagues or the Epistles of St. Paul; no longer could he relax his taut nerves in the pleasant warmth of her kindness and her good sense. "My mother always used to say," he writes in a note of farewell, "that I was very selfish, both Boy and Man, and I believe she was right— at least I know that I am always anxious to escape from anything of a painful nature, and find every excuse for doing so. Very few events could be more painful to me than your going, and therefore I am not unwilling to avoid wishing you good-bye. Then God bless you—As to health, let us hope for the best. The climate of the East Indies very often re-establishes it. I send you a Milton, which I have had a long time and often read in. I shall be most anxious to hear from you and promise to write. Adieu."

Then in the spring of 1836 he found himself in serious trouble over Mrs. Norton. She had been the central figure in his private life for the last five years. Either in his house or hers, they saw each other nearly every day; often for three hours at a time and often alone. She talked or listened to him about his political work; when he wanted to forget politics, they read poetry together, or flirted and gossiped. Such a relationship, innocent though in fact it might be, was bound to excite censorious comment. One man can steal a horse, says the proverb, while another cannot look over the hedge. Melbourne and Caroline belonged conspicuously to the second category. Both lived in the public eye: Melbourne because he was Prime Minister, Caroline because it was her nature so to do. Moreover, what with Lady Branden and the general amorous reputation of his family, Melbourne could not pay marked attention to a woman without people suspecting the worst. Nor was Caroline the type of woman to disarm their suspicions. She was showily beautiful, her conversation was the opposite of prudish and she had no sense of decorum. "Met Mrs. Norton at the French Ambassador's," notes the correct Lord Malmesbury in 1835. "She talked in a most extraordinary manner and kicked Lord Melbourne's hat over her head. The whole *corps diplomatique* were amazed." The world in general reacted to such exhibitions in the same way as the *corps diplomatique*: and disapproval mingled with their amazement. Indeed, Caroline had only maintained her precarious footing in respectable society in virtue of the fact that she had not broken its first fundamental law of conduct: she still lived under the same roof as her husband. As time passed, she found this growingly difficult.

The marriage had always been a dog-fight. Neither husband nor wife had the self-control to keep their wrongs to themselves. Gradually, parties were formed on each side. They interfered and made things worse. Caroline's supporters were the first to enter the fray. One evening in 1833, the Nortons had a worse row than usual. George Norton insisted on smoking a cigar in the drawing-room, though Caroline objected to the smell. Accordingly, she flounced upstairs and locked herself in her bedroom. Norton pursued after her, broke down the door, and, after blowing out the candle, proceeded to throw her and the furniture about in an alarming fashion. The next day she took refuge with her family who vehemently espoused her cause. However, things were patched up sufficiently for the Nortons and the Sheridan family—Caroline's sisters and her brother Brinsley—to go on a foreign tour together in the following year. As might have been expected, this only led to more trouble. Once again the worst explosion was occasioned by George Norton's smoking. One day, when driving with his wife in a small closed carriage, he puffed away at a hookah regardless of her entreaties. She tore the mouthpiece from his lips and flung it out of the window; he clutched her so violently by the throat that, in fear of her life, she jumped from the carriage and ran back to her relations. Outraged to see their sister treated in this way, they returned to England, George Norton's implacable enemies who never lost a chance of working up Caroline against him. Now it was his turn to seek for sympathy among his relations. He found it, and especially from Miss Vaughan, an elderly spinster connection of his, to whom he had always taken pains to make himself pleasant as he hoped she might leave him her fortune. Stirred up by Miss Vaughan on the one hand and the Sheridans on the other, the feeling between husband and wife began to increase to a bitterness that made rupture inevitable. It did not come at once only because George Norton was too unstable easily to take decisive action about anything; and because Caroline, partly out of concern for her reputation and her children, and partly out of genuine softheartedness, shrank when it came to the point, from pushing matters to their extreme conclusion. Some uneasy months followed of recurrent quarrels, apologies, and reconciliations. Each time the quarrel was sharper and the reconciliation more half-hearted. In April, 1836, the final break came. Its occasion—a dispute as to whether or not the children should be allowed to pay a visit to Caroline's brother—seems trivial enough. Perhaps George Norton had already thought of the plan by which he hoped he might at once disembarrass himself of his wife and also improve his wretched financial position. Why not take advantage of Caroline's notorious indiscretion to get a divorce and make the co-respondent pay him large damages? He therefore turned her out of the house, packed his children off to his relations, and set about looking for a likely co-respondent. Several celebrated names occurred to him as possible candidates for this important role. For a time his mind wavered between Shelley's corsair friend Trelawny, Harrison Ainsworth, the novelist, and the young Duke of Devonshire. Then an even more spectacular alternative presented itself to his mind; the Prime Minister himself. It is doubtful whether this was George Norton's own idea or—as was commonly rumoured—it was suggested to him by wire-pullers from the underworld of the Tory Party, who saw in the divorce case a means of discrediting the Whig Government. How George Norton thought he was going to get away with it is hard to imagine. For, up till the very day Caroline left him, he had taken pains to keep on particularly good terms with Melbourne—even better than with Caroline's other rich admirers. So far from objecting to the intimacy, he had ushered Melbourne up to visit her in her bedroom when she was ill and escorted her to South Street when she was going to pay a call there. However, he was intoxicated by the prospect of the fortune he was likely to get if he did contrive to win his case; alternatively, he thought Melbourne, for the sake of avoiding a public scandal, might pay up handsomely in order to persuade him to withdraw it. In either case he fancied he stood to win. He proceeded, therefore, to file a petition, accusing him of criminal connection with his wife.

The general sensation stirred can be imagined. It is

not every day that the Prime Minister of England is publicly accused of adultery with a reigning beauty. The gutter-press of the day resounded with articles in which spicy scandalous rumours were nicely blended with pious reflections on the deplorable prevalence of vice in high places. All this was more agreeable for the news-paper reader than for the parties concerned. Caroline was consternated. It looked like the end of all her ambitions. In those days, divorce meant complete social ruin for a woman. Even if she were exonerated, her good name would be tarnished. Her children, whom she loved with all the unbridled force of her emotional nature, were cut off from her, and in the hands of the odious Nortons. Reports reached her that they ill-treated them. Her dramatic imagination exaggerated these reports till she was nearly out of her mind. Alas, misfortune did not make her prudent! Indeed, it served still further to weaken her self-control and provide a new channel for the expression of her instinct for theatrical gesture. She proclaimed her wrongs at the top of her voice; she did her best to put herself in the wrong with George Norton by writing him letters imploring his forgiveness if he would take her back; she even rushed down to the country house where her children were confined, only to have them torn screaming from her arms and herself thrust ignominiously from the gates. At the same time, she failed to take the opportunity to mend her broken reputation by adopting a soberer and more retired style of living. Instead—either from pride or a desperate longing to forget her troubles—she shocked people by continuing to dine out and to go to parties, gorgeously dressed in pink satin and black lace, and laughing and talking with feverish vivacity.

The one person she could not risk being seen with was Melbourne. However, she communicated with him in a series of letters in which cries of anguish, denunciations of the Nortons, and appeals for comfort and advice were frantically mingled. Poor Melbourne, he must have rued the day he first called at her house! No pleasure he had found there could compensate for the trouble it was now causing him. He had chiefly enjoyed his relationship to Caroline as a delightful distraction from the disturbances of his political life. Now it turned out to be involving him in disturbance itself. And a much more disagreeable kind of disturbance. For it was one that stirred his sense of guilt. Through his own indiscretion, he had done harm to the reputation of his Government and brought acute distress upon a woman he was very fond of. He did not, indeed, look on himself as primarily to blame for the failure of the Norton marriage. To his shrewd and worldly-wise eyes it seemed to have been grossly mismanaged from the start. No doubt George Norton was the villain of the piece. Melbourne's personal experience of him made him certain of this. Norton had proved shockingly unsatisfactory at his job; quarrelsome, shifty, grossly unpunctual and conceitedly imperious to any word of correction. "I know very well that a man of that description," Melbourne told Caroline, "who is fully persuaded that he is about to do something extremely well is on the point of committing some irretrievable error or of falling into some most ridiculous absurdity." As to Norton's behaviour at home, Melbourne saw quite enough of it to realize that all Caroline's complaints were justified. All the same, he did not think she went the right way about dealing with him. Not thus would his mother have tackled a troublesome husband. Caroline was at once too violent and too weak; lost her temper too quickly and too readily forgave an injury. "The fact is he is a stupid brute," he said to Lord Holland, "and she has not the temper nor the dissimulation needed to manage him." Further, he thought that living with Norton had lowered her standards of behaviour so that she had grown content to let her marriage degenerate into a condition of continuous sordid squabble that must end in catastrophe. For he had no doubt that a breach was a catastrophe. Far more clearly than Caroline he recognized how fatal it would be for her reputation openly to be separated from her husband. All along Melbourne had urged her to put up with anything in order to keep the home together. As he wrote to her in his first letter after the final quarrel. "I hardly know what to write to you, or what comfort to offer. You know as well as I do, that the best course is to keep yourself tranquil, and not to give way to feelings of passion which, God knows, are too natural to be easily resisted. This conduct upon his part seems perfectly unaccountable, and, depend upon it, being as you are, in the right, it will be made ultimately to appear, whatever temporary misrepresentations may prevail. You cannot have better or more affectionate advisers than you have with you upon the spot, who are well acquainted with the circumstances of the case and with the characters of those with whom they have to deal. You know that

I have always counselled you to bear everything and remain to the last. I thought it for the best."

He still thought it for the best. Soon he was pressing her to try and make things up again—even after he got the news that George Norton was trying to find grounds for a divorce. "Never, to be sure, was there such conduct. To set on foot that sort of inquiry without the slightest real ground for it! But it does not surprise me. I have always known that there was a mixture of folly and violence which might lead to any absurdity or injustice. You know so well my opinion that it is unnecessary for me to repeat it. I have always told you that a woman should never part from her husband whilst she can remain with him. This is generally the case; particularly in such a case as yours, that is, in the case of a young, handsome woman of lively imagination, fond of company and conversation, and whose celebrity and superiority has necessarily created many enemies. Depend upon it, if a reconciliation is feasible there can be no doubt of the prudence of it." In spite of all, to make it up would be the best for Caroline, best for her children—and of course best both for Melbourne himself and for the Whig Party.

When all hope of reconciliation was over, Melbourne concentrated on comforting Caroline and trying to persuade her to keep her head. "I hope you will not take it ill," he said, "if I implore you to try at least to be calm under these trials. You know that whatever is alleged (if it be alleged) is utterly false, and what is false can rarely be made to appear true." And again, "Keep up your spirits; agitate yourself as little as possible; do not be too anxious about rumours and the opinion of the world." Alas, such advice, sensible though it was, had no effect on a woman like Caroline. Rather, it roused her exasperated nerves, to an outburst of irritation. To her his whole tone only showed that he was cold and selfish and did not enter into her feelings. How could he expect her to be calm? Nor did she like it when he said that other people agreed with him. What did he mean by talking of her concerns to other people. Was it not shockingly disloyal of him? Gently, and with the patience born of long experience of similar temperamental explosions in his own home, he defended himself. "You describe me very truly when you say that I am always more annoyed that there is a row than sorry for the persons engaged in it. But, after all, you know you can count on me." Indeed, Caroline was wildly mistaken in thinking that he did not feel for her. On the contrary, as the time for the trial approached, the matter began to prey on his mind till he became actually ill from disgust and apprehension. The idea of any woman he was fond of being involved in the squalor of a public lawsuit on such a subject was almost unbearable to his chivalrous heart. Caroline wrote describing an interview with her lawyers. She had found it odious: they had been so cold-blooded about the affair, so obviously ready under an air of superficial politeness to believe her guilty, and, she cried once more, Melbourne did not realize her sufferings! He was feeling so worked up by now that this time he burst out in reply, "I have received your letter," he said, "and given such instruction as I trust will be for the best. I do not wonder at the impression made upon you. I knew it would be so, and therefore I was most unwilling to have the interview take place at all. All the attorneys I have ever seen have the same manner: hard, cold, incredulous, distrustful, sarcastic, sneering. They are said to be conversant in the worst part of human nature, and with the most discreditable transactions. They have so many falsehoods told them, that they place confidence in none.

"I have sent your note, having read it. I daresay you think me unfeeling; but I declare that since I first heard I was proceeded against I have suffered more intensely than I ever did in my life. I had neither sleep nor appetite, and I attributed the whole of my illness (at least the severity of it) to the uneasiness of my mind. Now what is this uneasiness for? Not for my own character because, as you justly say, the imputation upon me is as nothing. It is not for the political consequences to myself, although I deeply feel the consequences that my indiscretion may bring upon those who are attached to me or follow my fortunes. The real and principal object of my anxiety and solicitude is you, and the situation in which you have been so unjustly placed by the circumstances which have taken place."

It is likely that his passionate desire to convince her of his sympathy made him exaggerate a little. He cannot have suffered so profoundly as at the crisis of his marriage. But he was older now, he could stand these strains less well: and perhaps it is true that never before had he felt his nerves so wretchedly upset. Certainly it is the first occasion in this phase of his life that we find people saying that he looked depressed.

Meanwhile he asked the King if he should resign; he was willing to if it was thought proper. The King said no.

He suspected the whole affair of being an underhand political plot: and with all his faults, William IV was not the type of man to connive at underhand plots. Nor had his own private life been of a kind to make him take a censorious view of Melbourne's alleged misconduct. The Duke of Wellington also took steps to let Melbourne know that he saw no cause for resignation. On the contrary, he said he would refuse to take office in any Government that might be formed as a result of it. He too was not the man to be particular in such matters. Besides he was very anxious to dissociate himself from the intrigues of his shadier supporters.

The case came up for trial on 23rd June. Public excitement was tremendous. Couriers waited all day ready to carry the news of the verdict to every important capital in Europe. From early morning, the law courts were besieged by huge crowds trying to get seats: so much so that the Attorney General, Sir John Campbell, who was appearing for Melbourne, had considerable difficulty in pushing his way through the throng. During the whole day before he had been feeling acutely apprehensive. Who knew what apparently damning evidence George Norton might have contrived to concoct in order to gain his ends? Campbell need not have worried. Dickens was to satirize the case a year or two later in the *Pickwick Papers*: and in fact, the proceedings did turn out to be a scene of grotesque Dickensian farce. Hogarthian rather: for much of the evidence offered was of too scandalous a kind to find a place on the chaste pages of a Victorian novel. Melbourne and Caroline were not present, though Melbourne sent an affidavit asserting his innocence. George Norton could not by law go into the witness box himself. Instead, he relied on the evidence of a handful of servants once in his employ, whom he had tracked down after months of search in the underworld of London and then persuaded by means of lavish bribes to come forward on his behalf. They were of a type to cast a lurid light on the character of life below stairs in the Norton household. Two were women who had been discharged on account of their indiscreet familiarities with members of His Majesty's Brigade of Guards; while the chief male witness was a groom called Fluke who had been dismissed for his habitual drunkenness. Fluke was an engaging character. It was reported that he had refused at the last moment to come to court unless he was brought in a chaise and four, and was given both chicken and duckling for breakfast before starting.

"I had had a drop too much," he confided to the court, when relating an incident in his evidence.

"You like to speak the truth sometimes?" said Campbell sarcastically. "You took a drop too much, eh?" Fluke resented the tone of his remark.

"I don't know who does not. We are all alike for that, masters and servants," he answered.

"How often did you take a drop too much while in Mrs. Norton's service?" asked Campbell.

"What Sir, during four years service!" exclaimed the astonished Fluke. "You have put a very heavy question!" It also transpired during his examination that Fluke had spent the last weeks living at a public house on the Norton family estate and had had several interviews with George Norton. The chief documentary evidence brought forward were three notes from Melbourne. The first ran, "I will call about quarter-past four. Yours, Melbourne."

The second, "How are you? I shall not be able to come today. I shall tomorrow."

The third, "No House today: I will call after the levee. If you wish it later I will let you know."

Norton's Counsel did what he could with these unpromising documents. He said they showed "a great and unwarrantable degree of affection," because they did not begin My Dear Mrs. Norton, and added, "there may be latent love like latent heat in the midst of icy coldness." This mysterious and imaginative reflection failed to make the impression on the court which its author desired. The proceedings, which lasted for nearly thirteen hours, were frequently interrupted by bursts of uproarious laughter. Campbell called no witnesses for the defence. Instead, rising at six o'clock and continuing till the candles guttered low in their sockets, he demolished the evidence offered on behalf of the plaintiff in a speech which all present agreed to be one of the most brilliant exhibitions of legal wit and eloquence ever heard in an English Court of Justice. The case ended just before midnight: the Jury acquitted Melbourne without leaving the box. The verdict was received with thunderous applause. Late as it was, Campbell went down to the House of Commons, where the news of his success had preceded him, and was met with another great outburst of cheering. Even the bitterest Tory did not dare to question the justice of the verdict. "As far as I can see," said one acidly, "Melbourne had more opportunities than any man ever had before and made no use of them."

On the whole the Prime Minister's reputation was affected wonderfully little by the affair. The newspapers indeed, on the morning after the trial, maintained the lofty and censorious tone which, as self-appointed guardians of public morality, they had assumed throughout. *The Times*, though it accepted the verdict, reproved Caroline's conduct as "imprudent, indiscreet, and undignified, and the very last we should hold up as an example to an English wife". As for Melbourne, a man who could waste his own and the lady's time on such "contemptible and unnecessary frivolities" was, it said, utterly unfit for his high office.

This view does not seem to have been shared by any one in the world of politics and fashion in which Melbourne lived: while, as might have been expected, his own relations, little as they cared for Mrs. Norton—why must William always involve himself with such impossible women?—rallied round him with all that sense of family solidarity which was characteristic of them. "The whole thing seems to leave the lady in a position where, with a little protection, she may do very well," wrote Frederick Lamb to his sister Emily. "We know them for *canaille*, but we must help her as well as we can. Do not let William think himself invulnerable for having got off again this time. No man's luck can go further."

William did not think himself invulnerable. No doubt it was a great load off his mind. The night of the trial, walking home by Storey's Gate, he saw a young lawyer of his acquaintance staring curiously at Mrs. Norton's house. Melbourne touched him on the shoulder. "What does this mean, Mr. Solicitor?" he asked with a roguish look. But he did not feel so carefree as to imagine he could risk resuming his intimacy with Caroline on anything like the old terms. It was sad; for he had grown in his loneliness to depend on her very much. But it was inevitable. All the same, he still felt responsible for her and very much concerned about her future prospects. Those were not bright. In spite of the fact that she had been exonerated, the trial was a disaster for her. It cut her off indefinitely from her children: and, for all that Frederick Lamb might say to the contrary, it struck a dangerous blow at her precarious social position. Many people still thought her guilty; at the best, she had shown herself extremely indiscreet. Nor did her flamboyant personality enable her to play the role of innocent, injured woman in such a way as to disarm the suspicions of the censorious. Besides, she was very poor. Legally everything she possessed down to her very jewels belonged to George Norton, even if she got a legal separation from him: and he was prepared to claim all his legal rights. Melbourne was all the more worried about her because for some time after the trial he did not hear a word from her, though he had written more than once. He began to wonder if she had not turned against him as one of the authors of her troubles. At last she did answer, miserable and bitter indeed, but against Norton, not himself. He replied in a series of letters in which are apparent the mingled strains of his feelings in regard to her: regret, affection, pity, a sense of personal responsibility and chivalrous indignation with Norton.

"Well, come what may, I will never again from silence or any other symptom think that you can mean anything

unkind or averse to me. I have already told you that most
of the bitterness which I have felt during this affair was on
your account. I do not think your application to Norton
was judicious.[1] Every communication elates him and
encourages him to persevere in his brutality. You ought
to know him better than I do and must do so. But you
seem to me to be hardly aware what a gnome he is, how
perfectly earthy and bestial. He is possessed of a devil, and
that the immensest and basest fiend that disgraces the
infernal regions. In my opinion he has made the whole
matter subservient to his pecuniary interests. . . . Now that
he has nobody to advise or control or soothe him, what
follies or what abominable conduct he may pursue it is
impossible to conjecture. I pity you about the children.
. . . It is most melancholy not to know where they are or
with whom. I have never mentioned money to you. I
hardly like to do it now. Your feelings have been so
galled that they have naturally become very sore and
sensitive. I know how you might take it. I have had,
at times, a great mind to send you some but I feared to
do so. As I trust we are now upon terms of confidential
and affectionate friendship, I venture to say that you have
only to express a wish and it shall be instantly complied
with. I miss you. I miss your society and conversation
every day at the hours at which I was accustomed to enjoy
it: and when you say that your place can be easily
supplied, you indulge in a little vanity and self-conceit.
You know well enough that there is nobody who can fill
your place. . . . I saw Brinsley and his wife the other
night at Lord Hertford's. I thought him rather cold.

[1] This appears to have been an application for money.

None of them seemed really glad to see me, except Charles. But there is no reason why they should be. If they went upon my principle, or rather my practice of disliking those who cause trouble, uneasiness, vexation, without considering why they do it, they certainly would not rejoice in my presence."

Towards the end of the year his private life was disturbed by yet another shock. For some months, Augustus Lamb's health had shown signs of breaking up. The attacks from which he has suffered since a child came oftener and more violently. In spite of all his other preoccupations, Melbourne had watched over him as carefully as he could: had him with him when he was working, and sat in his room for hours together observing vigilantly every varying symptom of his condition. One evening in November they were together and Melbourne was writing when Augustus suddenly said, "I wish you would give me some franks that I may write to people who have been kind in their enquiries." Words and tone were those of a sane, mature man: Melbourne's pen dropped from his hand in astonishment. "I cannot give any notion of what I felt," he related, "for I believe it to be, as it proved, the summons they call the lightening before death. In a few hours he was gone." Melbourne's words are calm and he went back to work at once, to all outward appearance his usual smiling self. But Augustus was his only child, and he had loved him with the ardour of a starved and tender heart. The event cast a greyer shadow on the last months of 1836.

There was nothing to dissipate it in his professional life. The Government continued, as it had for some months past, to jolt and creak along its accustomed round, checked and harassed as before by King and Peers, Irish and Radicals. The King's moods were various. Violently out of temper during August, he was sufficiently softened by November to send his Ministers an invitation to dinner, accompanied by the alarming proviso that he expected them each to drink two bottles of wine. In December, however, he had turned against them once more: and, though his experiences in 1834 had taught him not to try and get rid of them on his own initiative, he remained for the rest of his reign hostile. The House of Lords, too, was very obstreperous. It threw out the Irish Church Bill at the end of 1836; mainly because it still objected to the clause appropriating Church revenue to secular purposes. Melbourne took the opportunity to persuade his colleagues to drop this clause. The House of Lords was not sufficiently pacified to pass the Bill; and the Irish were very much annoyed. One evening in December sitting at Lord Sefton's, Creevey told Melbourne that he had heard O'Connell was likely to stop supporting the Government.

"God!" remarked Melbourne with placid interest. "It's a curious thing—two or three people have said the same thing to me."—and then after a pause, "God, perhaps it is so!" Creevey was amazed at the detachment with which the Prime Minister seemed to contemplate an event that must lead to the downfall of his Government. In fact O'Connell still preferred the Whigs to the Tories and so did not withdraw his support. His followers, however, were displeased. So were the Radicals. Every concession to the opposition made them harder to control. Meanwhile the Government appeared so weak that moderate opinion in the country was veering more and more round to Peel. The effect of all this was to exhaust the patience of Ministers to breaking point. John Russell began periodically threatening resignation again; and from the beginning of 1836 there was a growing party in the Cabinet who wanted to stop compromise, even if it meant that the Government went out. Melbourne felt a good deal of sympathy with them. The strain of accommodating himself to the King's temper and what he called "Peel's low creeping policy" was becoming more than he could bear. But his view of the general political situation had not altered, and against his private inclinations he still thought the Whigs ought to stick on. "A Minister has no more right to treat a case as desperate than a physician," he remarked, "events are too uncertain and results differ too much from anticipation, to permit such conduct." As late as May, 1837, he is still telling John Russell that he feared lest the fall of the Whigs might throw the country into a dangerous chaos. All the same, he cannot have thought the Government able to hang on much longer.

If it should fall, Melbourne's career might well seem to have come to its end. The Whig wave was spent, the Tories were likely to be in for a considerable time. Melbourne was fifty-seven, and old for his years: it was improbable that he would be Prime Minister again. Dawning late, his difficult, frustrated, unrewarding day of eminence looked as if it would soon be over. In fact his unpredictable fate had yet one more surprise in store for him. The most brilliant phase of his whole history was just round the corner.

Chapter V

THE QUEEN: FIRST
PHASE

(1)

IN THE MIDDLE of May, 1837, political circles in
London were thrown into fresh agitation by an
unforeseen event. King William IV fell dangerously
ill. After several weeks hovering between life and death,
he breathed his last in the early hours of 20th June. At
nine o'clock of the same morning the Prime Minister,
in the full dress uniform of a Privy Councillor, arrived
at Kensington Palace to pay his respects to the new
Queen. He was ushered into a small room where he
found himself alone in the presence of a round-cheeked,
blue-eyed little figure, dressed very plainly in deep
mourning, who with an air at once childish and regal
held out her hand for him to kiss. In artless words and a
sweet, clear treble, she told Melbourne that she wished
him and his colleagues to continue in office; and then
listened with attention, while he read to her the speech
he had written for her to make later in the morning to the
Privy Council. He asked if she would like to be supported
by the chief officers of her realm on entering the room

at this, her first public appearance as a sovereign. The Queen replied, at once and with composure, No—she preferred to come in alone. Melbourne then kissed hands again and withdrew. A short time before the Council, he returned in case she wanted any further advice as to how to conduct herself at it. He need hardly have bothered. Once or twice, the Queen was observed to look enquiringly at her Prime Minister as if in doubt what to do next; but for the most part, she amazed all beholders by the modest and graceful self-possession with which, in the face of a large and august audience, she went through the stately ceremonies of her in-auguration. After dinner that night, Melbourne came back once more for an hour's leisurely talk with her. "I had a very important and very *comfortable* conversation with him," wrote the Queen in her diary that evening.

It was to be the first of many such. The eighteen-year-old Queen needed someone to instruct her as to how to conduct herself in her new and difficult role. In the ordinary way this would have been done by some responsible and experienced person appointed as con-fidential secretary for the purpose. It was not easy, however, to find the right man; for if he were intelligent enough for the work, he was likely to have ideas of his own about political affairs which might well conflict with those of the Government. The last thing Melbourne wanted was an independent power behind the Throne. Nor did he intend, if he could help it, that the new monarch should be as hostile to the Government as the old had been. All these considerations made him decide to take on the secretary's work himself. This meant that

QUEEN VICTORIA

he saw the Queen constantly. He visited her at least twice a day: she saw him alone in her own private sitting-room where she received no other visitor. They also communicated by letter, he wrote to her and she wrote to him sometimes as often as three times a day. Three or four times a week at least he dined. Whoever the guests might be, Melbourne sat on the Queen's left, and after dinner she spent most of her time talking to him. A month or two later she went to take up residence at Windsor. But this change did not mean any break in their association. Melbourne wrote as often as ever and at greater length. He also went down to stay. There, in addition to the daily conference and evening relaxation with each other, he would accompany her out riding. Altogether it can be calculated that in these first years of her reign Melbourne spent four or five hours of every day talking or writing to his royal mistress. No doubt he felt it his duty to do so; but he was not the man to carry out a duty so rigorously, if it went against his inclinations. As a matter of fact, all his inclinations were in its favour; what had begun as a duty very soon turned into an intense pleasure. These months saw the birth and quick maturing of the most precious personal relationship that he had known since the first happy days of his marriage with Caroline thirty-two years before.

It was a very different sort of relationship. For apart from their unlikeness in age and situation, the two women involved were so different. The young Queen's personality, however, was just as compelling as Caroline's and, in its own way, as exceptional. Not that she was complex or eccentric. On the contrary, her simple and formidable character was compounded of a few basic and universal elements. By nature she was almost all the things that the typical woman is alleged to be by those who have the temerity to generalize on the subject; instinctive, personal, unintellectual, partizan, interested in detail, viewing things in the concrete rather than the abstract, and with a profound natural reverence for the secure and the respectable. With these common qualities of her sex, the Queen possessed also those of her age. Like most of the eighteen-year-old girls who were her subjects, she was innocent and enthusiastic, enjoyed dancing and dress, set store by anniversaries and mementoes and celebrations, blushed and burst out laughing, bubbled over with sentiment for her pet dog and her old home. And not in any particularly refined or rarefied way; though regal, she was not aristocratic as the English understand the term. The healthy, homely German blood which coursed through her veins had imparted a commonplace, even a bourgeois tinge to her taste. But if her nature was normal, her character was not. It was too abnormally high-powered for one thing. Her enjoyments were more rapturous than the average girl's, her sentimentality more unbridled, her interest in detail more inexhaustible, her partizanship more violent, her innocence more dewy. Some strain in her—once again it may have come from Germany—had endowed her with an extravagant force of temperament; so that the ordinary in her was magnified to a degree where it became extraordinary.

To this startling fervour of feeling she added a startling simplicity of vision. Through her childlike eyes she saw the world as naively, literally and absolutely as a child. All facts came fresh to her. "To hear the people speaking German and to see the German soldiers, etc. seemed to me so singular," she notes a year or two later, on her first visit to Germany. Her judgments were as simple as her vision. They were often shrewd, but never subtle and never tentative. Her mind was incapable of entertaining a doubt or a half shade. Things were frivolous or serious, sad or cheerful, right or wrong. Particularly right or wrong: childish vision went along with a child's ruthless unsleeping moralism. And its ruthless candour, too: as a little girl, it was noticed that though rebellious and passionate, the Princess could always be trusted to be rigidly truthful. At eighteen she was just as incapable of simulating a feeling or telling a lie. As she spoke, so she acted. The most formidably extreme of all her extreme qualities was her strength of character. Here she was not childish, nor feminine—if indeed weakness be a feminine characteristic. No one was ever less the creature of whim or vacillating impulse. Once she had made up her mind what she ought to do, she adhered inflexibly to it, however hard it might be for her and whether other people liked it or not. It was not in her to compromise. If other people were wrong, it would be wrong of her to give in to them.

The peculiarities of her nature had been sharpened by the circumstances of her upbringing. Her mother, the Duchess of Kent, suspicious and jealous of her royal in-laws, was determined that her daughter should not fall under their influence. The result was that the Princess spent her childhood in a strange, conventual seclusion, almost entirely in the company of women—notably her mother and her governess, Baroness Lehzen, who regulated and supervised every hour of her day. She was never allowed to be alone; she slept in her mother's room: never did she see anyone by herself except her mother and governess: if she kept a diary it had always to be shown to Lehzen. Very few grown-up visitors came to the house; and except for the daughter of her mother's secretary, or on the rare occasions when her German cousins came to stay, she did not have the chance of playing with other children. No window on the ordinary humdrum world was ever opened to let a whiff of fresh air into the soft, stifling atmosphere of meticulous feminine triviality and gushing feminine emotion which pervaded Kensington Palace.

But if her childhood was secluded, it was not obscure. As the future Queen of England, the Princess realized she was a personage of unequalled importance; and, as such, treated differently from other children. People did not bow and curtsey to other children: other children were not taught singing and dancing, as she was, by the most famous public performers in the world: other children were not prepared for Confirmation by the Archbishop of Canterbury himself. And with the glory of great position she was early introduced to its troubles. Uneasy lies the head that wears a crown, says the poet; and the head destined for a crown is hardly more comfortable. The four years before her accession, the Princess was the centre of a continuous turmoil of intrigue and conflict. There was the conflict between the King and her mother. The Duchess of Kent, a short, stout, foolish woman, rustling self-importantly about in velvet and ostrich plumes, was intoxicated by the idea of herself as mother to a future monarch; all the more because she considered she had never been treated by the English Royal Family with the respect due to her. Accordingly, at the same time that she strove to keep her daughter from them, she was always making efforts to bring her into prominence on her own; demanded that the Fleet should fire a salute in her daughter's honour when she was at the seaside, and paraded her round the country on official visits without getting the King's permission. She also intrigued with disaffected politicians, notably Durham, with the vague idea of creating a sort of Princess's Party in Parliament. The irascible William IV reacted violently against these proceedings of his sister-in-law. He forbade the Navy to fire a salute and incessantly abused the Duchess to his Ministers. On one of the rare occasions when she paid him a visit, he suddenly rose at the end of dinner and denounced her to the company in unmeasured and naval terms for deliberately keeping his beloved niece from him. The poor little Princess burst into tears of embarrassment. Thus early was she aware of herself as a bone of contention.

The King was not the only person trying to get control over her. Her uncle, Leopold, King of the Belgians, was a far-sighted statesman well aware of the political advantages of having a niece on the throne of powerful England. At his visits, therefore, and in a series of letters in which political advice, pious aspirations and demonstrations of highflown affection were

LORD M.

artfully blended, he sought to get her under his influence.
The Princess did not resent this, for Uncle Leopold was
always tactful; but she realized that his views were not
always the same as her mother's or her Uncle William's,
and that she must be careful how far she committed
herself to them. This added another complication to the
already complex situation in which she found herself.

There was a more disturbing complication to face
nearer home. Life at Kensington Palace, to outward
appearance so tranquil, was in reality a scene of strife.
On the one side stood the Duchess and her confidential
secretary, Sir John Conroy, an intriguing vulgarian who
saw in his position the means to advancement. He had
found the friendless Duchess an easy prey and she soon
became completely dominated by him. It was he who
instigated her progresses and political *démarches*. Opposed to him was Baroness Lehzen, who rightly thought
that his activities were not in the best interest of her
royal charge. Her hostility was sharpened by the fact
that Conroy together with the Duchess's maid of
honour, Lady Flora Hastings, made fun of her German
passion for caraway seeds. Friction between the two
factions cooped up together in the segregated Palace was
continuous and, though the occasions of dispute were
trifling enough, they were the symptoms of a bitter
animosity which poisoned the whole atmosphere which
the young Princess breathed.

Such an upbringing, at once so strictly regulated and
emotionally so disturbed, would have crushed an
ordinary girl. It served to reveal that the Princess was
very far from ordinary: for her character only gained

strength from the ordeal. All the same, it profoundly affected her. On the one hand, the fact that she was so cut off from the world increased her *naiveté*. On the other, consciousness of her royal position increased her innate self-confidence. She took for granted that it was her natural right to be obeyed. So far, education had served to intensify the qualities with which she was born. But it also curiously modified them. The quarrels and hidden plots of which she found herself the centre undermined her sense of security; so that the spontaneous candour of her nature was checked and she became cautious and distrustful. Distrustful, too, of the person with whom a child should feel safest—of her own mother! For the Princess did not take the Duchess of Kent's side in her endless quarrels. William IV had been kind to her; now and again she complained violently that she was not allowed to see more of her uncle. About Conroy she felt even more strongly. Indeed, she actually hated him: and her hatred chilled any affection which she may have had for her mother. What made her feel so strongly on the subject is mysterious. Scandal had it that Conroy and the Duchess were lovers, and that the Princess had discovered them in each other's arms. There is no reliable evidence for this sensational story. What is more sure is that the Duchess and Conroy did plot to have the Princess's time for coming of age delayed so that, should William IV die while she was still in her 'teens, the Duchess might become Regent with Conroy as the power behind the throne. If the Princess found this out, it was quite enough to put her into a passion of righteous wrath. Anyway, whatever the cause, for

two or three years she had been forced to live on outwardly submissive and affectionate terms with people she
distrusted and disliked. The consequence was that,
continually on her guard and unable to give voice to the
angry emotions that boiled within her, she had employed
all her extraordinary power of will in teaching herself
to be precociously self-controlled, precociously prudent
and precociously secretive. Since she was incapable of
saying what she did not think, she learned to say nothing
at all; and to bide her time. Altogether, nature and
circumstances had combined to make the eighteen-year-
old girl who ascended to the Throne of England in
July, 1837, an extraordinary and paradoxical mixture:
blending a child's simplicity and a child's uninhibited
violence of feeling with the self-command of a mature
woman and the unhesitating authority of a born
monarch.

This last quality showed itself at once, and alarmingly.
"Since it has pleased providence to place me in this
situation," runs the entry in her diary on the day of her
accession, "I shall do my utmost to fulfill my duty towards my country; I am very young and perhaps in
many, though not all things, inexperienced. But I am
sure that very few have more real good will and more
real desire to do what is fit and right than I have." There
was no doubt in her mind that one particular course of
action was fit and right. It was all over for the Duchess
of Kent and her schemes. Already, when William IV lay
dying, the Princess had taken the opportunity to have a
blazing row about Conroy with her mother; with the
result that the Duchess, so rumour ran, asserted her

parental rights and locked her daughter up in her room. It was foolish of her, she always was foolish. On her accession the Queen took action. Conroy was given a annuity but banished from her presence, and the Duchess put firmly in her place. She asked, so the story runs, if there was anything she could do for her daughter. "I should like to be left alone," replied the Queen. Not only did she order that her bed should be removed out of the Duchess's room at once, but she also had dinner by herself. However, she did not attempt to rely completely on her own resources. Instinctively she looked about for someone to guide her steps through the unknown world in which she found herself. This came partly from consciousness of her own inexperience, but still more from her extreme femininity, a femininity which made her, for all her strength of will, the reverse of independent-minded in coming to a judgment on general and impersonal matters. The fact that she was a woman also meant she sought for her guide among the male sex. For the time being indeed, sex in its extreme manifestations was latent in her. She was emotionally at the schoolgirl stage, looking less for a lover than for a hero, for some wise, benignant, fatherly figure on whom she could pour out all her youthful capacity for admiration. Other girls find such a man in some sympathetic schoolmaster or kindly clergyman: Queen Victoria found it in her Prime Minister.

Indeed, no one could have filled the role better. For in addition to being wise and benignant, he was also extremely handsome, an accomplished master in the art of pleasing women, and one of the most fascinating talkers in Europe. As a matter of fact the Queen does not seem to have wholly realized how much of his attraction for her was due to these less serious qualities. In her diary she harps on his moral virtues; "a most truly honest, straightforward and noble-minded man," she notes, "there are not many like him in this world of deceit." Above all, not Sir John Conroy she implies! And certainly, after Conroy it must have been pleasant to deal with someone who was a gentleman in the highest sense of that old-fashioned word. But all Melbourne's virtues could not have made the impression on her that they did, had they not been enhanced by his dark, charming eyes, his virile elegance and his light ironic sweetness. After all, it was soon to appear that she much preferred him to the praiseworthy Sir Robert Peel, as in later years she was to prefer Disraeli to Gladstone. These are not the sentiments of one who, whatever her avowed principles, does in fact set solemn conscientious virtue above the charms and the graces. Perhaps, like many of the professionally respectable, Queen Victoria felt unexpectedly exhilarated by the company of those who looked on the moral law in a more light-hearted spirit than she was able to do herself. Whatever the reason, Melbourne did exactly satisfy the Queen's emotional needs at this phase in her development. He became the object of her schoolgirl hero-worship; and this, like everything else about her, was more single-mindedly extreme than an ordinary school-girl could feel. People noticed that her eyes followed him wherever he went and that, if he left the room, an involuntary sigh escaped her lips.

He was equally drawn to her. Now that he was cut

off from Mrs. Norton there was no woman in his life: and he could not do without one. No longer, however, did he wish to take on the role of lover, even in the most platonic sense of the word: he was too old. On the other hand, with age, his frustrated paternal instinct more and more felt the need of an outlet. He had reached the stage in life when a man of his type tends to turn for emotional satisfaction to a daughter; to someone to whom he can be a mentor—Melbourne had always liked being a mentor—and on whom he can lavish a tenderness that involves none of the ardours and tempests inseparable from most love affairs. The Queen supplied his requirements. Artless youth had always appealed to him; and in this instance its attraction was enhanced by worldly position. A young Queen is in herself a romantic personage, especially to a man with Melbourne's imaginative sense of the poetry of history. Exquisitely he appreciated the incongruous contrast provided by the childish figure and the august, venerable role it was called upon to play. Moreover, apart from her age and her situation, the Queen's character was one in itself to attract him. In most ways, no doubt, she was wonderfully unlike Caroline Lamb and Caroline Norton. But she did share with them the distinctive temperamental quality which had always appealed to him in women; the vitality, the positiveness, the high-hearted unhesitating response to life which were at once an entertainment to his own subtle melancholy scepticism and also its needed antidote. She added to them also an innocent straightforwardness which the other women in his life had not provided and which was infinitely refreshing to a spirit wearied and disillusioned by over fifty years' experience of the great world. "She is the honestest person I have ever known," he once said. "The only difficulty is to make her see that you cannot always go straight forward, that you must go round about sometimes." Finally, he responded to her charm. For the Queen had charm; especially at eighteen years old before the soft contours of her immature character had been hardened by care and power; the charm of her ingenuousness and her dignity, her literalness and her enthusiasm, her composure and her unselfconsciousness, her childish gravity and her childlike sense of fun, all mingling together in a comical, delicious Alice in Wonderland-like blend. Melbourne had the trained taste to savour its quality to the full. The Queen amused him and touched him and stirred his admiration and won his heart. For though his feeling for her was not so rapturous and unbridled as was hers for him, yet it went far deeper. He had been born with an intense gift for affection, but it had been starved of its proper fulfilment during a life-time; so that now, with a reckless completeness, he poured it all out on her. At once his sovereign, his daughter and the last love of his life, Queen Victoria inspired Melbourne with a sentiment tenderer if not more vehement than he had ever felt before.

As he felt, so he appeared. "I have seen the Queen with her Prime Minister," reported the sharp-eyed Princess Lieven in July. "When he is with her he looks loving, contented, a little pleased with himself; respectful, at his ease, as if accustomed to take first place in the circle, and dreamy and gay—all mixed up together." Other people made similar observations. So intimate an association between monarch and first Minister was too unusual not to stir comment. But the comments were kindly. The relationship was too obviously and too charmingly innocent for people to want to be malicious about it. They made jokes, but they were good-natured jokes. "I hope you are amused at the report of Lord Melbourne being likely to marry the Queen," writes Lady Grey laughingly to Creevey. "For my part I have no objection."

It was the climax of Melbourne's career. Never had he been so eminent; and never had he been so admired. It was right this should be so. For it was the first and only time that the public and private strains in him were working to harmony at one end. As we have seen, he was not primarily a public character. In spite of the fact that he became Prime Minister of England, he remained to the end of his days a detached spectator, a little outside the political scene. His nature fulfilled itself most significantly and most profoundly in personal relationships; and especially with women. Now fate had willed that his duty as Prime Minister should involve him in a close personal relationship with a woman: so that at last he was able to put his whole self into his professional and official work.

It also happened to be the phase of his life in which we know most about him. The Queen kept a diary. With typical self-command she managed, in spite of all the distractions of her new life, to spend time every evening meticulously recording the happenings of the day. The most important happening was always her hours with Melbourne: with the consequence that we find in her pages an intimate day-to-day account of him, such as we get nowhere else. It is a wonderfully vivid account too. For the Queen was a born reporter. Her untiring interest in life and her taste for detail made her notice so much; while her literalness, her candour and her careful accuracy stopped her from colouring or altering what she noticed, in any way. When she came to describe Lord M.—so she always referred to him—the intensity of her feeling increased her natural powers. She observed him with the closeness of a Boswell. Indeed, there are moments when the Queen does oddly remind us of Boswell; an innocent schoolgirl Boswell, but with the same surprising mixture of *naiveté* and perceptiveness, unselfconscious enthusiasm and native shrewdness. Inevitably her picture has its limitations. She does not give us the whole Melbourne; but, rather, the bowdlerized version of him, which was all he was able, with propriety, to present to her view. Melbourne could not swear or lounge about, or put his feet up on the sofa at Buckingham Palace as he could at Brooks's Club. Instead, seated upright on a stiff little chair, he listened and replied to her quietly and in terms which he took care to keep strictly decorous. The matter of his talk was similarly modified. His "dashing opinions", his paradoxes and audacities appear in softened form. Nor could he exhibit to her either the depths of his scepticism, or the full freedom of his moral views. "He is so truly excellent and moral," exclaims the Queen in lyrical approval, "he has such a strong feeling against immorality and wickedness!"

All this meant his imposing such a change on his habits and manners that people both then and since have wondered that he did not feel himself intolerably irked

and cramped. How could he, they ask, after the sophisticated ease of social life at Holland and Devonshire House,
put up with the mixture of nursery simplicity and court
stiffness which surrounded the Queen? In point of fact,
he does not seem to have minded it a bit. He had had
enough of Holland and Devonshire Houses to last him a
life-time. He was glad of a change. The nursery atmosphere soothed and refreshed his spirit inexpressibly. As
for the court stiffness, Melbourne was so practised a man
of the world, so supple to respond to an alteration in
social atmosphere, that he adapted himself to it without
difficulty or effort.

Nor, in fact, did he have to suppress any essential
characteristics of his personality. Shakespeare is unmistakably Shakespeare, even in Bowdler's version: Melbourne
is unmistakably Melbourne, even when seen through the
eyes of the eighteen-year-old Queen Victoria. Some
important aspects of his nature, indeed, found scope to
show themselves in her company as they did not find it
at Holland House. Mankind relaxes in the nursery:
Melbourne could give rein there to his sensitive tenderness, his taste for gay, whimsical nonsense, and his playful
interest in little things in a way that is not revealed in any
other descriptions of him. These things were just as
characteristic of him, as his oaths and his paradoxes.
Moreover, the basic attitude to life that came out in his
talks with the Queen is the same as that in his letters to his
colleagues, though it is less trenchantly expressed. Even
the moralism she noticed in him was not an inconsistency.
No doubt he thought it right to impress orthodox moral
views upon her: for experience under George IV and

William IV had taught him that it was much better for the monarchy that it should be respectable. Besides he appreciated the charm of her innocence so affectionately that he shrank from the idea of its being tarnished. Yet when it came to advising her as to what she ought to think or do in particular and practical issues, he did not take an uncomfortably moral line. She disliked Lord Lyndhurst, she once said to him, because he was a bad man. "Do you dislike all bad men?" said Melbourne, amused, "for that comprises a large number!" He was always for tolerance: always he warned her against expecting too much from anyone or anything. While, over the whole texture of his talk sparkled, though with a tempered gleam, the light of his irrepressible irony.

The Queen did not always perceive its presence. But that only adds to the reader's fun. It is impossible not to smile at the contrast between the joyous ambiguity of some of Melbourne's remarks and the artless gravity with which they are recorded. The subject of the new railroads comes up. "People who talk much of railroads and bridges are generally Liberals," says Melbourne: conscientiously the Queen notes down this valuable item of political information. Or the conversation turned on the Irvingite sect who proclaimed that they had been vouchsafed a divine revelation; "People should be quite sure," said Melbourne, "when they have any of these revelations from *what* quarter they come!" Once again the Queen wrote his words down as an important point to be remembered. Or, "I observed to Lord Melbourne," she writes, "that there were not many good preachers. He replied in the affirmative and added, 'But there are not

many good anything', which is *very true*!" One day she
asked him if she ought to go to church twice on Sunday,
and he answered that it was unnecessary. "George III,
Lord M. says, never went twice though a strict man, and
was not at all for these puritanical notions; and he is the
man, Lord M. says, to look to in all these matters."

More often, however, the Queen realizes when Melbourne is saying something amusing and laughs delightedly in response. But she is not always clear as to
what exactly she is laughing at. All she knows for certain
is that Lord M. is being "funny". "Spoke of my having
got a letter from Feodore"—her cousin who had just
returned home after paying the Queen a visit—"Lord M.
said funnily, 'When these people get back among their
children they do not dress, and there is nothing so bad for
a woman';" or, discussing young Lord Douro's engagement, "They said Lord Douro had been out shopping
with the young lady; Lord M. said, 'Shopping is very
demonstrative', which made us all laugh": or, "He
examined my bouquet and talked of forcing flowers, and
said in his funny way, 'Forcing flowers is questionable'."

One is tempted to go on quoting for ever. Indeed, the
story of Melbourne's relation with the Queen confronts
his biographer with a peculiar difficulty. Up till then
he has had to construct his image of his subject's personality from scraps of information scattered few and far
between, over political diaries, reports of public speeches
and the records of ministerial negotiations. Now,
suddenly, he is presented with a document, every para-
graph of which contains something to enrich and
amplify his portrait. He longs to put everything in. But

to do so would mean including so much that the proportion of his general design would be fatally distorted. All he can do is, as it were, to let the reader look over his shoulder while, pausing now and again, he turns the pages of the Queen's diary.

There the idyllic tale of their first years together unfolds itself. For idyllic it is. There is something tranquil and garden-like about its atmosphere; and fresh too. Melbourne at this stage of his history has been aptly and beautifully described as an "Autumn rose". But he is an autumn rose blooming miraculously in springtime, the green, budding springtime of the new Victorian epoch, all ribbons and muslin frills and girlish smiles and tears and blushes and propriety. Vernal sunshine softly irradiates the stately background of court ceremonial, against which move the two figures entrancedly absorbed in each other; the distinguished elderly gentleman bending forward in respectful devotion and the child Queen gazing rapt and eager up at him; and now her brows are knit with the effort of concentration as she tries to grasp some point in the British Constitution which he is explaining to her, and now she breaks into a peal of laughter, showing her little rosy gums, as he makes one of his unexpected comical remarks, and he responding, throws back his head in one of his own rollicking laughs. Sometimes the scene is Buckingham Palace, sometimes battlemented Windsor: for a week or two in October, 1837, it is the incongruously exotic flamboyance of George IV's pavilion at Brighton. We see the pair in the morning alone in her little sitting-room—she in a chair, he in another "or on a sofa close to me"; we see them

cantering together through the turfy glades of Richmond
or Windsor Parks; we see them in the evening bent over
the chessboard or seated at a lamp-lit table beneath the
shadows of the high palace ceiling, looking at albums of
prints representing historical figures, or after paintings
by Old Masters. There were the great public occasions
too; the Military Review at Windsor Park where from a
carriage he watched her riding in flowing habit and with
bright, proud glance down the red-coated lines of troops;
and the Eton festival of Montem when they drove down
together to be welcomed by the boys gallantly tricked
out in military uniform and Cavalier fancy dress; and
the opening of Parliament when she read her speech
from the throne and he stood at its steps listening; and,
above all, the Coronation. Melbourne carried the Sword
of State in the procession. "He looked awkward and
uncouth," said the young Disraeli, satirically observing
the scene, "with his coronet cocked over his nose and his
robes under his feet, holding the Sword of State like a
butcher." But not thus did the Queen see him. "My
excellent Lord Melbourne who stood very close to me
during the whole ceremony was completely overcome
. . . he gave me *such* a kind, and I may say, *fatherly* look."

For however crowded and official the scene she is
describing, he is always in the picture, and more often
than not in its centre. She noticed every fleeting nuance
of his moods, every typical detail of his appearance,
habits and manner; the odd, comical grimaces he made
expressive of disgust or amusement; the size of his
appetite, "He has eaten three chops and a grouse for
breakfast," she relates on one occasion; his description

of his room, "all wax and ink, where I sit up to my neck in books"; the fact that he is wearing a new olive-green velvet waistcoat; how absent-minded he became when tired and overworked—suddenly going off to sleep in company, or talking to himself in an unintelligible murmur so that at first she finds herself looking round, thinking that he is addressing her; his old-fashioned way of pronouncing his words, "goold" and "Room" for gold and Rome. Above all, she notices what he says. Nine-tenths of the diary is a record of Melbourne's conversation.

It was of a very varied kind. Much of it was necessarily about business. Every day he brought her the news of what was happening in Cabinet and Parliament; how John Russell was making difficulties about the ballot question, or Brougham trying to trip up the Government in debate in the House of Lords. There was the foreign news too: a hitch was occurring in our relations with Portugal, or there was trouble arising in our Jamaican and Canadian Colonies. To make these things clear, generally entailed some account of previous events, and explanation of the wider issues involved. Melbourne found himself giving informal instruction to the Queen about the working of the English political system, or the recent history of the Continent. He also put her in the know about the characters of the public men, English and foreign, she might have to deal with. "John Russell," he said, "has feeling but he don't show it, his manner is rather short"; Lord Grey had not a bad temper but flew into a passion when you first told him anything; "The Duke of Wellington is amazingly sensible to attention.

Nothing pleases him so much as when one asks his opinion about anything"; "Lord Stanley is a man of great abilities but says things out of place and just what he ought not to say"; "Lord Howick has a fretful, uneasy temper, but is better than he used to be"; M. Sebastiani, the French Ambassador, "slow and pompous, but clear and clever"; Don Migual di Alava, the Spanish General, had "that very open, honest manner which is never to be trusted".

Melbourne was, in fact, giving her a thorough political education. He did it very well, explaining things in a brief, colloquial, simple way which was easy for her to understand and not at all boring; and often illuminating his point by some lively anecdote which helped her to remember it. He was also careful not to appear to condescend to her ignorance. Alike in his talk and his letters, he addresses her on terms of equality and with an implied respect for her judgment. The substance of what he said was also adapted to suit her special requirements. He did not try to give her a political philosophy; there is nothing in the diaries about the theory of constitutional monarchy, or the trend and deeper significance of world events. The Queen's mind, Melbourne realized, was too concrete to grasp such things and besides, though he much enjoyed speculating about them himself, he had long ago given up thinking it served any useful purpose. What the Queen needed, in his view, was practical guidance as to what line she ought to pursue in the conduct of day to day business. This mainly meant for Melbourne any line which kept things running smoothly. To help her achieve this end he sought all the time to cultivate two qualities in her. The first was good will. If the Queen could be persuaded to like a man or, at any rate, to see his point of view, she would find him easier to get on with. In consequence, though Melbourne always told her frankly what he thought about people, his tone in speaking of them, except in a few instances like that of Don Migual di Alava, was friendly. He says what he can in their favour. And the few general maxims that do fall from his lips are on the side of sympathetic tolerance. "If people are made to do what they dislike, you must allow for a little ill-humour"; and "everything works for the best, even the worst intentions"; and "it is idle to talk to people of their faults, for, if they knew them, they wouldn't commit them"; and "if you want to influence a person you must not begin by reprimanding him". This last also illustrates the second quality he sought to instil into her, which was tact—this all the more perhaps because he realized that it is rarely found in young and truthful people. Clumsiness, he thought, was often as fatal as ill will. Emphatically he quotes to her the French saying, "C'est les maladroits qui sont malheureux".

He does allow his tone to grow sharper when he talks about doctrinaires and doctrinaire schemes, especially radical ones. Wilberforce, he told her, was actuated by good opinions, "but they were very uncomfortable opinions for those he acted with," and he could not bear the proposal to establish Normal schools for educating schoolmasters. "You will see, they will breed the most conceited set of blockheads ever known," he exclaimed, "and will be of no use whatever. . . . Walter Scott was quite right when he said 'Why bother the poor? Leave them alone'." Even these caustic remarks, however, went along with his wish to impress upon her the necessity to make things easier for other people. The type of school-master likely to be produced by the Normal schools would only create quarrelling and discontent; the poor should not be bothered because it was of the first importance that nobody should be bothered: it was mistaken of Wilberforce to insist on his principles, if this involved disregarding the difficulty in which they might involve his colleagues. For, as he told the Queen, "Nobody should be troublesome: they should be made to realize that it is the worst thing there is."

He was her social as well as her political tutor. The Queen felt herself in need of one. Both in conversation and in letters she asked his advice about every detail of her social life. Who should she ask to meet Sir Robert Peel? Was the Duke of Sussex likely to get on with Lord and Lady Cowley? Was she to grant Lord Amelius Beauclerk's request that the aides-de-camps be permitted to wear sashes with their court uniforms? She could not have found anyone who could help her better than Melbourne in solving these thorny problems. Natural talent assisted by a life-time of experience had made him an expert authority on English aristocratic and fashionable life; its traditions and factions and cliques and customs. Moreover, he was prepared to put the whole of his knowledge at her disposal. In the midst of all his other activities he always found time to give full answers to her queries. Lord and Lady Lansdowne, he said, would be very suitable people to meet Sir Robert Peel, but not

Lord and Lady Cowley to meet the Duke of Sussex—
he disliked Tories too much. As for Lord Amelius and
his sash, Melbourne swept the request aside. "It was
always refused by the old King as absurd and ridiculous;
as it is—particularly considering Lord Amelius' figure,"
he remarked tartly. Sometimes Melbourne proffered
advice on his own initiative. The Russian Ambassador,
he writes, will be offended if he is not asked to dinner
soon, and an official called Skinner may be hurt if his
wife does not receive an invitation—"she is, Lord
Melbourne understands, a vulgar woman, but it may be
as well to keep him in a good humour."

The Queen was more seriously concerned about her
duties as guardian of social morality. Anxiously she asked
Melbourne what plays were suitable for her to see, and
whether she should allow Mrs. Gore, the fashionable
novelist, to dedicate a book to her; and, more generally,
should she receive people with bad moral characters at
Court. Melbourne was equally fitted to advise her on
these subjects. For though easygoing by nature, he had
learned by bitter personal experience how foolish it was
to disregard the opinion of the world and how important
to keep up the right kind of appearance. His advice
shows that he had always kept two objects in mind. On
the one hand, the Queen should not appear so censorious
as to get herself disliked. On the other, she must do
nothing that might compromise the dignity of the
Crown or tarnish her reputation for virtue. As a matter
of fact, there was not much danger of this. Instinctively
she leaned to the strict side. On several occasions we are
presented with the unusual spectacle of an old gentleman

recommending a young lady not to be quite so nervous of doing something improper. The Queen need not fear, Melbourne said, that Sheridan Knowles' plays were too shocking for her to see, not even one called *The Love Chase*. On the more general question, he thought anyone should be permitted to go to Court who had not been proved guilty of immorality in a law court; "It is better to go according to what has been determined by a Court of Justice and, if there was nothing against them there, to receive and not enquire what their early lives have been." On the whole, however, he clearly thought her strictness was a fault on the right side. He will have a look at Mrs. Gore's book, he tells her, for "Your Majesty is always right to be cautious in such matters." And he was extremely pleased when she told him she thought that it would be improper for her to dance the waltz. "I think you are quite right," he said eagerly, "it is quite right!" Indeed, he took some steps of his own to stiffen Court etiquette. The maids of honour complained that Lord Melbourne would not allow them to walk unchaperoned on the terrace of Windsor for fear of making a bad impression on the populace watching them from below, and though Lady Holland was one of his oldest friends, he desired her not to come to Court, as he feared that the presence there of a divorcée, however distinguished and elderly, might be bad for the Queen's good name.

As the Queen and he got to know each other better, her reserve began gradually to thaw, and she found herself consulting him about intimate and private difficulties. She found the complexities of religious dogma very bewildering. Did Lord Melbourne think this mattered? For herself she felt that one could get oneself inextricably puzzled about such questions and thought it wrong to let this happen. Melbourne agreed: "It is best to believe what is in the Scriptures without considering *what* Christ's nature was. For that is not comprehensible; the Trinity is not comprehensible." The Queen was relieved. "This is all just as *I* feel. . . . Lord M's feeling is so *right, just* and *enlightened*." She felt all the more wholeheartedly comforted because Melbourne, whatever his own doubts, never showed any sign of wishing to weaken her faith. On the contrary he told her that a good Christian did not allow himself to brood on insoluble problems, such, for instance, as how was the existence of evil to be reconciled with the idea of a good and omnipotent God. Melbourne had grown into a very different man from the clever and iconoclastic youth who had taken an impish pleasure in undermining Caroline's beliefs during the first years of his marriage. It was not only that he would now have felt it cruel to disillusion the Queen, but also that his love for her stirred the depths of his heart and imagination in such a way as to set vibrating within him that mystical strain that no doubts could ever completely eradicate. We find him reminding her to remember to make her private devotions before her Coronation: and, at one of their early interviews, he read earnestly aloud to her a passage of scripture about the young Solomon, which he thought might bring home to her mind the spiritual significance of her royal position: "And now, O Lord my God, thou hast made thy servant king instead of David my father; and

I am but a little child: I know not how to go out or come in. And thy servant is in the midst of thy people which thou hast chosen, a great people, that cannot be numbered nor counted for multitude. Give therefore thy servant an understanding heart to judge thy people, that I may discern between good and bad: for who is able to judge this thy so great people?"

The ancient solemn words roused an echo in the Queen's heart. Strong character though she was, there were moments when her confidence failed her at the thought of the magnitude of her responsibilities. Sometimes she felt utterly unfit for her station, she told Melbourne. "Never think that," he answered reassuringly. "Try to do your best and leave the rest to fate . . . it never does when people think of what they ought to do and of what they do do."

She consulted him about other personal problems too. Her shyness for instance: she felt so nervous in company, she confided to him, and did not know what to say to people. Melbourne said that the longer one stood thinking, the worse it was. Better to say something commonplace and foolish than nothing at all! He was equally understanding about her difficulties with her mother. These had not ceased with her accession. The Duchess of Kent, indeed, soon lost any hope she may ever have entertained of exercising political influence over her daughter. The Queen's treatment of her made it too painfully clear that such hopes were vain. The Duchess still remained at Court for appearances sake: but she was assigned apartments far away from the Queen's; mother and daughter met, as a rule, only in public, at dinner or in the drawing-room; if the Duchess wanted to see her alone she had first to send a message requesting an interview. All these arrangements showed the Queen's prudence. But the Duchess not unnaturally felt herself deeply injured by them. Her ample bosom seethed with wounded pride, disappointed ambition and furious jealousy of the two people, Melbourne and Lehzen, whom she considered responsible for her exclusion. And since, unlike her daughter, she was not self-controlled, these emotions found vent in word and action. To have the prestige of her position, if not its power, might be some consolation. She therefore wrote a letter, addressed for some confused reason of her own to the Speaker of the House of Commons, demanding to be given the rank and precedence of the Queen Mother. In time this request reached the Queen who refused it point blank. "It would do my mother no good," she said coldly, "and offend my aunts." The Duchess also relieved her outraged feelings when she was in her daughter's company by saying offensive things to her, disguised as words of warning and advice. One evening she would tell her she thought she had got into the habit of drinking too much wine; on another that she was letting down her dignity by going so often to the theatre. "Mama is always plaguing me," exclaimed the Queen irritably. Meanwhile, the Duchess proclaimed her wrongs to anyone who would listen to her. "There is no future for me, I no longer count for anything," she lamented frantically to Princess Lieven. "For eighteen years this child has been the sole object of my life, and now she is taken from me." Her friends joined their voices to hers. Conroy, in particular, went round London announcing that the Queen had broken her mother's heart by her cruelty. These remarks were repeated to the Queen and added yet further to her annoyance. It was not made less by the news that the Duchess had, by irresponsibly overspending, got herself into financial difficulties which might involve her in a lawsuit extremely discreditable to the reputation of the royal family. The Queen poured this, and the rest of the long tale of her mother's misdoings, into Melbourne's ears, beseeching his advice and clamouring for his sympathy.

He found it was easy to give. He had already had a lot of trouble with the Duchess himself. It had begun during William IV's reign. Her political intrigues were a nuisance to him, so was her extravagance. The Duchess never seemed to have enough money for her needs and had no scruple in asking for more. She also demanded furniture for her house and jobs and honours for her friends, especially, of course, for Conroy. When she was not bothering Melbourne to do something for her, she was quarrelling with him. William IV she looked on as her active enemy, and Melbourne, as his Prime Minister, came in for a share of her hostility. If she was peculiarly annoyed with her brother-in-law she would refuse to receive communications from Melbourne on the ground that he, too, must be working against her. Melbourne did not allow himself to be moved by her goings on. Rows between members of the royal family in his view were as undesirable as were every other sort of row. He pursued his usual policy of pacification and strove both to bring the Duchess on to better terms with the King, and to keep on good terms with her himself. When William IV proposed forcibly removing the Princess from the care of her rebellious mother, Melbourne persuaded him to give up the scheme. And he discouraged the King from proposing any suitor for the Princess who was likely to be displeasing to the Duchess. Himself, he presented a front of urbane courtesy to her attacks and caprices and, though he generally found himself compelled to refuse her requests, tried to soften his refusals by presenting them agreeably clothed in a cloud of respectful compliment. On one occasion, for example, we find the Duchess asking that Conroy should be given a job at the Treasury. Melbourne answered that he feared Conroy had not sufficient experience, but added, "I lament this. But from my knowledge of your Highness's exalted character and patriotic feelings I cannot but anticipate with some confidence that your Royal Highness will appreciate the motives by which I have been actuated." It is unlikely that he felt quite so confident as he professed himself. Finally, during the last months of William IV's life, the Duchess increased his poor opinion of her by her intrigues to get herself appointed Regent. Ineffectively she tried to deceive him into thinking that it was the Princess's wish that this should be done.

Such experience disposed him to listen sympathetically to the Queen's complaints. He began to think that he had been mistaken, he told her, in persuading William IV not to remove her from the Duchess's protection. Indeed he did not try to disguise his opinion of her mother from the Queen. So far from objecting to this, the Queen seems to have found it an exhilarating relief. Together they discussed the Duchess's defects with zest and a startling candour. "Talked of my dislike of Mama," runs one entry. "Lord M. said that she was a liar and a hypocrite." "I never saw so foolish a woman," said Melbourne on another occasion; "Which," comments the Queen, "is very true, and we both laughed!" Melbourne also pointed out that the Duchess felt no shame in changing her mind and contradicting one day what she had said another. "This is, alas, too true, and a sad reality it is!" noted the Queen in a tone of melancholy satisfaction. Melbourne agreed that it would be a great mistake for the Duchess to be involved in a lawsuit; but he did not think that this would stop her embarking on it or appearing in court to give evidence. For as he remarked, "Ladies are very fond of law and of appearing in courts of justice and before magistrates." As for her pretensions to higher rank and precedence, he thought them, he said, a parcel of nonsense. The Queen told him that her mother publicly signalized the varying degrees of favour in which she held the Baroness Lehzen by sometimes bowing to her and sometimes refusing to do so. "As if her doing so or not were such a great thing!" observed Melbourne with amusement. "It is too absurd!"

All the same, he always worked to improve relations between mother and daughter. The Duchess, he used to say, was not primarily to blame for her worst indiscretions. Always they could be traced back to Conroy's influence. Moreover, he said that it would make a very bad impression on the public if the Queen was known to be openly at war with her mother. He urged her, however much she might be provoked, to behave to her with studious civility. And if she did shows signs of softening and made a friendly gesture to the Duchess—sent her a special invitation to a party or dinner—Melbourne hastened to tell her how much it pleased him.

These gestures occurred rarely. Even Melbourne could not persuade the Queen habitually to act so much against the grain of her feeling. But his talks with her about her mother, the sympathetic understanding he showed over this long-hidden and central trouble of her life, bound her to him with an added closeness. "As for the confidence of the Crown," she exclaims, "God knows! No *Minister*, no *friend* EVER possessed it so entirely as this truly excellent Lord Melbourne possesses mine!"

Melbourne's lessons in statesmanship and in personal and social behaviour took place mainly during his official morning visits. At other times the Queen and he talked for pleasure and about every sort of subject. Even then Melbourne was often educating her, though not deliberately. He discoursed to her about literature. The authors he singled out for special mention throw a revealing light on his own taste. As might have been expected, he admired Dr. Johnson's works. "They have deep feeling," he said, "and deep knowledge of human nature." Among poets he put Racine first for beauty of taste and sentiment. It was characteristic of the classic and cosmopolitan nature of Whig culture that Melbourne, unlike the Victorians who followed him, could appreciate Racine. This same Augustan purity of taste qualified his admiration of Shakespeare, though he enjoyed him so intensely. *Hamlet* was one of the finest of Shakespeare's plays, he told the Queen, but he thought its end awkward and horrid. As for *King Lear*, "I have always thought Lear a foolish old man," said Lord M.

They talked about the other arts as well. The Queen was fond of music, Melbourne not so much so. He had never cultivated a taste for it when he was young, he said regretfully. However, she noticed that he listened to her own singing with absorbed attention—this perhaps was evidence of his interest in her rather than his interest in music—and that he venerated Mozart. When the Queen said that she found the music of Don Giovanni old-fashioned, Melbourne clasped his hands and cast up his eyes in astonishment. Indeed he had far too much native aesthetic sensibility not to realize what music could mean to people, even if he did not respond to it intensely himself. "She has not much feeling for the beautiful," he remarked to the Queen about some lady of their acquaintance, "she praises the opera without feeling." He was more at home with pictures. In harmony with his liking for Racine and Mozart, he preferred the classic and ideal nobility of the High Renaissance Italian artists to the realism of Flanders. It did not surprise him that the Italians should never tire of painting the Holy Family. "After all," he said, "a woman and child is the most beautiful subject one could have."

Foreign nations, their characters and habits, were another subject of their talks. The Queen picked up some curious information from Melbourne about them. The

fact that the Indians burned their widows, for instance—
"not a good custom," Melbourne said: and he explained
that the natives in New Zealand, though a fine race, had
one unfortunate fault. "They eat men; and they say it is
impossible to break them of it; they say it is the best
thing!" The Queen was a little worried because
Melbourne laughed so much at the Germans, to whom
she felt bound by the tie of kinship. She told him she
thought he disliked them. Laughing more than ever,
he denied it. "I have a great opinion of their talents, but
not of their beauty," he explained. Melbourne's
favourite theme of instruction, however, was history.
Here it was that he blended useful information and
entertainment most brilliantly. He conveyed to her
easily and tersely the essential facts she ought to know
about the Conquest of Canada or the Civil War, or
whatever other famous events came up in the conversation, and made them live for her by the vivid way he
described the characters involved. His view of these was
characteristic. As always, he spoke up for Henry VIII;
"those women bothered him so," he remarked surprisingly
when speaking of Henry VIII's treatment of his wives.
But he condemned the cruelty of Edward III; and
deplored religious bigotry, alike in Protestant Edward VI,
Popish Mary and the rationalist Spanish statesmen who
had lately suppressed the monasteries and turned the
monks out to earn their living on the land: "To those
accustomed to pass their lives in prayer, to be told to dig
is hard," Melbourne observed with an ironical commonsense. Among foreign statesmen he praised the moderate
Sully, but spoke disapprovingly of Richelieu and

Mazarin: "Shocking fellows!" said Melbourne. He also made the past alive by his knowledge of the manners of past periods. Conditions at the Court of Queen Elizabeth were so primitive, he related, that gentlemen and Maids of Honour slept in the same room only divided from each other by a partition that did not reach the ceiling. The Queen was much amused to hear that the Maids of Honour petitioned that it should be made higher in order to stop the gentlemen climbing up and looking over. "It was a very right feeling of the Maids of Honour!" said Melbourne with his usual laugh. One evening he looked through a volume of Lodge's portraits with her. These gave him an opportunity of telling her about Raleigh and Hobbes, and Leibniz, and Addison, and other eminent persons. The Queen was enthralled. "I wish I had time to write down all the clever observations about *all*. It is quite a *delight* for me to hear him speak about these things; he has such *stores* of knowledge; such a wonderful memory; he knows about everybody and everything; *who* they were, and *what* they did; and he imparts his knowledge in such a kind and agreeable manner; it does me a *world* of good; and his conversations always improve one greatly."

It was even more interesting and delightful when they got on to more recent times and he talked about what he remembered himself, the social and political history of the last fifty years; about George III and his sons, and Mrs. Fitzherbert and Pitt—"a tall, thin man with a red face who drank amazingly"—and Fox and the Hollands and Madame de Stael with her square countenance and "fine full arms which she was fond of showing", and

Byron and the lovely Duchess of Rutland, and the rest of the statesmen and wits and beauties who had made brilliant the distant past of his youth. As the Queen listened, the florid ghosts of the dead world of the Regency rose for a brief hour before her mental eye, to haunt the decorous salons of early Victorian Buckingham Palace. Through the midst of them moved the ghost of the young Melbourne himself. His reminiscences of social life turned often into personal reminiscences; of his childhood and his schooldays at Eton, where he wore his hair long—"How handsome he must have looked!" thought the Queen—of Cambridge, Brocket and Melbourne House. The Queen was inquisitive about everything connected with him, asked him endlessly about his home, his mother, his brothers and sisters. Above all, she was extremely inquisitive about the woman he had loved, his wife. She could not very well ask him about her directly; but she picked up any information she could from others; notably the Duchess of Sutherland, who told her some such strange and shocking stories about Caroline Lamb, as to arouse all her royal indignation on behalf of her hero. "What a dreadful thing that his wife should have embittered his life, which it should have been her pride to render a happy one," she exclaimed, ". . . he has now the greatest horror of any woman who is in any way eccentric or extraordinary, which shows how very much he must have suffered from such a wife!"

Indeed he had. An incident which occurred about this time recalls to us how acute his suffering had been. Melbourne's cousin, who was also Byron's widow, came to live in Windsor in the first months of 1838, and he went to call on her. They had not met for many years, not, so far as we know, since the anguished period of his married life, with which Byron had been so intimately connected: so that the sight of her brought it all fresh back to his mind. In spite of the fact that Caroline had been dead for years and that Melbourne's own heart was now absorbed in another object, he was, so Lady Byron noted, throughout the interview, in an uncontrollable state of emotion.

Melbourne's conversations with the Queen during their leisure hours were only instructive intermittently and, as it were, by chance. Much of the time, delighted for a blessed instant to forget the cares and boredom of public life, he talked simply to please; allowed his mind to saunter irresponsibly in whatever direction the changing mood of the moment might suggest; modulating at every turn from fact to fancy, the playful to the pensive, the serious to the trivial, from cooking to history, from religion to feminine fashions. Even on this last subject he amazed the Queen by the unexpected extent of his knowledge. "Lord M. was very funny about caps and bonnets, he looked round the table and said, 'There is an amazing cargo of bonnets and things come from Paris I fancy. . . .' He spoke of Mademoiselle Laure; we laughed very much and asked him how he knew about her; 'They tell me of her,' he added, 'and I fancy she has beautiful things'." Melbourne's taste in clothes was fanciful, he told the Queen; he disliked dresses made of shot silk—"like chameleons, it looks so faithless." Fanciful or not, his opinions on dress inspired as much respect in the Queen as did all his other opinions. "He is so natural and funny and nice about toilette, and has very good taste I think," she writes. She notes his reaction to any change she might make in her appearance. "Lord M. observed my sleeves, which were very long, with astonishment and said, 'Amazing sleeves!'" She was also interested to hear what he thought of her pets. The grey parrot seems to have pleased him most. One day the Queen found him talking to it alone. "It is a sociable bird," he explained. About her dogs he was less appreciative: so little that for once she actually felt annoyed with him. "Lord M. said that Islay was a dull dog, which really makes me quite angry, for Islay is such a darling!" and she refused to agree that Dashy had crooked legs. Together they lifted Dashy on to the table and watched him lap up a saucer of tea. "I wonder if lapping is a pleasant sensation," mused Melbourne. "It is a thing we have never felt."

Thus whimsically and gaily their conversations wandered on. Now Melbourne would be telling her of his feelings towards children; how he liked their company if he could talk to them in his own way, but found it a bore when they were brought in to be made much of; now he was admitting that he had never finished Wordsworth's *Excursion*—"But I have bought the book," he said, "it is amazing when you leave a book on the table, how much you know what is in it without reading it;" now describing how he often interviewed people when he was in bed in the morning, because he got up late and thought that they would rather see him in bed than not at all; now he was explaining why he avoided having much to do with artists, "a waspish set of people"; now giving his reason for taking two apples at dessert, even if he did not think he was likely to eat more than one, "I like to have the power of doing so." Did not he have the power equally when the apples were in the dish, asked the Queen with characteristic and literal simplicity? "Not the full power," he replied humorously. Or they compared their views on Christian names— "Louisa is a fastidious name," said Melbourne; or on faces with large features—"I like large features," he told her—"People with small features and *squeeny* noses never do anything;" or on the song of birds, which Melbourne thought overrated; "I can never admire the singing of birds. There is no melody in it. It is so shrill. That is all humbug: it is mere poetry." Unexpectedly, however, he liked the noise of rooks. "The rooks are my delight," he observed gazing dreamily out of the windows at them as they swooped and hovered and multitudinously cawed amid the yellowing October trees. Was it some Proustian memory of childhood days in the Brocket fields that spoke to him in the sound? Or something romantically poignant and haunting in its wild harshness? For, as always, romantic sentiment mingled strangely in Melbourne with sceptical good sense and, even while he mocked at it, disturbed his heart. The Queen scolded him on one occasion for risking his life by standing under a tree during a thunderstorm. His answer to her sums up both this fundamental duality in his nature, and his ironical awareness of it. "It is a hundred to one that you are not struck," he said rationally, but then—his mind moving to contemplate the contingency in the light of imagination, "It's a sublime death!" he added.

He said the words with a smile; but it might have been with a tear. The heightened key of feeling in which he now lived kept his emotions always close to the surface, so that at the slightest touch they welled over. Easily and often the unbidden tears would fill his eyes; at an act of generosity, a word of gratitude, a tale of bereavement, at the pathos of old age, at the Duke of Wellington's chivalrous friendliness to an old opponent, at the sight of the Queen taking affectionate farewell of her uncle or her thoughtful kindness to the veterans of Waterloo. For, of course, he was most easily touched if she was involved. When she had a fall from her horse riding in the Park, Melbourne was thrown into an extraordinary agitation. He grew dead-white and "Are you sure you are not hurt?" he asked her again and again, as they rode home, "Are you really not the worse?" Most deeply and significant-ly was he moved during her Coronation when it came to his turn to go through the ceremony of paying homage. It was indeed, in a very special sense, a sacra-mental act for him; the eloquent symbol of that tender and sacred relationship which was now the centre of his existence. Beneath the immemorial arches of the Abbey the girl-Queen sat on her throne, her brows surmounted by the great gleaming Crown of State. Melbourne approached to kneel and kiss her hand. His fingers lingered on hers in an involuntary pressure. She re-turned it; he looked up: she saw his dark eyes shining with tears.

Tears of devotion; tears of joy too! For Melbourne's feeling for the Queen had released his emotional nature, so long frustrated of proper fulfilment, in such a way as to flood his spirit with a dreamlike happiness unknown to him since his far away youth; and which was all the more intoxicating because it came so unexpectedly and in the evening of his life, many years after he must have given up hoping for anything of the kind.

Alas! It did not remain long unclouded. It could not. For it depended on circumstances of their nature transitory. The Queen was growing more confident every month: as she gained confidence, she revealed herself more freely. With the result that Melbourne began to discover that she could be a source of anxiety as well as pleasure. She had the defects of her qualities. Feminine devotedness went along with feminine prejudice, regal dignity with regal imperiousness, moral strictness with intolerance, a child's simplicity with a child's unreasonableness. Further, force of character together with violence of feeling disposed her to be on occasion self-willed and headstrong. Her accession to the Throne strengthened these tendencies in her. It is hard not to grow a little headstrong and imperious if you are treated by everyone you meet as the most important person alive. Altogether by the summer of 1838 the Queen's character was beginning to display itself in a manner incompatible with an atmosphere of perfect ease and serenity.

Her change of temper was visible in her appearance:

213

she was looking bolder and more discontented people said. It was also apparent in her growing sense of what was due to her royal position. The etiquette of the Court, fairly slack at the start of her reign, was now tightened up by the Queen's especial desire. If anyone deviated from it, even in some detail, she noticed it at once and signified her displeasure by a sharp, irate glance. What did the Duchess of Cambridge mean, she asked angrily, by asking her to her ball and then not coming down to meet her at the door? She was indignant, too, with anyone who showed signs of trying to thwart or manage her. Her Uncle Leopold had gone on writing to her about politics. Now he was dismayed to find that his careful, tactful, considered advice met, as often as not, with a decided snub from the Queen. More sharply did she snub her mother. "I told Lord Melbourne," she writes, "that I had carried my point with Mama about coming up to my room without asking. She was angry at first. I had to remind her *who I was*!" Melbourne was a little alarmed by so formidable a display of royal character. "Quite right," he replied nervously. "But it is very disagreeable doing so." The triumphant tone in which the Queen relates the incident suggests that she had not found it so disagreeable. On another occasion Melbourne had difficulty in persuading her from formally rebuking the Duchess of Sutherland for asking Conroy to her house. He often found himself trying to curb her. "For God's sake don't do that Ma'am!" people would hear him saying in agitated tones. Sometimes she obeyed him: often she did not. Indeed he sometimes incurred her displeasure himself. Not that she liked him less. But her very affection for him made her more and more exacting in her demands on his time and attention. She hated him to be away from her. "He *ought* to be near me, it is his place," she wrote in her diary. She commanded him—he was indeed willing enough to obey her in this—to join her four or five minutes after she left the dinner table, instead of lingering for half-an-hour's relaxation over the port wine; she scolded him for being late in his visits; if he failed to come owing to the pressure of public work, she was seriously annoyed. One evening he excused himself for not having looked in at a party at Buckingham Palace because he had been working till eleven o'clock and thought it too late. The Queen did not accept this as a reasonable excuse. "He could have come perfectly well," she said. The harassed Melbourne tried to make up for such lapses by patient reasonable letters of apologetic explanation. "Lord Melbourne presents his humble duty to Your Majesty, and cannot express how deeply concerned he is to find himself restrained from obeying Your Majesty's commands, and repairing without delay to Brighton. Both his duty and his inclination would prompt him to do this without a moment's delay, if he did not find it incumbent upon him to represent to Your Majesty the very important circumstances which require his presence for two or three days longer in London. The Session of Parliament approaches; the questions which are to be considered and prepared are of the most appalling magnitude, and of the greatest difficulty. Many of Your Majesty's servants, who fill the most important offices, are compelled by domestic calamity to be absent, and it is absolutely necessary that there should be some general super-intendence of the measures to be proposed, and some consideration of the arrangements to be made. Lord Melbourne assures Your Majesty that he would not delay in London if he did not feel it to be absolutely necessary to Your Majesty's service. . . ."

Indeed, he could not find it in his heart to feel annoyed with her even for a moment. It was her stomach, he told her comfortingly, which made her feel out of temper—that and the strain of the life she was living, so unnatural for a young girl. She hoped he was right. Certainly she did feel nervous, as never before. It was this, she told him, that made her need him so much; this was why she was so unreasonably cross if he did not come. "I am so very sorry," he replied. "I will take care and come another time." Did she not worry him dreadfully, she would ask him? "Oh no, never!" he would hasten to assure her with earnest, affectionate kindness. As a matter of fact, she worried him a good deal: and, what mattered more, he was beginning to be a little frightened of her. Rightly; that extraordinary and tameless force of personality which was going to make her a great Queen of England was something Melbourne could not in the long run control. Already the ignorant eighteen-year-old girl was gaining the upper hand over the elderly statesman, in spite of all his charm and diplomatic skill and the prestige of his experience. She might listen to him and love him: but once she had made up her mind to do something, she did it—whether he wanted her to or not.

THE QUEEN: FIRST PHASE

This became dramatically apparent in the early months of 1839. The Duchess of Kent had a Maid of Honour called Lady Flora Hastings. The Queen had never liked her, partly for the simple reason that she was her mother's Maid of Honour, and still more because she knew her to be an intimate friend of Conroy's. So intimate indeed that at this very time there were some scandalous and light-hearted jokes going round the Court, arising from the fact that the two had travelled down together from Scotland in the same carriage. Whether the Queen had heard these jokes is unknown. But it is likely that she had for, in February, she and Baroness Lehzen were interested to notice that Lady Flora's figure was changing shape: and immediately their minds leaped forward to suspect a very discreditable cause for this phenomenon. When the Queen discovered that these suspicions were shared both by two of the Court ladies and by the Court physician, Sir James Clarke, she was convinced they were justified. "We have no doubt that she is— to use the plain words—with child!" she wrote in her diary in a blaze of righteous wrath: "the horrid cause of all this is the monster and demon incarnate, whose name I forbear to mention." With the Queen, to feel was to act. Such goings on must not be condoned: something must be done. Melbourne was consulted as to what it should be. As might have been expected, he recommended doing nothing at all. Whether Lady Flora was guilty or not—and Melbourne had no special reason for believing her innocent—the situation was clearly an extremely awkward one: and it would be better to wait and see what happened. But the Queen and her ladies were in far too militant a mood to be checked in this manner. The sight of Lady Flora flaunting it shamelessly about the Court in a condition more interesting than reputable was more than they could bear. "Mama is here with her amiable and virtuous lady!" the Queen wrote in her diary with bitter sarcasm after an evening party at the Palace. Accounts are somewhat confused as to what happened next, but the upshot was that Lady Flora was reluctantly forced to submit to a medical examination by Clarke and another doctor. The examination proved that the alteration in her figure was due to other causes and her character was completely exonerated.

Events, however, did not end here. By this time the story had reached the ears of Lady Flora's brother, Lord Hastings, who, not unnaturally, was furious at the insulting way his sister had been treated. Supported by his mother, the Dowager Lady Hastings, he besieged Melbourne with a demand for redress. The scandal, he said, must be traced back to its source and its author exposed. Meanwhile, Clarke should be dismissed. Melbourne was in a very uncomfortable position. As a just and generous man he could not but understand Lord Hastings's anger on his injured sister's behalf. On the other hand, he knew that closer investigation might well disclose that a prime instigator of the whole proceedings had been the Queen herself. To save her from annoyance and to maintain the good reputation of the Crown, he was prepared to sacrifice Lady Flora or anyone else. He therefore wrote off to the Hastings family in a curt, snubbing tone, saying that the incident was closed and that there could be no question of opening it again. Beside himself with frustrated rage, Lord Hastings resolved to make the whole matter public and sent the correspondence to the newspaper. The fat was now in the fire. The more scurrilous journals made the most of the story; disaffected politicians did all they could to make the scandal resound more loudly; and a wave of public indignation surged up in favour of Lady Flora. It was not until the Duke of Wellington intervened to lend all the weight of his venerable reputation to the cause of pacification that the outcry began to die down. But irretrievable harm had been done. Though the Queen's full responsibility in the matter was not known, yet she had been enough implicated to get a bad name. In the space of a week or two, her early popularity had vanished.

It is a very odd story: and one of the oddest things about it is the behaviour of Melbourne. Why, when he clearly realized that it was better to do nothing at all, did he not see to it from the start that nothing was done? Why, since he was an experienced man of the world peculiarly equipped, it would have seemed, to deal with delicate situations of this kind, did he defer to the judgment of an excited girl of eighteen and her almost equally excited German governess? The only plausible explanation is that he was powerless to do anything else. The Queen was shocked as only a youthful moralist can be shocked; and the violence of this shock combined with her age-old horror of Conroy to rouse her to a pitch of indignation into which she concentrated the full strength of her personality. Faced by it, Melbourne was too rattled to dare to make a decisive stand. Instead he temporized; while he temporized, the Queen acted. Afterwards he could only passively watch events rushing to their catastrophic end. He was at length forced by the conduct of the Hastings family into taking hasty action in order to conceal the Queen's responsibility in the affair. But even then, he was still so flustered that he acted with unwise violence and so made matters worse. The Queen's accounts of her talks with him during these weeks reveal him in a state of mind at once unsettled and fatalistic, typical of a man who knows that, through his own weakness, he has failed to assert himself when he should have done so. Sometimes he seems to be making light of the matter: jokingly he suggests that Lady Flora should be married off to one of his supporters as a way out of the difficulty. "I laughed excessively," commented the Queen, "for Lady Flora has neither riches nor beauty nor anything!" Most of the time, however, Melbourne appeared subdued and anxious. Well he might. He wanted the Queen to do well more than anything else in life. Now, for the first time, she was doing badly and, as he would have been the first to admit, it was largely through his own fault.

(3)

There was little in the political situation to cheer him up. At first the Queen's accession had proved slightly to the advantage of the Whigs. It was more comfortable to have an engaging young Queen on their side than a grumpy old King against them. Moreover, some of the general good will that was felt for the

Queen extended itself to the Prime Minister with whom she was so closely identified. Otherwise, the position of the Government was unaltered. A weak ministry of the middle way, threatened perpetually by the House of Lords on the one hand and on the other by the Radicals, it still maintained a precarious existence, partly by the favour of O'Connell and his Irish followers who thought they would do worse under the Tories, and partly through the connivance of Peel, who was biding his time till he thought he had the country sufficiently on his side for him to be able to come in at the head of a strong Tory administration. Melbourne, too, continued to pursue his policy of tacking and balancing, making concessions in turn to the right and to the left according as to which seemed likely to be the greater nuisance if thwarted. Himself, he disliked change as much as ever; and always opposed it as far as he could, in small things as much as in big. "Whenever you meddle with these ancient rights and jurisdictions it appears to me that for the sake of remedying comparatively insignificant abuses you create new ones and always produce considerable discontent," he observed to someone who proposed reforming the financial administration of the Duchy of Cornwall. "Delay" and "postpone" were still his favourite words, if any political project was under discussion. In one respect only was he changed from the year before. His determination to keep in office had grown stiffer than ever. For party loyalty and fear of revolution were now reinforced by a new and more powerful motive. He realized that going out would entail his own separation from the Queen, and in consequence the end of his chief satisfaction in life. He endeavoured to persuade his colleagues that they really had a respectable majority of the country behind them, so that it was positively their duty to go on in office as long as they could. And even if this was not so, he had made up his mind not to budge till he was forced. "I am for standing our ground, even with the majority of one," he told the Cabinet in the spring of 1838. All the same, he was in reality far too clear-sighted not to recognize that in fact the Government might fall at any time. A crisis on a major issue, and the Peers or the Radicals or the Irish could upset the whole apple-cart in the course of one debate. Besides, there was always the risk that the Government might come to pieces from within. His colleagues had not the same motive as himself for clinging to office: none of them had the luck to be an object of royal hero-worship. On the other hand, there were those among them who did not think that all reforms were nonsense; and so felt it ignominious and frustrating to be continually prevented from carrying them out. Further, this sense of frustration made them quarrelsome. A Government that feels itself ineffective loses its *esprit de corps*. Melbourne did all he could to keep his ministry a friendly, manageable group. However awkward the Radicals made themselves, he absolutely refused to placate them by giving them office: still more firmly he rejected the proposals that Durham should be admitted to the Government again. "It is impossible to be with him," he declared, "without perceiving not only that he can do no business, but that no business can be done where he is."

As a matter of fact Melbourne found his existing Ministers troublesome enough. Nothing could make Glenelg competent, Palmerston prudent, or John Russell flexible and tactful. As in William IV's days, it was John Russell who especially minded having to compromise with the Tories. Apart from the fact that he genuinely believed in a policy of moderate reform, his priggish, doctrinaire habit of mind made him morbidly sensitive to any accusation of inconsistency. He could hardly bear it if he heard that the Radicals were saying he was not true to liberal principles. The Secretary at War, Lord Howick, son of the famous Earl Grey, had also begun to be a cause of trouble. Angular, high-minded, energetic, and with a perverse propensity to look for faults in his own side, he was always interfering with his colleagues' business; scolding Melbourne for inertia, or protesting against the inefficiency of Glenelg. If his protests were unheeded, he threatened to resign. His natural intransigence was increased by the fact that he was religious in the new-fangled earnest, strenuous fashion, much deplored by Melbourne in his conversations with Queen Victoria. Many others of his generation were too. It was something to which Melbourne was so unaccustomed in young men that it bewildered him. "All young people are growing mad about religion," he lamented. What, he asked, was he to think of Hobhouse who distrusted a man's political opinions because he lived a loose life? The more the Victorian age got into its swing, the less comfortable did Melbourne feel in it.

However, in spite of these difficulties, political affairs

jogged along for the next year or so without running into any fatal trouble. A certain amount of legislation was put forward, notably three Bills dealing with Ireland. Like similar Bills in the past, they all came in for some drastic modification in the House of Lords. But only one, the Irish Corporation Bill, had to be dropped. The Poor Law Act and the Tithe Bill passed, though the Government found itself forced at last to give up the idea of appropriating any of the Irish Church revenues for secular purposes. This did not bother Melbourne who, for some time past, had been against it. He was a little more worried by John Russell who, in the autumn of 1838, decided that the Reform Bill of 1832 represented the furthest final limit in the extension of the franchise which his principles permitted him to accept, and insisted on declaring this in public. The Radicals who looked on the 1832 Bill as a mere first step on the golden road to full democracy protested violently; and John Russell was nicknamed "Finality Jack".

The end of the year was troubled by the first rumblings of a more formidable threat to Melbourne's peace of mind. This time it was Radical not Finality Jack who was the cause of disturbance. For some time past trouble had been brewing in Canada. It was split into two provinces, Upper and Lower Canada. In neither did the Colonists consider that they had enough to say in governing their own country. In Lower Canada feeling was made worse by the fact that the majority of the inhabitants were agricultural French Catholics who violently resented being ruled as they thought in the interests of mercantile English Protestants. The only cure for these evils was a drastic change in the constitutional system. If the Canadians were to be prevented from leaving the Empire, as the United States had done, they must be given some sort of self-government. A far-sighted English Government should have realized this and begun to think out a scheme by which it might be achieved. The existing English Government had not thought out such a scheme. It was altogether too big a job for the ineffective Glenelg; nor was Melbourne the man to supply the deficiencies of his Colonial Secretary. Such energy as he possessed was fully occupied in keeping the Cabinet quiet and the Queen happy. Moreover, he was in these matters, as in so many others, a figure from the past; a survivor from the eighteenth century when people did not bother much about the Empire. When it came to the point, he did in fact boggle at the idea of losing Canada; but he had no vision of the glories of a future British Commonwealth to inspire him to devise plans for preventing it. It is likely, too, that the failure of Catholic emancipation to pacify the Irish made him sceptical about the good which there was to be gained from making concessions to the Canadians. Anyway, for whatever reason, nothing was done and the situation in Canada steadily deteriorated, till early in 1838 both provinces rebelled. The rebellion in the Upper province was put down fairly easily by the Lieutenant-Governor, Sir Francis Head. His methods of doing so, however, were thought indefensibly unconventional, and when he came home, he went to see the Prime Minister in order to complain that he had not been thanked for his success as he thought he deserved to be. He found Melbourne shaving. "I saved the Colony!" cried Head. "And so you did," answered Melbourne placably; and went on shaving. After a minute or two he put down his razor and turned round. "But, you see, you're such a damned odd fellow!" he commented. Head's outraged feelings were not soothed by this reception. However, since Upper Canada was now quiet this was not, from Melbourne's point of view, of much consequence. The trouble in Lower Canada was more serious, and needed more drastic treatment. Accordingly the Government suspended its constitution and decided to send out a Minister armed with special and dictatorial powers to deal with it. Who should it be? After a vain attempt to persuade Spencer to come out of his retirement, Melbourne turned to Durham. This was a very different kind of choice. Not that it was a bad one. Autocratic and independent, Durham was far better suited to be a dictator than a Cabinet Minister. What was more important, he was, unlike Melbourne, a man of the new age with a vision, rare among his contemporaries, of England's possibilities as an imperial power. This, however, was not why Melbourne chose him. He had always had a low opinion of Durham. Now he told the Queen that he thought him a man of not even second-rate ability. The fact was that, as usual, Durham had been making trouble. Frustrated once more of a post in the Government, Radical Jack had begun to foment discontent among his Radical followers. Yet again, Melbourne thought the best way to deal with him was to get him out of the country. Another reason for sending him to Canada was that his mission there was certain to involve arbitrary and despotic actions of a kind likely to annoy the democratically-minded Radicals. They would be more ready, Melbourne considered, to swallow these if the despot in question was their hero Durham. The fact that he thought Durham third-rate does not seem to have worried him. Colonial affairs were not important enough in Melbourne's eyes to require a first-rate man.

Altogether the appointment was an ill-considered affair, and reveals where Melbourne was weak as a statesman. He was soon punished for his weakness. For, though Durham's appointment turned out to be to the advantage of Canada in the long run, it brought nothing but trouble to the Prime Minister. As might have been expected, Durham proved to be just as tiresome to him on the one side of the Atlantic as he had been on the other. From the moment he landed he behaved with a lordly disregard alike of the feelings of his party and the opinion of his countrymen. Every despatch that arrived from Canada after he had got there contained something to worry Melbourne. To begin with, in order to impress the Canadians and please himself Durham arranged that his first official appearance among them should be marked by an unexampled and spectacular magnificence. He took so much luggage that it took two days to get it on shore; then, attended by a huge retinue, he made his entry in an elaborate silver-laced uniform and riding on a superb white charger. All this, as Melbourne expected, shocked the English who thought that they would have to pay for it out of taxes. They were still more shocked when they learned that Durham appointed to important posts two men, Turton and Gibbon Wakefield, of notoriously bad private character. Wakefield had been in prison for three years for abducting a young girl, while Turton had been involved in a peculiarly sordid divorce case. Melbourne, who had specially asked Durham not to bring them into public prominence, was furious. "Considering feeling here, it is really inconceivable that Durham should think it necessary to compose his Council of two such men," he lamented to the Queen, clasping his hands and casting his eyes to heaven. He wrote, and in his most trenchant style, told Durham what he thought of him. "It is incredible that a man of common sense should show such an ignorance or such a disregard of public feeling and opinion as you have done in the selection of these gentlemen. If their abilities and powers were superhuman they would not counterbalance the discredit of their characters. They will materially weaken us; they will cause every act of your Government to be viewed with a jealousy and suspicion to which they would not otherwise have been exposed. I rely, therefore, upon your assurance that you will not give Mr. Wakefield any public appointment whatever, that his name will not appear in any public documents; and that you will not put forward Mr. Turton in any more prominent situation, or place him in any other post of trust or dignity. . . . Only consider how you injure your own private character by the association of such men with yourself and your family. Only consider how you injure the Queen, whose age and character demand some respect and reverence." This last sentence reveals the true cause of Melbourne's agitation. For him the one dominating consideration in deciding any course of action was how it might affect the position of the Queen. Durham, in neglecting this, had committed the sin for which there was no forgiveness.

In spite of Melbourne's words he continued to neglect it. He kept on Wakefield and Turton and did not answer Melbourne's letters. Instead, without informing anyone in England of his purpose, he proceeded to break the law. The rebellion had now been suppressed; what then should be done with the ringleaders? To try them for treason in the ordinary way would be unwise, for no Canadian jury could be trusted to convict them. Durham, therefore, had them transported by his own arbitrary ordinance to the Bermudas, a region outside his jurisdiction. There was something to be said for his action, but it was technically illegal. As such, it gave an opportunity to the enemies of the Government for which they had been waiting. The Tory lawyers leapt to the attack. Their protests were reinforced by a formidable assistant. For the last year or two Brougham had been bursting to avenge himself on the Whigs for having turned him out. During the last two sessions of Parliament he had quarrelled incessantly with Melbourne in debate. Now he came forward as champion of the age-old and lawful liberties of British subjects, and delivered a terrific philippic in his finest manner in the House of Lords demanding that Durham's ordinance should be disallowed. Melbourne listened to him with an expression of contemptuous calm on his countenance. "If I had said anything," he remarked later, "the fellow would have gone stark staring mad." Afterwards he rose to make the official reply for the Government. Durham, he said, was in an extremely difficult situation and the House should wait for more information before taking action. But he himself was too annoyed with Durham to put up a very strong fight; all the more because Durham had issued his ordinance without consulting him and had not condescended to answer his request for a full explanation after he had done it. The Duke of Wellington and the rest of the Tories rallied to Brougham's support. In face of their representations the Government gave in and disallowed the ordinance. When he got the news Durham resigned in a rage; but before he left he relieved his feelings by issuing a public declaration in which he denounced the Government for betraying him and pointed out to the Canadians how much they were losing in being deprived of the only British statesman, namely himself, who had their interests at heart. He must have secretly hoped, said Melbourne irritably, to create so much bad feeling that rebellion would break out again as soon as he left.

The Government awaited his return with trepidation. If this was the sort of thing he said in Canada, what was he not going to say when he got to England? Their fears turned out to be unjustified. The strain of idealism which was intermingled so strangely with Durham's egotism and ill temper rose for once to dominate his actions. His imagination had been fired by a new conception of the relations between England and her dependents; and with the help of the disreputable Turton and Wakefield he was evolving a bold and brilliant scheme for giving self-government to Canada. By the time he reached England his temper was sufficiently under control to realize that the success of this scheme depended on making up his quarrel with Melbourne. He did not behave in an actively friendly manner to him—this could hardly be expected—but neither did he start a campaign of vengeance. Melbourne was not the man to refuse an overture of peace, however guarded. Moreover, he had now begun to discover more about Durham's conduct in Canada: and he realized that intolerably though he had conducted himself to the Government at home, in Canada he had done pretty well. Melbourne, therefore, did all he could to persuade his infuriated colleagues not to exacerbate Durham's wrath by telling him what they thought of him. "Whether Durham's resignation was right or wrong is a question which may be viewed in different lights and upon which there may fairly be much difference of opinion," he said. "His provocation was great, and though I think he brought it upon himself by his rash and imprudent manner of doing things in themselves right, it required much patience and forbearance to submit to it." Melbourne had been the more able to recover his temper with Durham because, though he disliked him thoroughly, he was not afraid of him. "It is very odd to see the terror that Durham inspires," he said. Hysterical *prima donnas*, however gifted, were to the placid and worldly-wise Melbourne always a trifle ridiculous. When all was said and done, he could not bring himself to respect Durham. "What he did was often right, but always so done as to be totally indefensible"; thus he sums up his final judgment on the episode.

Later historians have not always agreed with him.

Melbourne has come in for a good deal of scolding from them because he did not put up a stronger fight for Durham and his ordinance. These strictures are unjustified. Melbourne must indeed be blamed for sending out Durham in the first place. It is not right to appoint a man you distrust to an important public job abroad just because it will ease the political situation at home to get him out of the way. But once the appointment was made Melbourne could not be expected to behave otherwise than he did. After all he did not share Durham's grandiloquent imperial dreams: so far as we know, Durham had never deigned to expound them to him. On the other hand, he thought that to fight to the death for Durham would almost certainly mean the fall of the Government. Melbourne's devotion to the Queen and his fear of civil strife united to convince him that his first duty was to keep the Government in. Moreover, as he saw it, Durham had forfeited all claim to extraordinary support from his colleagues by sinning deliberately and repeatedly against what Melbourne had all his life considered the first obligation of a statesman; personal loyalty to his party, his leader; and, in this instance, to his Sovereign as well. It was not from want of warning either. Melbourne had been writing to Durham for months telling him how mistakenly he thought he was behaving: and Durham had paid no attention whatever. Why then should Melbourne imperil the existence of the Government for Durham's sake? Since he was responsible for his appointment he was prepared to make a speech in the House of Lords saying what he truthfully could in his defence, but after that he would act as seemed best for his Government as a whole. Privately he cursed himself for sending Durham. "The fact is," he said, "that his mission is the greatest scrape and the greatest blunder we have committed."

It certainly weakened the little confidence people still had in the Whigs. Up till the middle of 1838 Melbourne had been able to feel fairly cheerful about their position. He even began to wonder if the Government might not be able to totter along indefinitely, as it had under William IV. No doubt it was a bore if they had not a comfortable majority: but they must make the best of it. "Equality of Parties makes government doubtful and difficult," he said soothingly to John Russell in August, "but it cannot be helped. It is a contingency that may happen, and has happened." Two months later he was not feeling so sanguine. "I am sure that there are some times of trouble approaching for which Your Majesty must hold yourself prepared," he wrote to the Queen; "Your Majesty is too well acquainted with the nature of human affairs not to be aware that they cannot very long go on as quietly as they have gone for the last sixteen months." Indeed, with the coming of autumn things had begun to take a turn for the worse. All the forces making for the downfall of the Government were getting stronger. The Tories were growing more popular, the Radicals more recalcitrant, the Irish more uncertain-tempered, while the members of the Cabinet squabbled more than ever. Sometimes it was about personalities. Glenelg did something stupid, and then Howick and John Russell began saying they would resign if Melbourne did not get rid of him at once. Melbourne, unwilling to be bullied, refused, and the squabbles sputtered on till in February, 1839, Glenelg resigned of his own accord. More often the quarrels were about policy. In order to win back the confidence of the Radicals, somebody proposed a progressive sounding measure; a Bill for educational reform, for instance, or for introducing the secret ballot. Melbourne opposed both, partly because he was always inclined to oppose changes, and partly because he wanted to do nothing that would exacerbate the Tories. As a matter of fact he had always been against educational reform. About the ballot his record had not been so consistent. In principle he was against it. But it was not a matter which he cared much about, and a year or two before he had toyed with the idea of adopting it in order to please the Radicals: at any rate it might be made an open question, on which ministers could vote as they pleased. This device, as a way of avoiding Cabinet quarrels, appealed to Melbourne. In 1839 he came out definitely against the ballot. Equally he resisted a movement inspired by the Evangelicals to enforce the suppression of the slave trade more rigorously. No doubt it was still carried on to some extent but he did not see how this could be helped. "It is impossible," he remarked in a spirit of chilling realism, "not to feel and to expect that religion, morality, law, eloquence, cruisers, will all be ineffectual when opposed to a profit of a cent per cent and more."

The end of 1838 was disturbed by the first mutterings of a more formidable agitation. The price of food had recently gone up with the result that the working class were restive and discontented as they had not been for several years. Liberal-minded people now seized on this discontent as a reason to demand a reform which they had long desired; the repeal, or at any rate the modification, of the laws which controlled the price of corn. The more advanced members of the Cabinet agreed with them. Not so Melbourne: he could hardly be expected to, for the repeal of the Corn Laws involved a change almost as revolutionary as the Reform Bill itself. Indeed, it was its economic counterpart. It meant that the landed gentry of England would lose that economic predominance on which their political influence ultimately rested. The country would be run rather in the interest of the new urban and manufacturing community which was drawn predominantly from the middle and lower classes. For this reason Melbourne, wholly a man of the old régime, was bound to dislike it. "I doubt whether property or the institutions of the country can stand it," he said. Still more was he against it just because it was a major issue and was, therefore, bound to involve a major conflict. Never, so long as he could help it, was the country to be disturbed by a row like the row over the Reform Bill. "Depend upon it," he said sharply to John Russell, "any advantage that can be gained is not worth the danger and evil of the struggle, by which alone it can be carried. . . . We shall only carry it by the same means as we carried the Reform Bill, and I am not for being the instrument or amongst the instruments of another similar performance!" He employed his usual stonewalling tactics; objected, temporized, procrastinated. His colleagues were not sufficiently united on the question to defeat him. For the moment it too was dropped. Meanwhile he sought to soothe the Corn Law reformers of the country in any way he could; scotched a movement from the Right to check the development of the Trades Union movement, and instructed ministers to use extreme tact in replying to anti-Corn Law propaganda. He says to one who showed him the speech he was going to make on the subject, " I should not consider it very conciliatory. It is reproval and condemnation, and there is in it a good deal of sarcasm. The middle and lower orders are very touchy and, above all things, hate to be sneered at." For all that his political ideas were old-fashioned, Melbourne's perception of his countrymen's characteristic weaknesses was as acute and as up to date as ever.

For the time being then, Melbourne had managed to get his way and keep going. But the effort of doing so made the early months of 1839 a dreadfully wearing and anxious time for him, especially as these political difficulties coincided with the trouble about Lady Flora Hastings. He was less able to stand the strain too, because for the last month he had not been at all well. Physically old before his time, his health had begun to deteriorate. "I am listless and ill and unable to do anything, or think— which does not suit the time," he said to Lady Holland. He could not sleep, he could not digest easily. His health reacted on his spirits. To his dismay he found that natural buoyancy which had carried him through so much trouble beginning to desert him. Melbourne, who for so long had been the most cheerful member of the Government, was now noticeably the most depressed. "I do not know what the deuce is the matter with me!" he sighed to the Queen.

(4)

In the ordinary course of things all this should have made him want to go out of office. In fact he did consider it. He was always talking about Charles V and Diocletian and other eminent persons who had chosen to retire from places of power to enjoy the peaceful pleasures of private life. After all, he had never been very enthusiastic about being Prime Minister. He did not like work, and he did not believe in power. Indeed, he would have been thankful to go—had it not been for the Queen. He hated parting from her and he hated giving her pain by doing so. For the very idea of losing him filled her with a sort of panic. It was not just that she minded being deprived of his company. She was convinced that without him she would be plunged back into the dreadful situation in which she had lived before she came to the Throne; alone in a dangerous universe without a soul she could consult and surrounded by secret enemies. The political situation presented itself to her in simple terms. On the one side was a great and good man, Lord Melbourne, who was always right about everything; on the other, a loathsome mixture of sinister Tories, revolutionary Radicals and weak treacherous Whigs. In all the Government quarrels she was his passionate partizan. How could creatures like Howick and John Russell dare to question the will of their noble leader? Melbourne listened to her, soothed her, assured her that he would stay in while it was humanly possible. But he cannot have thought this would be for much longer. In fact his downfall did come in May, 1839.

LORD M.

Trouble had arisen in Jamaica in consequence of the emancipation of the slaves there. Some Radicals thought the Government so feeble and illiberal in the matter that they refused to support them, with the result that the Government only avoided being beaten in the House of Commons by five votes. This was the smallest majority it had ever had: clearly its position had deteriorated to a point on which it could no longer deceive itself into thinking that it possessed the confidence of the country sufficiently to continue as its official leaders. Even Melbourne recognized it was time to go out of office.

He had reckoned without the Queen, however. On 7th May she got a letter from him announcing his resignation in terms whose restrained formality could not conceal the passionate regret that filled his heart. "Lord Melbourne is certain that Your Majesty will not deem him too presuming if he expresses his fear that this decision will be both painful and embarrassing to Your Majesty, but Your Majesty will meet this crisis with that firmness which belongs to your character, and with that rectitude and sincerity which will carry Your Majesty through all difficulties. It will also be greatly painful for Lord Melbourne to quit the service of a Mistress who has treated him with such unvarying kindness and unlimited confidence, but in whatever station he may be placed he will always feel the deepest anxiety for Your Majesty's interests and happiness and will do the utmost in his power to promote and secure them." A few hours later he came to say good-bye. The interview was extremely distressing. It was a moment before they could trust themselves to speak. Overcome with emotion the Queen kept his hand clasped in hers. Then, "You will not forsake me?" she sobbed out at last. Melbourne, his eyes brimming with tears, gave her a long, pitying, loving look. "Oh no," he replied. Within a few minutes she was in such floods of tears that for the time being all he could do was to speak any words of sympathy that occurred to him and leave her to collect herself, returning later in the day in order to discuss details of her future. In the interim he wrote recommending her to send for the Duke of Wellington and, if he refused office, to accept Sir Robert Peel instead. He added that he feared he must give up dining with her while negotiations were proceeding lest she should be suspected of intriguing against her new ministers. "Lord Melbourne," he ended, "felt his attendance upon Your Majesty to be at once the greatest honour and pleasure of his life, and Your Majesty may believe that he will most severely and deeply feel the change." The Duke of Wellington arrived the next day and, as Melbourne expected, recommended that the Queen should send for Peel. Peel came the same afternoon. He made a bad impression. A stiff, male, professional person, ill at ease in the company alike of royalty and of young girls, he gazed awkwardly at the ground, and replied to the Queen's questions with cold formality. "Oh!" wrote the Queen, "how different, how dreadfully different to that frank, open, natural and most kind warm manner of Lord Melbourne!" Nor were his words more reassuring than his manner. At the close of the interview he suggested that the Queen should change some of the appointments in the Royal Household in order to show her confidence in the new

Government. This stirred her besetting fear. Was he
meaning to set spies upon her? She demurred. Peel
took his leave. The Queen wrote off to Melbourne
describing what had happened and asking his advice.
Melbourne read what she said about the Household
appointments with anxious feelings. His sole aim was to
make things easy for her: and indeed, for this very
reason, he had already told her that a new Government
should not mean a complete change in her Household;
her Ladies at any rate would most likely be left alone.
She need not be frightened lest she should be left without
any old friends. But equally he did not want her to get on
the wrong side of her new ministers by making demands
on them which they might think unreasonable. Accordingly, he wrote her a long letter saying that though he
thought her in the right about her Household, it was not
a matter of the first importance; she had better compromise over it rather than risk an open break with Peel.
He was all the more anxious to avoid this because of his
old fear of political impasse. If a hitch occurred which
made it impossible for either of the great Parties to form
a Government, then a situation might be created in which,
for want of an alternative, a Radical revolutionary
movement might sweep the country and gain control.
Meanwhile, in the last part of his letter he did his best
to bring round the Queen to a more favourable view of
Peel. Though he did not care for him personally, he
knew it was vital the Queen should learn to get on with
him as, sometime or other, he was almost certain to
become her First Minister. Melbourne had tried to
bring them together before now. Once at a royal party

he had vainly tried to persuade Peel to come up and talk to her. Now he told her, "Lord Melbourne earnestly entreats Your Majesty not to suffer yourself to be affected by any faultiness of manner which you may observe. Depend upon it, there is no personal hostility to Lord Melbourne nor any bitter feelings against him. Sir Robert is the most cautious and reserved of mankind. Nobody seems to Lord Melbourne to know him, but he is not therefore deceitful or dishonest. Many a very false man has a very open sincere manner, and vice versa. . . ." The Queen wrote back thanking him warmly for his letter, saying that he was a father to her and that she would follow his advice in every respect.

She may have meant to; but in fact she did nothing of the kind. As over Lady Flora, she had got the bit between her teeth. When Peel arrived the next morning, trouble broke out at once. It was over the question of the Court Ladies. The Queen said that she was willing that the male members of her Court should be changed, but not the ladies. Peel was taken aback. The Court Ladies were all married to Whigs. As the head of a minority Government, he felt, not unnaturally, that he could not afford to take the risk of having the Court against him. If the Queen stuck to her point, he said, he was not at all sure he could take office; he must talk the matter over with the Duke of Wellington. His words had an electrifying affect upon the Queen. Who was he to think he could bully the ruler of England in this fashion? The wrath of outraged majesty rose to reinforce the will to resist already implanted in her by her fear of spies. Nor was this all. As she listened to his chilly protests an unexpected gleam of hope flashed through her mind. If Sir Robert Peel refused to take office, why then, Lord Melbourne might come back! Afire with mingled fury and exultation, she rushed to the writing table to pour forth to him an account of her interview with Peel. So beside herself was she that, forgetful alike of royal etiquette and of the rules of English composition, she burst out suddenly after a line or two from the third into the first person. "The Queen writes one line to prepare Lord Melbourne for what *may* happen in a very few hours. Sir Robert Peel has behaved very ill, and has insisted on my giving up my Ladies, to which I replied that I never would consent, and I never saw a man so frightened. He said he must go to the Duke of Wellington and consult with him, when both would return, and he said this must suspend all further proceedings, and he asked whether I should be ready to receive a decision, which I said I should; he was quite perturbed—but this is *infamous*. I said, besides many other things, that if he or the Duke of Wellington had been at the head of the Government when I came to the Throne, perhaps there might have been a few more Tory Ladies, but that then if you had come into Office you would never have *dreamt* of changing them. I was calm but very decided, and I think you would have been pleased to see my composure and great firmness; the Queen of England will not submit to such trickery. Keep yourself in readiness, for you may soon be wanted."

He very soon was. In vain the Duke of Wellington pleaded with her. In vain Peel suggested that she should give up just a few ladies; only those whose husbands were actually in Parliament. The Queen was adamant. "The Queen maintains *all* her ladies," she wrote to Melbourne, "—and it is her Prime Minister who will cut a sorry figure if he resigns on this." Melbourne was so agitated by her communications that he came to see her. Passionately she adjured him to back her: she trusted him, she said, to return to her if Peel stood out.

Melbourne felt painfully divided. On the face of it, it seemed his duty alike to his Party and to the Queen herself that he should advise her to give in to Peel. There was no chance of any Whig Government lasting long now: it could not be in the best interests of the Party that it should be dragged back, as the result of a court intrigue, only to submit to a second and more ignominious defeat, within a few months. Further, the Queen's reputation was likely to suffer if people thought she was taking an arbitrary and partizan political line. But if Melbourne's conscience told him to go, his heart ardently urged him to stay. It went against his every tender and chivalrous instinct to desert her when she said she needed him: besides, he yearned for her company. It is indeed the measure of his self-sacrificing devotion to her that he had been able to make himself plead for Peel so strongly. Now he hesitated and said he must consult the Cabinet. The result of his consultation was unexpected. Though most of the ministers had wanted to resign more than Melbourne had, yet now they were out, they found they did not like it. Was not Melbourne, they said, going rather far in his efforts to help Peel? When they met, and Melbourne read aloud the Queen's letter to them, their doubts became certainties. As the

R   243

assembly of hard-bitten, middle-aged politicians listened
to her naive, touching beseechings they were swept by a
wave of sentimental loyalty. Never, never, they cried,
would they abandon such a Queen and such a woman!
All this was too much in tune with Melbourne's own
secret feelings for him to stand out any longer. He told
the Queen they would support her. She informed Peel
that she would not give in about the ladies, he thereupon
declined Office.

Melbourne did not feel very happy; and still less so
when he discovered from a memorandum of Peel's
that the Queen, carried away by the frenzy of battle, had
failed to give him a complete accurate account of the
proceedings. Peel, it appeared, had only asked for the
removal of some ladies, not all. Melbourne was sufficiently dismayed by this information to make an effort
through a third party to persuade Peel to come back
after all. "He must have it, he absolutely must have it,"
he exclaimed. However, Peel refused. In a mood mingling apprehension, fatalistic resignation and secret joy,
Melbourne found himself in office again. Meanwhile
he did what he could to ensure that any blame in the
matter might fall on himself rather than on the Queen.
He defended his conduct in the House of Lords with an
airy flippancy which shocked its more earnest-minded
members. He was callous, he said, to accusations that he
clung to office from ambition or avarice, "For, my
Lords," he remarked smiling and chuckling, "I don't
altogether deny the truth of any one of them."

He could have done. The Queen alone had made him
return. For the second time, and over a more important

issue, it had been demonstrated that if she put forth the full force of her will, she could get her way with Melbourne, even though he knew it was a mistake. In this he was true to his character as it reveals itself throughout his history. Personal obligations had always meant more to him than general principles just because he believed in them more. Moreover, coolly sensible though his judgment usually was, yet when his romantic heart was fully engaged, it ruled his head. The most powerful force in his life was his love for two women, his wife and the Queen. And, as the young Melbourne had disregarded every other consideration in order to stand by Caroline when she asked him to, so now the old Melbourne disregarded every other consideration in order to stand by Queen Victoria.

THE QUEEN: FIRST PHASE

```
╔══════════════════════════════════╗
║                                  ║
║           Chapter VI             ║
║                                  ║
║          THE QUEEN:              ║
║         SECOND PHASE             ║
║                                  ║
╚══════════════════════════════════╝
```

(1)

"AS THE negotiation with the Tories is quite at an end . . ." wrote Queen Victoria gaily to Melbourne on the evening of 10th May, 1839, "the Queen hopes Lord Melbourne will not object to dining with her on *Sunday*?" Lord Melbourne was very far from objecting. How much he had minded the idea of parting from the Queen can be measured by the extent of his joy when he discovered that after all he would not have to do so. Even though he felt in his heart that he had been wrong to take office again, his error had not been of so heinous a kind as unduly to disturb his robust and good-humoured conscience. He found it all the easier to disregard its voice because his fear lest the Queen should have made herself unpopular by her action had not been realized. On the contrary, the British public seemed to have been as much stirred as was the Cabinet by the spectacle of the young Queen alone and gallantly standing up for her rights against an army of experienced and middle-aged politicians. As she

246

drove to church on Sunday she was greeted by a crowd shouting "Bravo" and "The Queen for ever". Melbourne arrived to dine at the Palace in an unbridled state of high spirits such as he had not known for months. He laughed louder than ever, twisted his curly locks through his fingers, knit his brows in comical, extravagant frowns and murmured delightedly to himself. "I like what is joyous and agreeable," he ejaculated, "I hate what is disagreeable and melancholy." Entranced, the Queen listened to his words and observed his every movement: admired his hair in its picturesque disarray and gazed with amused surprise at his frowns. Melbourne caught her eye fixed on him. He smiled and rubbed his forehead. "Never mind. I was only knitting my brows," he explained. "I know it looks tremendous! But you should not judge by expression; very susceptible people constantly change expression." His conversation that evening was at its most fascinating, ranging absorbingly and whimsically from the ballet to medieval troubadours, from the troubadours to the art of cooking, from cooking to the character of King Francis I of France. "He was the first who introduced that gaiety; he was the first King who had that gay liberty which has since been practised," he said snapping his fingers and laughing.

Melbourne would have been in even higher spirits had he been able to foresee the future. For his reprieve was to last for pretty well two years; and with it the old intimacy. Once more we open the Queen's diary to watch the day to day close-up moving picture of her relationship with him. All seems as before; the daily companionship and daily correspondence, the visits to

Windsor, the rides in the Park, the evenings spent looking at prints, the hours of business and of relaxation, the mingling, shimmering, enchanted flow of entertaining instruction and ironical wisdom and delicate sentiment and carefree fanciful fun. Now we see him sitting for his portrait on horseback—very comical he looked, the Queen thought, in a white top hat astride a wooden block—now in the Royal Box at the opera, whither she had inveigled him rather against his will—"That is too bad, rather a bore," he exclaimed in murmured protest when the audience insisted on an encore—now taking a lesson from her in the game of Cup and Ball; "I do it with perfect steadiness, patience, perseverance and tranquillity, which is the only way to do anything," he remarked. As before, he is full of information about history and geography; "Catherine of Aragon was a sad, groaning, moaning woman," he remarked, and that the Spanish were unpopular on account of their sobriety, "Somehow or other sober nations do not get on well with other nations." As before, he is always startling her agreeably by his unexpected idiosyncrasies and opinions. On smoking, for example, "If I smell tobacco I swear, perhaps for half an hour," he told her; or on bad habits, "If you have a bad habit the best way to get out of it is to take your fill of it"; or on old people dancing, "I consider when old people begin to dance at a party all propriety is over"; or on early rising, "For recruiting the spirits there is nothing like lying a good while in bed"; or on fires, "I always have a fire when I am worried or annoyed; it's astonishing how it dissipates trouble!"; or on feminine beauty, "There's nothing men get so

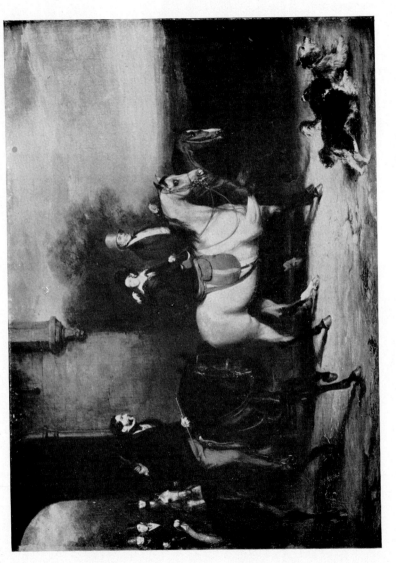

QUEEN VICTORIA AND LORD MELBOURNE
RIDING AT WINDSOR

tired of as a continued look of great beauty—very fine eyes for instance, nothing tires men so much as two very fine eyes"; or on foreign travel, "The first time you go to Paris, the Capital of Pleasures, you should spend four thousand pounds, it is not social not to"; or on gardens; it was natural that the Queen should be bored by the garden of Buckingham Palace, "For," he said, "a garden is a dull thing." His contempt for gardens did not extend to the flowers that grew in them. Every week there arrived for the Queen from Brocket a carefully chosen bouquet gathered from his own garden there. Their fresh fragrance symbolized the quality of his unchanging feeling for her; that feeling which so often brought the tears to his eyes and compelled him every now and then in the course of a conversation to bend forward and impulsively to kiss her hand.

All seemed as before! But in fact it was only now and again that he recaptured the unalloyed delight of two years earlier. Melbourne's second phase as Queen Victoria's Prime Minister was not quite so happy as his first had been. This was largely due to physical causes. The events of the spring had accelerated the decline of his health. Almost all the time he felt ill and tired: he suffered from lumbago and acute attacks of indigestion; the slightest worry kept him awake at night. Moreover, every month that passed he found he could do less. By the end of the year it had become too great an effort for him to give dinner parties or go out riding. Not only in the morning, but also in the evening he did as much of his work as he could in his dressing-room. The moment he got back from the office he would take off his cravat and put on his dressing-gown to ease his exhausted body. Philosophically he found diplomatic advantages in this change of régime. Having to go up so many stairs, he said, left his visitors breathless and thus forced to leave the initiative to him.

People noticed the change in him. He seemed to have aged years in a few months. "Lord Melbourne begins to look picturesquely old," remarked a Court lady. Nor was it only his appearance that showed a change. His growing weakness betrayed itself in his behaviour. Too fatigued to concentrate, he grew vaguer and more absent-minded than ever. Ladies sitting next to Lord Melbourne for the first time at dinner would be enchanted by the charm of his talk; then it would stop and he would begin murmuring and swearing to himself, or relapse into silent brooding which found vent in a remark wholly unconnected with the conversation round him. "Do you not consider," he suddenly asked, leaning across to address a shy young man opposite during dinner at Holland House, "that it was a most damnable act of Henry IV to change his religion with a view to securing the Crown?" Members of Brooks's Club were disconcerted to find Lord Melbourne standing in the hall remarking loudly to himself, "I will be hanged if I will do it for you, my lord." More than ever he was liable to go to sleep any time, anywhere; in the middle of an important Cabinet meeting, or talking to the Queen. During one evening's conversation with her he went to sleep three times. Gently, she teased him about it. "It is the sign of a composed mind," he replied humorously. Alas, this was not true. His health affected his nerves so that occasionally he would be swept by a sudden inexplicable fit of melancholy, during which he could not exert himself to speak, even when he was with his beloved Sovereign.

In fact he was too apathetic to do much about his health. Though he did not feel up to giving dinners himself, he dined out a great deal with other people, tiring himself by sitting up till two or three in the morning at John Russell's or Holland House, where on occasion he could still enchant the company by the breadth of his learning and the paradoxical wisdom of his discourse. And he ate more injudiciously than ever. "The stomach is the seat of health, strength, thought and life," he once said to the Queen; but he did not behave as if he thought so. Coming back from the House of Lords at four in the morning, he would consume a four-course meal and drink a whole bottle of Madeira; and the way he stuffed himself with pie and truffles and ices was enough to strain a constitution less impaired than his own. He felt guilty about this. Pork made him ill, he once informed the Queen after a night of in-digestion, but he never liked to own it. "What makes you own it now?" asked she. "A fit of conscience," sighed Melbourne. Conscience, however, was not powerful enough to make him change his habits. This was not primarily because he was too self-indulgent. At heart he did not believe any change of habits would make any difference. It was not illness but mortality, inescapable, omnipotent mortality, this was his enemy. He was like his mother. Magnificently youthful she had remained till late middle-age, he remembered, yet after sixty she had sunk rapidly. So was it happening to him. The Queen pressed him to take advice about his health. "That will not do any good," he said sadly. "It is age, and that constant care!"

(2)

He was right about the constant care. Here was another reason for low spirits. It was partly connected with his work. The political situation was more uncomfortable than it had been before the crisis of May. It looked much the same: the Whigs still pursued their trimming, balancing, middle way policy, making concessions now to the Right, now to the Left according as to which seemed likely to threaten its position the most: hedged about the Corn Laws in order to pacify the Radicals, gave way to Peel and the Tories about Jamaica and Ireland. Especially did they seek to placate the Tories because the tide of opinion in the country was now flowing more strongly than ever to the Right. However, this middle way policy now appeared ignominious, as it had not done before. Up till May of 1839 it could claim that it had the country behind it. Now the Government's position had been shown up as too weak for this to be possible. Furthermore, before May it was easier to justify concession on genuine political grounds. To Melbourne at any rate the Whigs had seemed the only alternative either to a dangerously Radical Government, or to a reactionary Government that might provoke revolutionary opposition. Now even Melbourne thought that there was not much danger of a revolution; most people feared it so little that they took for granted that the Whigs were just clinging to office for selfish reasons, surrendering to each side in turn merely in order to stay in, at whatever sacrifice of principle. As Melbourne wrote to John Russell, "By one set of people we are told that we are ruining ourselves and losing support by allying ourselves with the Radicals and the Roman Catholics: by another that we are producing the same effect by leaning too much to the Tories and Conservatives; probably both statements are true and we are losing credit on both sides." Himself, he did not much mind if they were. It mattered little to him that his Party's actions should ultimately be controlled by Peel, for at heart he agreed with Peel's policy. "I do not dislike the Tories," he told the Queen, "I think they are very much like the others: I do not care by whom I am supported; I consider them all as one; I do not care by whom I am helped as long as I am helped," he said laughing. Indeed, he had never been a Whig because he believed in Whig principles. His loyalty to his Party had been a personal loyalty. Now that it had come into conflict with the stronger personal loyalty he felt for the Queen, he threw it over without a tremor.

But, if he did not mind what people said about his Government, his colleagues did. The sense of their ignominious position was destroying what was left of the morale of his Government; with the result that they became increasingly irritable and unmanageable. More often than ever Howick objected, John Russell talked of resignation, Palmerston acted with ostentatious disregard of his colleagues. Nor did Melbourne feel up to managing them in the way he used to. He was too tired. He still went through the motions of being Prime Minister, read the State papers, wrote off innumerable little notes to his ministers. But in fact he exerted his will less and less. He did not give his full mind to affairs, evaded issues, shunned decisions, left the initiative to John Russell. Better make the Ballot an open question if this would help to keep the Cabinet together, he said; better give in to Peel about Jamaica if it would stop him raising the question of Canada! Better continue the old Poor Law Act for another year, rather than stir controversy by discussing a new one! Throughout his political life Melbourne had been accused of laziness—on the whole unjustly. But now he really was growing lazy. Fatigue made him yield to his instinctive desire to turn his back on disagreeable facts. But alas, it was seldom possible. Do what he would, the unending squabbles in his Cabinet worried him. It was not the attacks from outside but the internal dissensions that vexed him, he complained. All he could do was ineffectively to try and forget them and concentrate such energy and attention as remained to him on the Queen.

(3)

And even his hours with her were no longer the source of satisfaction they had been. He felt them too precarious for one thing; with the Government's position so weak, it seemed as if they might end any day. The sunshine of his happiness was fading to an evening glow over which stretched the ever lengthening shadow of his imminent parting from her. Further, the troubles that had a little clouded them in the early part of the year had not passed away. The Hastings affair was not over yet. Though the populace might cheer the Queen, there was still a good deal of hostility to her in high society. "Mrs. Melbourne," shouted a gentleman in coarse, mocking tones as the Queen and her Prime Minister stepped forth on to the balcony at Ascot, and as she drove down the Course the sound of hissing made itself heard; two fashionable ladies, the Duchess of Montrose and Lady Sarah Ingestre, were protesting their disapproval. The Queen was furious. "Those two abominable women ought to be flogged!" she burst out to Melbourne. He strove to imbue her with some of his own ironical indifference to public opinion. Popularity is a capricious thing, he was always telling her: he urged her to try and ease the situation by making herself particularly pleasant to Lady Flora. The Queen was reluctant; how could she, she asked, be pleasant to someone she did not like? Worse was to come. In the beginning of June Lady Flora became dangerously ill. The tumour, which had given rise to such unfortunate interpretations, proved to be malignant: within a few weeks it was clear that she was dying. Melbourne was extremely concerned. It is a sign of his obsessed devotion to the Queen that even now he, usually the justest and most sympathetic of men, could not find it in his heart to be fair to those who threatened her peace of mind. Surely too much fuss had been made about the wrong done to Lady Flora, he said; no doubt inchastity was a shocking thing, but such things did happen in families. He was acutely anxious,

however, lest the Queen should damage her reputation
still further by incurring any accusation of heartlessness.
At first she had refused to believe Lady Flora was really
seriously ill: but he persuaded her all the same to stop
all entertainments at the Palace, to send frequent messages
asking how Lady Flora was, and to give orders that
everything possible should be done for her comfort.
Melbourne also pressed her herself to go and see Lady
Flora. Not unnaturally the Queen shrank from this
ordeal. But lack of courage was never one of her faults;
once Melbourne had convinced her that it was her duty,
she agreed—and, characteristically, decided to see her
alone. The interview took place on 27th June. The
dying woman, now a shadow of her former self, and
with the mark of her approaching end written on every
haggard feature, gazed at the childish figure of her
Sovereign with a ghastly fixed stare and, clutching at her
with a fevered hand, gasped out her thanks for the
kindness that had been shown her during her illness. In
the face of this, her first experience of death, the Queen's
hard-heartedness melted away in a mingled flood of awe,
pity and bewilderment. "Poor Lady Flora!" she kept on
repeating as she described the scene to Melbourne, "Poor
Lady Flora!" When, ten days later, Lady Flora died, the
Queen burst into a torrent of tears. Her death was
followed by a *détente*. Conroy left the Duchess of
Kent's service soon afterwards: and, freed from his
malignant influence, the Duchess became more friendly
towards her daughter. Melbourne's continuous efforts to
reconcile them were at last beginning to bear fruit. Also,
thanks to him, the Hastings episode had not ended so

badly for the Queen's good name as at one moment it seemed likely to do.

The Queen's political reputation was another worry to him. The events of May had given him a fright, for they revealed what an unbridled partizan she was. Since the Tories might come in at any time, it was vital that she should be ready to accept them in a spirit of good will. It would never do for her to be thought of as a Whig Queen. Rather late in the day, therefore, Melbourne set to work to implant in her the impartial and non-party point of view appropriate to a constitutional monarch. He also spent a good deal of time trying to make her like the Tories better, more especially Peel himself. Peel, he said, was reported to speak very highly of her; and his faults of manner were due to awkwardness and in-experience. "You must remember that he is a man not accustomed to talk to Kings . . . it is not like me; I have been brought up with Kings and Princes." The Queen was not placated. Peel, in her view, had been rude and presumptuous, and the Duke of Wellington not much better. She would rather have a Radical Government than the Tories, she told Melbourne. Horrified, he explained to her that, quite apart from their faults, the Radicals had not a chance of getting into power. They had little support in the country, and their Leader was the in-tolerable Durham. Besides, the Tories were not so bad. Personally, he had found them reasonable enough to do business with. Were not they always altering the Government Bills in the House of Lords? asked the Queen. "I do not know that those alterations did not do them good," answered Melbourne laughing. Moreover, he pointed out that it was not politic to quarrel with the Tories; how could she hope to exert any influence on them if she treated them as declared enemies? He strove to persuade her to be polite to the Tory ladies and now and again to ask important Tories to dinner. She did not want them, she replied, at least, not this year. "If you do that, you, as it were, cut them off," he said. "Flies are caught with honey, not with vinegar." These efforts to soften her were unsuccessful. Causes to her were indistinguishable from the people who supported them. Whigism meant Melbourne, whom she liked, Toryism meant Peel, whom she disliked. Patiently, throughout 1839 Melbourne went on trying to weaken her hostility. In vain: nine months later we find her telling him that the Opposition was to blame for everything that went wrong.

It was not the only thing that she was obstinate about. Greville, meeting Melbourne, congratulated him on his skill in keeping the Queen straight. "By God, I am at it morning, noon and night!" he exclaimed with feeling. Indeed, the strain of the last months had affected the Queen's nerves as well as his, making her moody, on edge and more self-willed than ever. Her rumpus with Peel had left her extremely touchy about her royal position. At the slightest suspicion that she was not being consulted about a political appointment or a matter of State, she rushed to her writing table to indict a long, heavily underlined letter, indignantly proclaiming her royal rights and demanding an explanation. "The Queen has been a good deal annoyed this evening," she wrote in August, "on Normanby's telling her that John Russell was coming to Town next Monday in order to change with him. Lord Melbourne never told the Queen that this was definitely settled; on the contrary, he said it would 'remain in our hands,' to use Lord Melbourne's own words, and only to be settled during the Vacation; considering all that the Queen has said on the subject to Lord Melbourne, and considering the great confidence the Queen has in Lord Melbourne, she thinks and feels he ought to have told her that this was settled, and not let the Queen be the last person to hear what is settled and done in her own name; Lord Melbourne will excuse the Queen's being a little eager about this, but it has happened once before that she learned from other people what had been decided on." Any criticism of herself, too, in Parliament or the Press roused her wrath. It ought to be stopped by law, she told Melbourne furiously.

At the same time that she grew more jealous of her privileges, she began to rebel against such obligations as bored her. Why must she have ministers down to stay at Windsor when it was more agreeable to be there alone with Melbourne? Sometimes she said she could hardly bear the tedium of her official duties. Melbourne dealt with her moods with characteristic skill, apologized for any oversight and took care to keep her more closely informed than before about the details of affairs: more than ever he speaks to her as to an equal in these matters. He was extremely sympathetic, too, about her boredom. After all, he himself was often bored by politics; how much more a girl of her age! "You lead rather an unnatural life for a young person," he said, "it is the life of a man."

But if he was sympathetic, he was also firm. The Queen must get used to being criticised, he told her, and still more must she simply force herself not to show temper. "I cannot help it," objected the Queen mutinously. "But you must," he insisted kindly, "I am sorry to be so peremptory." Nor was boredom, however natural, a justification for neglecting her duties. No doubt being a constitutional monarch was a tricky, troublesome job but "you must bear it, it is the lot that has been cast upon you; you have drawn that ticket." Anyway, he said soothingly, her irritation was most likely due to the summer heat; he recommended her to drink more wine in order to calm her nerves.

Whether the Queen took his advice is unknown. If she did it failed to have the desired effect. Her temper remained uncertain even with Melbourne himself. Outwardly in fun, but with a glint of irritation showing through, she would scold him for his sleeping and snoring, his fits of apathetic silence, his tendency to overeat. "I said to Lord Melbourne that I could not bear to hear that he thought so much of eating and drinking— that it is *low* to think of such things," she writes. And she made as much fuss as ever if she thought he was neglecting her; more often, too, because ill-health and pressure of work was making it harder for him to see as much of her as in the past. Why did he only spend two days a week at Windsor instead of five as he had in the previous year, she complained. Why did he leave her so early in the evening? What did he mean by writing to say that after all he would be unable to dine with her? "The Queen has received both Lord Melbourne's notes;

she was a good deal vexed at his not coming as she had begged him herself to do so, and as he wrote to say he would, and also as she thinks it right and of importance that Lord Melbourne should be here at large dinners; the Queen *insists* upon his coming to dinner tomorrow." Could it be that he did not enjoy dining with her, that he preferred dining at Holland House? She had grown jealous of any woman who was reported to be his friend, and particularly so of Lady Holland who, from what she heard, sounded the sort of woman of whom she strongly disapproved. Melbourne teased her by telling her that Lady Holland had criticised her for trying to make her ministers more religious. "A very good thing!" retorted the Queen, "she must be a bad person to think so." "She is a great enemy of religion, but one hopes she may be converted in her last hours," said Melbourne demurely. "That is too late!" asserted the Queen severely.

Nor was she altogether happy about Melbourne's own religious tone. Now that he knew her so well, he was not quite so careful as at first to keep up appearances in her presence; so that she began to wonder if he was, in fact, so pious as her first impressions had led her to suppose. Certainly he always seemed to find an excuse for not going to church; and why, she asked, when he did deign to come, did he fidget and sigh so much? Melbourne was amused. "It is right to sigh in church," he said, "He who despises not the sighing of a contrite heart. . . ." The Queen was a little shocked to hear the Liturgy quoted in this flippant fashion. "It is wrong to jest about such things," she protested. Melbourne denied that he jested about them. About other things he knew he did, perhaps too much—but never about religion. And he strenuously maintained that her first impressions of him were right, that there was nothing dubious about his view of religion. He admitted he did not like going to church, but this was for a highly creditable reason; "It is against my creed," he said with a twinkle, "I am a *quietist*; it is the creed which Fénélon embraced and which Madame Guyon taught. You are so perfect that you are exempt from all external ordinances." One wonders what the Queen can have made of this blissful account of Melbourne's spiritual state. But she was still too much under his spell to be anything but reassured.

All the same, their sparrings over religion were a symptom. As the Queen grew up she began to reveal herself as possessed of a point of view profoundly different from that of her Prime Minister: and now and again hints of this difference cast a fleeting shadow over the bright surface of their intercourse. The easygoing eighteenth century in the person of Melbourne found itself brought up with a bump against the stricter age of which the Queen was the representative. One day, for instance, he happened to say that people were not gay any more, they were too religious. "But that is quite right," said the Queen, "how can they be too much so?" "I think there will be a great deal of persecution in this country before long," explained Melbourne, "people interfering with one another about going to church, and so on." "The world is very bad," said the Queen sternly. "I do not see anything so very bad," Melbourne protested. Another time he told her that his nephew

Spencer Cowper was rather a rake, "which is quite refreshing to see." "It is melancholy," answered the Queen; and she spoke with shocked horror of the hard-drinking days of the Regency, and the scandalous dissipations of her royal uncles. Wistfully recalling the days of his easygoing youth Melbourne sought to soften the harshness of her judgment. "But they were jolly fellows . . ." he pleaded, "times have changed, but I do not know if they have improved."

Such moments of dissonance between them were slight and they did not last long. The Queen was so devoted to her Prime Minister that she felt overcome with remorse the instant after she had been the least disagreeable to him. "I fear I was sadly cross with Lord Melbourne," she wrote the evening after one of these small moments of friction. "It is shameful, I fear he felt it, for he did not sit down for himself as he generally does, but waited until I had told him to do so. I cannot think what possessed me for I love the dear, excellent man . . . and he is so kind and never minds my peevishness, but is so amiable and forgiving." Indeed he was. When she apologized for plaguing him, "That's a good thing," he said, "it keeps people from being ill." His good humour bound her for the time being yet closer to him. Again and again in the Diary she reproaches herself for her ill temper, again and again protests her gratitude and love for him. To all appearances Melbourne possessed her heart as much as ever.

And yet . . . there are signs that his company was not quite the ecstatic unfailing delight to her that it had been. It could even disappoint her. One evening in June she was actually forced to admit that she had found an evening spent in Lord Melbourne's company had been dull! This was partly due to his infirmities. On the evening in question Melbourne had been feeling too ill to talk much. But there were deeper and more powerful forces working within the Queen to make her dissatisfied. She was very normal; and normal girls do not find all the pleasure they want in life can be provided by talks with elderly statesmen, however delightful. Now that the first excitement of being Queen had worn off, she longed instinctively for fun and gaiety in the society of her own contemporaries. Further—and this lay at the root of her restlessness and moodiness—she was growing up. The stage of schoolgirl hero-worship was passing; and there had begun to stir uneasily within her the desire for a more mature emotional fulfilment. She was hardly conscious of it but, in fact, when any attractive young man appeared her spirits rose. At the end of May the youthful Grand Duke of Russia paid a visit to the English Court and was entertained with appropriate celebrations. The Red Drawing Room at Windsor shone with the light of a myriad candles as, to the seductive lilt of the violins, the Grand Duke and his retinue of dashing young nobles, their shapely figures resplendent in glittering uniforms, twirled and leapt and clicked their heels through the dance, with all the exuberance of their Slav temperaments. The Queen enjoyed herself wildly. How delightful it was to be whirled round in the Mazurka by the Grand Duke's strong arms, she noted. How they both laughed as he strove to guide her through the figures of a new German dance, the *Gross Vater*—and how

dreadfully flat and dull it seemed the evening after he left!
"I felt so sad to take leave of the dear amiable young man
whom (talking jokingly) I was a little in love with . . ."
she wrote in her diary. She confided her feeling of
flatness to Melbourne. "A young person like me must
sometimes have young people to laugh with," she said.
"Nothing so natural," replied Melbourne with tears in
his eyes.

The Grand Duke was only a forerunner. Early in
October two other young foreign princes arrived in
England; the Queen's cousins Ernest and Albert of
Coburg. King Leopold of the Belgians had for some
years past been working for a marriage between the
Queen and his nephew Albert. Three years earlier, while
William IV was still alive, Albert had been sent over for
her inspection. She had found him attractive enough at
any rate not to turn him down. Her accession to the
Throne, however, had put her off marriage for the time
being; and, with a comical assumption of maturity, she
had sought to delay making up her mind on the question
by telling her uncle that she did not think Albert was
sufficiently experienced and grown up for her to be able
to judge whether he was likely to be a fit mate for the
Queen of England. Accordingly he had been sent on an
educative tour of Europe under the tutelage of Leopold's
confidential adviser, Baron Stockmar. Now in 1839 it
was proposed he should return in order to give the
Queen a chance of making a decision. She still felt
reluctant. Dancing with the Grand Duke was one thing,
surrendering her independence to her husband was
another. Albert could come if he liked, she said, but he

must realize that she did not regard herself as in any way committed. Certainly, she insisted, there could be no question of her marrying anyone for two or three years.

One sight of Albert, however, and these maidenly hesitations vanished. "It was with some emotion that I beheld Albert—who is *beautiful*!" she wrote in her diary on the evening of his arrival; and in subsequent entries she proceeded with growing enthusiasm to enumerate the catalogue of his perfections; "His beautiful blue eyes and exquisite nose and such a pretty mouth with delicate moustaches and slight, very slight, whiskers." Two days in the company of such an Adonis and she was head over ears in love! On 13th October she told Melbourne that she had made up her mind to marry Albert. "You have?" said he. "I am very glad of it . . . you will be much more comfortable; for a woman can't stand alone for long in whatever situation she is," and he proceeded to discuss what steps should be taken to make the engagement public.

Throughout the interview his tone, though tender, was calm. This was remarkable seeing how readily as a rule he showed emotion. For now, if ever, he had reason to do so. Her words meant the end of that close intimate relationship which had become the centre and sunshine of his whole existence. Even if he stayed in office, even if he remained her chief confidential adviser, he was no longer the first man in her heart. But Melbourne loved the Queen so selflessly that he did not want her new-found happiness to be shadowed, though but for an instant, by any regret he might himself be feeling. Indeed, to see her so happy did, in a sense, make him happy too.

Reason as well as affection strengthened him to resign himself to the situation. The disturbances of the last year had left him with no doubt at all that it was for the Queen's good that she should marry. She had to have a guide: and he himself was not going to be able to fulfil the role much longer. He was getting too old. Besides, his Government might fall any day. Melbourne had never been one to shut his eyes to painful facts: tender-hearted though he was, his heart did not rule his head to the extent of making him sentimentally self-deceived. He might, against his better judgment, give in to some-one he loved, but he always realized that he was going against his better judgment, if he did so. Now he judged that the time had come when it was inevitable and right that he should lose the young Queen to a husband. Rigidly suppressing any indulgence in self-pity, he threw all his mind and energy into seeing that the transaction was effected as pleasantly and with as little fuss as possible.

The next few months were mainly occupied in settling the legal position of the Prince and making arrangements for the wedding. Both involved some ructions. The Opposition was in a cantankerous humour and sought to embarrass the Government by making every difficulty they could. There was a row because it was not cate-gorically stated in any official document that the Prince was a Protestant: there was a row because the Govern-ment, following precedent, asked that he should have an income of £50,000 a year. There was also a row over the question of his precedence. The Queen wanted him to have first place in the kingdom after herself. But her royal uncles, notably the Duke of Sussex, objected to this; and they were supported in their objections by the more factious section of the Tory Party. Melbourne did not show his old skill in dealing with these difficulties. Here we notice that he was losing his grip. Considering the strength of anti-Papal feeling in England, he should have taken more care to do nothing that might stir it up; and rather than run the risk of letting the Queen's wishes become a Party issue, he ought to have tried to settle the questions of the Prince's income and precedence in private consultation with the Opposition leaders before bringing it up in Parliament. Instead he let things slide and inertly trusted that all would go right on the day. The result was that they got out of hand. After some public and distressing wrangling, the Prince's income was reduced to £30,000 and the Bill establishing his precedence looked so likely to be defeated that Melbourne had hurriedly to withdraw it and arrange that the matter should be settled later by an Order in Council.

The Queen did not make his task any easier. Her engagement, though it had raised her spirits, had not softened her temper. On the contrary, she felt more indignant than ever with the Tories for their impudence in opposing her will. "As long as I live," she burst out to Melbourne, "I never will forgive those infernal scoundrels with Peel—nasty wretch—at their head;" and she alluded to one of the venerable prelates who had voted for reducing the Prince's income as "that *fiend*, the Bishop of Exeter!" On New Year's Day in her diary she solemnly recorded her thanks to God for delivering her from her enemies during the Government crisis of May. She added a petition; "From the Tories, good Lord deliver us."

THE QUEEN: SECOND PHASE

The controversy over the Prince's precedence especially aroused her wrath. Originally she wanted to make him King Consort by Act of Parliament. "For God's sake, Ma'am," exclaimed Melbourne, "let's have no more of it. If you get the English people into the way of making Kings, you will get them into the way of unmaking them!" With such an idea of what her husband's position ought to be, she was not likely to be pleased by the proposal that he should yield first place to her uncles. She would rather he had no legal precedence at all, she said, than one so ignominious. "Oh no!" said Melbourne with robust good sense, "That's the foolishest thing. You should always get what you can." In spite of his fatigue, he had not lost his skill in dealing with her. Mingling firmness, sympathy and a sort of gay tact, he generally managed to keep her in check. When one Sunday he got a letter from the Duke of Sussex asserting his claim to precedence over the Prince, "I did not show the Duke of Sussex's letter to Your Majesty before you went to church," he told her with a smile, "I thought it would discompose you for devotion." The Queen still responded to Melbourne's arts. Once again she apologized deeply to him for losing her temper and promised with a touching artlessness not to do it again.

It was not easy for her though. Being engaged is notoriously trying to the nerves; and struggle as she might, the Queen remained irritable. She was annoyed by the Duchess of Kent who had again begun bouncing into her apartments uninvited; she was annoyed by King Leopold who continued to plague her with unasked-for political advice; at times she could even be a little irritated by the Prince himself. Her relations with him at this time show what an extraordinary mixture the Queen was. There was no doubt that she was violently in love with him. In her diary she rapturously records every detail of his caresses, his kisses, his tender words. Yet, even in the full flood of youthful passion, she never forgot that she was Queen and must maintain her position as such, even in relation to the object of her adoration. She disliked the idea of his taking any part in political business. So far as the official organization of his life was concerned, she required him to submit to her will without question. She chose all the officers of his Household without consulting him, including his confidential secretary, a Mr. George Anson, who had once been secretary to Melbourne. The Prince protested. Not only did he object to being ruled in this way, but Anson's appointment in particular conflicted with his views. He thought the Crown should be a neutral moderating power and that a Royal Household should therefore be composed of people with no marked political affiliations. The Queen reacted sharply and unfavourably to these signs of independence in her future husband. So far as English politics were concerned, she had no confidence in the Prince's judgment. For all she knew he might, if left to himself, fall, in his ignorance, under the sinister influence of the Tories. He must learn to trust her to know what was best for him in these matters. She spoke her mind to him. Anson was appointed.

The outside world put her insistence down to the influence of Melbourne who was suspected of wishing to get the Prince into his power. It was true that Melbourne did not sympathize with the Prince's political ideas. The conception of a neutral moderating monarchy was likely, in his view, to lead to the Crown taking an active line independent of the Government; whereas, according to the orthodox English doctrine, it was the King's duty to back whatever Party was in power. Moreover, Melbourne feared that whatever his intentions the Prince would, in practice, tend to choose Tories as his servants. Foreign princes in his experience had an instinctive bias against English Liberals. "They think our Liberal influence rough and disagreeable," he told the Queen. All the same, when he heard that the Prince objected strongly to have Anson as his secretary, Melbourne told the Queen she ought to give in to him. It was not a good thing that a wife should domineer over a reluctant husband in this fashion. Further, Melbourne himself did not want to appear responsible for any step that might alienate the Prince from him. From the moment of the Queen's engagement he made it an important part of his business to get on good terms with the Prince.

At first he had to feel his way, for he knew little about him. "He seems a very agreeable young man," he wrote to John Russell. "Certainly he is a very good looking one—and as to character, that we must always take our chance of." It was a safe enough chance had Melbourne known it. The Prince was eminently, even alarmingly, respectable. This did not mean that he would necessarily be easy for Melbourne to get on with. In fact, the two men made a comical contrast to each other; Melbourne a casual, ironical, pleasure-loving Englishman of the eighteenth century world, the Prince a stiff, conscientious, serious-minded German, not above relaxing for an hour's innocent merriment in the bosom of his family, but with his spirit already shadowed by the anxious earnestness, so typical of the nineteenth century. His affinity with the Queen lay precisely on that side of her nature which had least in common with Melbourne's. She was sufficiently aware of this to get a little feminine fun by playing off her fiancé against her Prime Minister. The Prince, she said, thought she should not receive anyone at Court whose reputation was doubtful. "The Prince is much severer than me," she announced to Melbourne. Melbourne could not suppress his surprise and vexation. Not only did the Prince's views strike him as intolerant, but, considering the free and easy morals of the English aristocracy, they seemed likely to get the Queen into disfavour with some of her most influential subjects. "That is a very bad thing," he said bluntly. "Albert thinks I should set an example of propriety," pursued the Queen. Melbourne was still sufficiently ruffled to disclose the worldly-wise nature of his approach to social morality in a manner more frank that prudent. "That is shown by your own conduct," he blurted out, "character can be attended to when people are of no consequence. But it will not do when people are of a very high rank." A day or two later the Queen laughingly told Melbourne that she feared he did not like Albert so much as he would, if he were not so strict. By this time Melbourne had recovered his self-command. "Oh no! I highly respect him," he answered discreetly.

Sometimes it was his turn to tease the Queen. She said triumphantly that Albert did not care for fashionable beauties, indeed that in general he took no interest in women. From what he had seen of royal princes, Melbourne judged this to be improbable. "That will come later," he mischievously remarked. The Queen was so outraged by the implication of these words that he hastily withdrew them and later took occasion to reassure her by telling her that from what he had observed of the Prince he seemed in these respects to be a glorious exception to the general run of young men.

When the Prince was actually present, Melbourne seems to have taken more pains to curb his tongue. Even so, now and again a remark slipped out which revealed the gulf between their points of view. One evening in Windsor, they were playing a letter game. Melbourne was given the word "pleasure" to guess. "It is not a *common* thing," explained the Prince in order to help him. "Is it truth or honesty?" enquired Melbourne.

"This made us all laugh," says the Queen relating the incident: and, in fact, whatever fundamental difference there might be between them, Melbourne and the Prince during these months contrived to get on pleasantly enough together. Melbourne's manner to the Prince was remarked on as perfect in its blending of respectful politeness with informal ease. The Prince responded to it: he speaks of Melbourne always as a kindly distinguished old gentleman devoted to the Queen's service. Melbourne reciprocated his goodwill. The difficulty of the Prince's position as a young foreigner suddenly pitchforked into the intricate hurly-burly of English public life stirred his sympathy: and he took pains to give him hints as how best to conduct himself in it. As he got to know him better, too, his opinion of him steadily improved. Melbourne meant what he said when he told the Queen that he respected the Prince. No doubt he was a bit of a prig like most Germans, but he was clearly a good young man who could be trusted to make the Queen happy. Since her happiness mattered to Melbourne more than anything else in the world, he felt growingly friendly towards the Prince.

This confidence in her future happiness may have helped him to keep up an appearance of good spirits. Certainly he managed wonderfully to do so. The accounts of him during the last weeks of her engagement are all sparkling and sunshiny. It was as though he was determined to extract every ounce of pleasure from his last days with her as an unmarried woman. Her diary is as full as ever of his conversation, and though once or twice he refers to his fatigue and depression, for the most part he is at his most delighted and delightful. He cajoled her into asking the Duke of Wellington to her wedding in spite of the shameful way she considered he had behaved over the Prince's precedence: he gave her his views on Scottish history—"There are too many Jameses and all murdered, the Scottish are a dreadful people;" he gaily gossiped to her about the appearance of her ladies, "Miss Montague," he observed, "has a peculiar way of carrying her nose;" he expatiated on the splendour of the new coat he was having made for the wedding. "I expect it will be the thing most observed," remarked Melbourne humorously.

One evening three days before the wedding he allowed his deeper feelings a little more play. The Queen noticed that his manner was unusually affectionate, even for him. She told him that she felt nervous. He comforted and encouraged her. "Depend upon it, it's right to marry," he said; "if ever there was a situation that formed an exception, it was yours; it's in human nature, it's natural to marry; the other is a very unnatural state of things; it's a great *change*—it has its inconveniences. . . . After all," he continued, "how anybody in your situation can have a moment's tranquillity!—a young person cast in this situation is very unnatural. There was a beautiful account in a Scotch paper of your first going to prorogue Parliament; 'I stood close to her, to see a young person surrounded by Ministers and Judges and rendered prematurely grave was almost melancholy'; 'a large searching eye, an open anxious nostril, and a firm mouth' . . . a very true representation," he said, "can't be a finer physiognomy." The Queen smiled at his earnestness. "I am sure none of your friends are as fond of you as I am," she said. "I believe it," he answered. He spoke with deep emotion.

On 11th February the great day came. The Prime Minister was observed to be much affected, as he stood in his smart new coat watching the ceremony. Afterwards, at Buckingham Palace, when she had changed her dress, she sent for him for a final private interview. He kissed her hand. They remained a moment or two talking of how well everything had gone off. "You look very tired," said the Queen anxiously. Once more he gave her a long, loving look. His hand clasped in hers,

"God bless you Ma'am," he said. Then the Prince appeared. Together he and the Queen went downstairs and drove away.

(5)

Meanwhile the Government muddled its way ineffectively and uncomfortably along, frustrated by the Tories, sniped at by the Radicals and disturbed by the wranglings of its own members, notably Howick. At last in June he was so exasperated that he resigned. Melbourne accepted his resignation with easy indifference and made Macaulay minister in his stead. This made for a more peaceful atmosphere: for Macaulay was not temperamental. But neither was he restful. Brilliant, dogmatic, voluble and tireless, he at once dazed and dazzled his colleagues by the uninterrupted flow of his discourse. "I wish I was as cocksure about anything," said Melbourne, "as Macaulay is about everything!" However, he was not bored by Macaulay. On the contrary he sat listening to him "with an air of complacency and as if for instruction." Melbourne was unusually ready to tolerate monologists, so long as there was something original about them. This propensity got him into trouble about this time. In the summer, Robert Owen, celebrated in history as a pioneer of socialism, had persuaded him to present him officially at Court. It was surprising that Melbourne should have agreed because Owen, in addition to being universally recognized as one of the greatest bores alive, was a militant Left Wing atheist who had taken a leading part in attacking Melbourne for his treatment of the Dorset labourers. However, Melbourne never disliked anyone for attacking him, and had a strong objection to punishing a man, otherwise harmless, simply because he held unorthodox opinions. His respectable contemporaries did not share this view: presentation at Court, in their view, implied approval of a man's ideas. Melbourne was violently criticised for his action by important people at Court and by his opponents in the House of Lords. Though professing himself sorry if he had acted without due consideration, he took these attacks very lightly. "I beg to assure you," he wrote to a correspondent, "that you may most safely and in the most decisive manner contradict the notion that there may be any approbation on my part of Mr. Owen's opinions. . . . I have more than once heard Mr. Owen's statements and I have always told him that his doctrines appeared to be the most absurd, and he himself one of the most foolish men I ever conversed with. I always considered that his principles were too ridiculous to be dangerous." In Parliament, after a few perfunctory words of explanation and apology, he proceeded to air his views on the subject of free speech in general. It was no good advocating it, he said, on the ground that it led in the end to truth prevailing: mankind was far too foolish for that. But on the other hand he thought repression equally useless, for it was impossible to make it effective.

These characteristic and inconclusive reflections showed that Melbourne had not lost his taste for speculation. However, less than ever did this influence his practical activities as a statesman. These were solely directed to

LORD M.

keeping the Government together until such time as he judged the Queen had learned to manage without his help. To achieve this end he employed his old tactics of combined obstruction and concession. Two important new measures were introduced during the latter part of 1839; one for an Education Bill and one for establishing the Penny Post. Melbourne did not believe in either. The Penny Post would do no good, he told the Queen: but he thought it sufficiently uncontroversial to be ready to back it in order to please his colleagues. There is an amusing account of Rowland Hill, the chief promoter of the measure, coming to coach him for his speech in the debate on the subject. He found Melbourne in his dressing room; and, running through the chief points, mentioned a Mr. Warburton who had views on the matter. "Warburton, Warburton," said Melbourne, "he is one of your moral force men isn't he? I can understand your physical force man, but as to your moral force men I'll be damned if I know what they mean!" A few minutes later Hill was shown into another room while Melbourne interviewed Lord Lichfield, the Postmaster General who opposed the Bill because, oddly, he thought that the Post Office buildings would collapse under the weight of letters likely to be put in them, if postage became so cheap. Melbourne soothed him. "Lichfield has been here," he remarked to Hill after ushering the excited Postmaster General out of the room. "I cannot think why a man cannot talk of Penny Postage without going into a passion!"

Melbourne made more difficulties about the Education Bill. Not only did he disbelieve in educational schemes

278

as such, but he rightly thought that they always raised
trouble with the Church, who considered that no one
else should have any control over them. Howick was
still in the Government when the question was first
discussed. "Thank God there are some things which
even you cannot stop, and this is one of them!" he broke
out furiously to Melbourne. Melbourne merely smiled
and went on making objections. As he expected, the
Church, supported by the Tory Party, did oppose the
Government Bill violently. In the end a compromise
was reached which left the control of education in
Church hands.

The year 1839 also saw a slight revival of these civil
disturbances which had marked the Reform period. That
same economic distress that had led to the anti-Corn Law
agitation also gave birth to the semi-revolutionary
Chartist Movement. During May there was serious
rioting in Birmingham, and at Newport in November.
Melbourne dealt with the new disturbances as he had
with the old: he advocated vigorous repression but only
within the limits of the existing law. The ringleaders of
the riots ought to be hanged, he said. On the other hand
he was against John Russell's proposal that the Government should be given extraordinary powers to seize
arms, etc. On the whole, however, he took the whole
affair much more calmly than in 1831. When, on
10th August, the Cabinet was told that the Chartists were
organizing a mass protest movement in support of their
demands and that it was scheduled to start on 12th August,
"God bless my soul," said Melbourne breezily, "that
is the day after tomorrow! It is time for us to be looking

about us." Clearly he had at last come to the conclusion that there was not much danger of bloody revolution breaking out in England. He was quite right. Lawlessness was easily stamped out. But the deterioration in the economic situation continued: and Melbourne did worry about this, especially as he thought it was likely to get worse and saw no way of stopping it. However, he still was determined to try and stay in office. Apart from anything else, the Queen was always asking him to: and he had told her he would. He preferred, however, that the outside world should not know this, for fear they might blame her for it. Let it be thought, rather, that he was doing it to please those members of his Party who were enjoying the sweets of office. "No one supposes I want to go on," he said, "but I must think of those poor fellows who would have to put down their broughams." By the spring of 1840 there did not seem any immediate danger that they would have to. The disturbances were over, the Radicals were losing heart. For the time being, at any rate, it looked as if things were settling down.

However, Melbourne was not fated to feel easy for long. In the summer a new crisis loomed up. This time it was over foreign affairs. These had never been one of Melbourne's major preoccupations up till now. Not that he neglected them. The subject interested him—he was the only member of the Cabinet except Palmerston who really understood it, said a foreign observer—and anyway he was not allowed to forget about it by his brother Fred Lamb, now British Representative in Vienna, and who distrusted Palmerston even more than he did himself. Both brothers were against his militant pro-Liberalism:

they wanted to combine with Austria to create a middle force that might hold the balance between Russia and France. However, Melbourne was not prepared to try and enforce this view on his obstreperous Foreign Secretary. Once he had resigned himself to taking Palmerston back in 1835, he seems to have come to the conclusion that he had better let him run foreign policy as he wanted. For one thing, he knew he could not stop him, and for another it was a great saving of trouble. All he could do was to keep a vigilant eye on him and intervene from time to time to check his more perilous extravagances of word and action. Breezy and combative, Palmerston continued to pursue his liberalizing policy; backed the Constitutional Party in Spain and Portugal, encouraged Liberal Movements in Central Europe, hauled foreign monarchs and statesmen over the coals when he caught them doing anything that struck him as unusually tyrannical. None of this was much to Melbourne's liking. Palmerston did not seem to realize that "the worst thing in the world was to be troublesome." Besides, trouble abroad meant trouble at home, and trouble at home might easily lead to that downfall of the Government which it was Melbourne's chief aim to avoid. The situation at home always conditioned his view of the situation abroad. His first reaction to any proposal of Palmerston's is to ask him how it is to be defended in the House of Lords. His own advice to him was always on the side of caution. It is extraordinary how many sentences in his frequent letters began with the phrase, "For God's sake don't. . . ." He stopped Palmerston seizing the island of Goa from the Portugnese in 1839 because they had not kept their promise to put down the slave trade; in 1836 he warned him about getting entangled in grandiose schemes for moulding the future of Asia. "The Black Sea and the Caucasus and those great empires enflame the imagination wonderfully," he remarked ironically. He was also always suspicious of coming to any international agreement which committed England to some definite course of action in the future. "It may be necessary to defend Turkey," he says on one occasion, "but I should not like to be bound to defend her. Our policy is to have our hands free. . . ." And again when commenting on the French proposal for a comprehensive treaty of mutual defence, "Treaties of this comprehensive character are very dangerous transactions. They rarely answer the purpose for which they were formed and they often involve consequences which are in no respect foreseen." Melbourne realized, as Palmerston did not, that the English, however progressive and idealistic, liked their foreign policy to be cheap. They might cheer the spectacle of a foreign people rightly struggling to be free; the last thing they wanted was to spend money or soldiers in helping them to win the struggle. Melbourne, therefore, objected to Palmerston's tendency to speak strongly, because he knew he seldom had the power to enforce his words by strong action. What was the good of scolding the Czar for addressing his Polish subjects in offensive terms; much the Czar would care! And why promise to see that the Spanish gave generous terms to the Basques when there was no means of ensuring that they carried out these terms? Why encourage the Circassians

282

and the Serbs to resist their oppressors when England had neither the intention nor the means actively to help them in their fight? The only consequence of such conduct was to irritate England's enemies without alarming them, and to leave her friends with the impression that she was either perfidious or ineffective.

All the same, in spite of these causes of disagreement, Palmerston and Melbourne did not get on so badly. For one thing, personal relations between them were easy. They had a family connection: Palmerston, who for many years it was suspected, had been Emily Cowper's lover, married her in 1839. Further, he and Melbourne were natives of the same fashionable Whig world, both talked the same blunt, flippant, male Whig language. Plain-spoken though their letters to each other are, they are also good-humoured. Neither was offended by the other's frankness. Further, each respected the other enough to make concessions. More often than not Palmerston listened to Melbourne's advice and modified his policy accordingly. On his side Melbourne, whatever he might say to Palmerston in private, loyally supported him in public. He always refused to hold any communication with foreign representatives who tried to negotiate with him behind Palmerston's back, and when Holland or John Russell grumbled to him about Palmerston, Melbourne replied that he thought he was doing well. He meant it, too. Melbourne had the open-mindedness of his scepticism. So long as Palmerston's risky-seeming policy did not get the Government into serious trouble, Melbourne was willing enough to give it his approval.

Altogether Melbourne had not found much to worry

about in foreign affairs during the first five years of his Premiership. Alas, in the summer of 1840 he did. Trouble arose in the Middle East. It had been brewing some time. Early in the 'thirties Mehemet Ali, the powerful Pasha of Egypt, rebelled against His Suzerain, the corrupt and feeble Sultan of Turkey. The consequence was a long drawn out conflict between them which seemed likely to end in the victory of Mehemet Ali and the break up of the Turkish Empire. Palmerston was horrified at such a prospect. For he saw the Turkish Empire as a necessary bulwark against the rival ambitions of France and Russia to dominate the Eastern Mediterranean.

Accordingly, in the autumn of 1839, he set to work to persuade the great powers to agree to a treaty by which they pledged themselves to help the Sultan, by force if need be, to defeat Mehemet Ali. This proposal produced a new alignment of powers in Europe. Russia, Austria and Prussia agreed to it, but the French, who saw a chance of getting Egypt on her side if Mehemet Ali won, hung back. Undismayed Palmerston set to work to bully them into acquiescence. Here he found himself at odds with some of his colleagues. Two in particular, Holland and Clarendon, the new Lord Privy Seal, shrank from any idea of quarrelling with progressive France, more especially as they feared that Palmerston's policy might lead to increasing the power of the arch-reactionary, Russia. They wanted Palmerston to drop his plan. Melbourne, as so often, felt divided on the question. Though he diplomatically denied it to Holland, on the whole he thought Palmerston right; for Egypt dominated by

France would be a danger to England; and as for Russia, Melbourne had come to the conclusion that she was bound to get control of Turkey sooner or later. On the other hand, he wanted above all things to avoid a split in his own Government. He therefore took up his usual middle-way position and pleaded rather ineffectively with his colleagues for compromise. To the outside world he adopted his old tactics of agreeable evasiveness. In March, 1840, Guizot, the new French Ambassador, went to see him and expatiated with Gallic eloquence on the strength of his country's case. Melbourne, stretched out comfortably in an armchair, listened and laughed and seemed friendly and interested, and refused to commit himself in any way. In July, alarmed by Mehemet Ali's continued successes, Palmerston decided to force the issue. Since the French would not agree, he proposed making a treaty with the other powers, leaving them out. At once Holland and Clarendon said they would resign if such a proposal was accepted. Palmerston replied that he would resign if it was not accepted. "For God's sake," cried Melbourne, "let nobody resign or we'll have everybody resigning;" and he proceeded to try and persuade one side or the other to yield. In the end, Holland and Clarendon gave way and the Treaty was signed.

It was far from being the end of the trouble. The French were furious. Their excitable Prime Minister, Thiers—"he is a strange quicksilver man, this Thiers, he puts me in mind of Brougham," said Melbourne—fulminated threats of reprisal. It seemed possible that if the other powers went to the Sultan's help, France might go to the help of Mehemet Ali. For the first time for many years the shadow of a possible general war rose to brood darkly over the European scene. The result was an explosion in the English Cabinet. The pro-French party became frantic; and, what mattered much more, John Russell who had agreed to the Treaty, was now so frightened by the idea of war that he changed his mind. He wrote clamouring for some compromise with France before it was too late. So also did those respected grand old men of the Whig Party, Lord Spencer and the Duke of Bedford. Melbourne communicated their agitated expostulations to Palmerston who paid no attention whatever. The French were merely bluffing, he said cheerfully, they were not such fools as to embark on a war in which they were bound to do badly. Melbourne was unable to feel so confident. Hitherto he had managed to stop himself worrying; now he became seriously disturbed. It was all very well for Palmerston to say that the French would be silly to go on standing out, but people often were silly. "You calculate a little too much upon nations and individuals feeling reason, right and a just view of their own interest," he said crisply. Even if Palmerston were right about the French, the defeat of Mehemet Ali was likely to be a long job; and meanwhile the English Government might fall. However, Melbourne reflected gloomily, it was too late for England to back out now without disastrous loss of face. Besides, to do so would mean Palmerston's resignation and that also would bring about the downfall of the Government. No—there was nothing to do but go on as they had begun; and his own particular task was to hold country and Government together in the hope that the situation might improve. The country in general added little to his difficulties for the public was not fully awake to the crisis; and Melbourne safeguarded himself against any attack from the official opposition by going to see the Duke of Wellington and persuading him to promise his support. It was his own colleagues who were the trouble; Holland, John Russell who had begun again to talk of resigning, and, of course, Palmerston. In order to deal with them Melbourne pulled himself together to give such an exhibition of his diplomatic skill as had not been seen since the days of his prime. There was no longer any sign of his having lost his grip. Outwardly his old lazy, ironical self, he proceeded during two tense months to evade and temporize and pour oil, and now and again, genially but firmly, to read the riot act. Of course Palmerston was indiscreet, he told John Russell, but for John Russell to resign would only increase Palmerston's power. Of course John Russell and Holland were tiresome, he said to Palmerston—"Friends are generally more troublesome and often more hostile than adversaries," he remarked sardonically—but that was all the more reason for being cautious and circumspect. To both parties Melbourne insisted on the folly of doing anything that might break up the Government. If it fell, neither, he pointed out, would have a chance of getting their way in foreign affairs.

At first all his efforts appeared vain. Mehemet Ali did better and better, the French got angrier and angrier, John Russell went on threatening his resignation, Palmerston became more arrogantly intransigent than ever. Keeping him in order was the hardest part of

Melbourne's task; and secretly he found himself turning more and more against him. Why, oh why had Palmerston ever embarked on so dangerous a policy? "Never," he wrote sharply to him, "was a great measure undertaken upon a basis of support so slender and uncertain." Not that Palmerston was much more of a nuisance than Lord and Lady Holland, who, it was reported, were now repeating every Cabinet secret at their parties in Holland House, even when the French Ambassador was present.

Certainly it was a wearing time, especially for a frail and ageing man like Melbourne. The strain began to tell on him. He suffered continually from indigestion and lumbago; he lost his appetite and could hardly sleep at all. He kept awake, it was noticed, even during Cabinet meetings! In mid-September, a new element insinuated itself into the situation, to disturb him still further. The Queen intervened. Prompted by the Prince, who in turn was prompted by King Leopold, she became extremely suspicious of Palmerston's policy and began to bombard Melbourne with excited letters complaining that she was not consulted and pressing for accommodation with France before things came to a crisis. "The Queen really could not go through that *now*," she protested, "and it might make her *seriously ill* if she were to be kept in a state of agitation and excitement." Melbourne was extremely distressed. The Queen, as he knew to his cost, was likely to be just as unmanageable as Palmerston. Besides, the last thing he wanted to do was to upset her at the present moment, she was now several months gone with child. However, he kept his head, soothed her down with his usual skill and made use of her delicate condition as an argument to impose his will on Palmerston and John Russell. If they had an ounce of consideration for the Queen they simply must try to be moderate. Meanwhile, with light tact he suggested to the Hollands that they should cultivate discretion. "I know not what can be done except to take care that as little of political affairs transpires in conversation as possible;" he wrote to Lord Holland, "but this is inconsistent with a salon—which has many advantages and some disadvantages."

At last, his patience reaped its reward. The situation took a turn for the better. Helped by the British Fleet, the Sultan began to prevail over Mehemet Ali, and in France there were signs that Thiers, the leader of resistance to England, was losing support. Melbourne judged that the need for procrastinating was over. Now was the moment for strong action. Without consulting anyone, he therefore wrote off to King Leopold, who had constituted himself a sort of unofficial intermediary between England and the French King, Louis Philippe, a letter written in his most trenchant style, in which he said that if Thiers called up the army he, Melbourne, would summon Parliament and demand that England should take effective counter-measures. He assumed that this letter would be shown to Louis Philippe. It was: and the effect produced was instantaneous. The terrified Louis Philippe dismissed Thiers. Soon after news came that Acre, a principal fortress in Mehemet Ali's defences, had fallen to the Sultan. The danger of war was over. By the end of October the crisis was at an end.

(6)

A wave of relief swept over Melbourne. For a week or two he was like a boy escaped from school, bubbling over with laughter and high spirits. He had reason to be exhilarated as well as relieved, for England's success was partly due to him. The policy had been Palmerston's: but unless Melbourne, in spite of his own inner misgivings, had backed it so loyally and kept Queen and Cabinet in check, Palmerston would never have been able to carry it out. It had been a very trying time for Melbourne though, and left him—once the first exhilaration had worn off—frailer and older than ever: "Lord Melbourne is looking as old as the hills," said a court lady. He felt it too. Clearly he would not be up to going on with the work of a Prime Minister for much longer. In fact he did not have to. The year 1841 saw the final collapse of the Whig Government. The economic situation was its undoing. This got no better: with the result that the agitation to get rid of protective duties, more especially the Corn Laws, revived and intensified. More and more Government supporters went over to the anti-Corn Law side: more and more did ministers press that the Corn Laws should be modified if not repealed. Melbourne was still against this. He thought modification must lead ultimately to complete abolition: and he recognized—as some of his colleagues did not—that abolition must fatally undermine the rule of the English landed gentry. Melbourne continued to favour the rule of the English landed gentry. Further, he realized that raising the Corn Law issue also meant the end of the Whig Government.

It was bound to start a major political row: and the precarious balance which kept the Whigs in power could only be maintained, so long as it was not shaken by a major political row. Up till now Melbourne had tried to stave things off by suggesting that the Corn Laws, like the secret ballot, should be treated as an open question on which ministers could vote as they pleased. But this was no longer a possible way out; the question had become so important that the Government must make up its mind to give the country a definite united lead about it. Melbourne thought the matter over, listened to his colleagues' arguments—and gave way to the anti-Corn Law party. Airily he explained his position in the matter to the Queen. "I do *not*," he said, "go the length of those people who think the Corn Laws are against the Gospel and the spirit of Jesus Christ! I am against the political principles of many in this way. But I have always kept it open for me to change, if I should think it necessary." Indeed, his change over about the Corn Laws was not an inconsistency on his part. It had always been one of his principles that a wise statesman compromised with a movement once it had become too strong and too widespread to be checked without an explosion. He behaved over the Corn Laws as he had over the Reform Bill. All the same he could not bring himself to feel much interested in how they should be modified. It was the sort of practical subject that bored him to tears. Absent-minded and indifferent, he sat through one Cabinet meeting after another while his colleagues wrangled interminably about fixed duties and sliding scales. At last, in March, they came to an agreement and took their leave. As they went downstairs they heard the Prime Minister's voice calling to them: looking up they saw him leaning over the banisters: "Stop a bit," he said, "what did we decide? Is it to lower the price of bread, or isn't it? It doesn't matter which, but we must all say the same thing."

Indeed he seemed to take the whole crisis very lightly: and also the imminent eclipse of his Government which it portended. "Ten to one we shall not be in next year," he remarked cheerfully: and when Clarendon reported to him that Palmerston was said to be intriguing secretly with the Tories, he received the ominous news with detached ironical amusement. "It can't last—it's impossible this Government can go on!" he reflected aloud, chuckling and rubbing his hands. The fact was that he had at last resigned himself to the prospect of going out of office: and thought, characteristically, that it was best to make as little heavy weather over it as possible. After all, politics were not a subject that should be taken very seriously.

One serious task did however remain to him; to prepare the Queen for his exit. This was not so hard as it would have been once. For no longer was she going to be left alone. Indeed, one of the reasons that Melbourne gave way over the Corn Laws so easily was that his chief motive for staying in had been weakened by the Queen's marriage. During the last few months he had worked steadily to train the Prince for his future responsibilities as the Queen's personal adviser. It was not always easy; the Prince was so extremely unlike himself. "This damned morality will ruin everything!" Melbourne

exclaimed after the Prince had expressed some view that
struck him as peculiarly priggish. But his feelings about
the Prince, like so many of his other feelings, were
mixed. At the same time as he was irritated by him, he
was also impressed by him. And anyway he was careful
to hide his irritation. So successfully that the Prince told
his uncle that "Good Lord Melbourne" was the only one
of his wife's ministers that he really trusted. Melbourne
arranged for him to see all the foreign dispatches; and the
Prince would send them back to him accompanied by
long and detailed memoranda of his views about them.
Melbourne did not answer him in equal detail, in fact he
often did not answer him at all. But the Prince was
flattered to notice that he often acted as if he had modified
his views in consequence of the memoranda. Meanwhile,
Melbourne managed to get his own opinions through to
the Prince either in direct conversation or—more
tactfully—by saying a word to Anson or the Queen with
the intention that it should be passed on. He took pains,
too, in the course of his talks with the Queen to tell her
how intelligent and judicious he thought the Prince was.
With good effect: the Queen, as we have seen, had
started off with the idea of not allowing the Prince to
share in her political work. It was not just that she
wanted to keep power in her own hands; she also had an
uneasy feeling that political discussions might lead to
political disagreement; and that this would dissipate the
atmosphere of idyllic rapture which she desired to glow
round every moment that she spent in the loved one's
company. The Prince, however, preferred interesting
work to idyllic rapture, and complained to her about

his exclusion. The Queen rushed off to ask Melbourne's
advice. Was he tempted to back her up in her resolution
to keep the Prince out of politics? He might well have
been, for politics were the one subject concerning which
he kept his old exclusive position with her. But if he was
tempted, he resisted. His love was self-sacrificing and
unpossessive. Earnestly he pressed her to consult the
Prince more: disagreements, he said, were less dangerous
to married happiness than secretiveness, for secretiveness
led to distrust. At first the Queen demurred; but as time
passed she began to come round. It was inevitable she
should. By nature she tended always to look up to some
man as her chief authority in all matters; and who should
it be but her husband? Already he was modifying her
outlook in other ways. Fancy the Queen talking about
botany and tree-planting! said the Ladies of the Household; before the Prince came she did not know one plant
from another! And what about her new-found taste for
sacred music? Clearly all these changes came from the
Prince. About people, she was not so ready to follow
his lead. The Prince wanted to invite learned men and
scientists to the Palace in order that he might enjoy the
benefit of improving talks with them. This prospect did
not appeal to the Queen. She was too ignorant for such
talk, she said. She consulted Melbourne, who, for once,
found himself baffled. Even he did not know how to
make the Queen enjoy the company of scientists.
In general, however, she began to defer more and
more to the Prince's opinions. These soon included
his political opinions. His influence already showed
itself powerful at the time of the Syrian crisis. By the

spring of 1841 it had consolidated itself even further.

It was still not to be compared with Melbourne's, however. For the time being the Queen still turned to Melbourne before anyone else. This, he realized, was going to be a difficulty if the Government fell. For one thing, the Queen indicated that she wanted to go on keeping in touch with him afterwards. Though he must have longed for her to do so, yet he knew quite well that it was not the custom of the British Constitution for the Sovereign to be in habitual communication with the Leader of the Opposition behind the back of her Prime Minister. Some compromise must be found. Would it be possible for the Queen, if for once in a way she felt particular need of his advice, to tell the Prince who would tell Anson who would tell Melbourne? His advice would then be passed back through the same devious channel. The Prince thought this an excellent idea. Not so the Queen: she said categorically that she must be allowed to communicate with Lord Melbourne directly. Melbourne, who knew her in this mood, bowed to her words. Then there was the vexatious question of the Queen's Ladies to be settled. By now, Melbourne was convinced that the original quarrel over it had been an error which would have ended disastrously had not Peel agreed to give in rather than to have a public row about it. The same mistake must not be made again, and the best thing would be to get the matter arranged beforehand. Once more with the help of the Prince, a secret negotiation was opened with Peel, by which it was tacitly agreed that he should not demand the dismissal of the Ladies, but that the Queen should ask those few who were most

connected with the Whigs to send in their resignations
when the Tories came in. Melbourne also asked Anson
to try and indicate to Peel the importance of being patient
with the Queen. Last time he had been too hasty. "He
didn't give the Queen time to come round," he said
"you should always give people time to come round."

He had done what he could to smooth the way for the
new Government. Late in May the crash came. The
Whigs were defeated over the Budget. They did not
go out straight away because they could not make up their
minds whether to resign or to advise the Queen to
dissolve Parliament. If she dissolved Parliament, there
would be an election at once and they might have a
better chance of winning it: if they resigned, the Queen
would send for Peel who would then be in a position
to have an election when he thought it suited him best.
All the same Melbourne was for resignation. He judged
that the Government would be defeated in any case, and
he very much disliked the idea of an election fought, as it
certainly would be, on the issue of the Corn Laws; for it
was likely to be a violent contest which roused popular
passions in the way he most disliked. "No terms," he
said, "can express my horror, my detestation, my
absolute loathing of the attempt to enlist religious
feelings against the Corn Laws." More important, he
thought that the Queen was for the time being so
identified with himself and the Whigs that she would
be looked on as a partizan in the election and that this
would make her unpopular. Melbourne was not going
to recommend any policy, whatever its other advantages,
that ran the slightest risk of making the Queen

unpopular. She did not agree, all she wanted was to help the Whigs. John Russell and others took the same view. For a week or two the question was undecided; people began to wonder if the Whigs were not intending to stick on, in spite of their defeat. "Why is Lord Melbourne like a *very* serious young lady?" said a wit of the time. "Because he won't go out *at all*." At last after a lot of arguing and letter-writing, Melbourne bowed to the will of his Sovereign and colleagues. Another Government defeat was followed by the dissolution of Parliament; in August an election took place. As Melbourne had prophesied, the Whigs were soundly beaten. Parliament met again at the end of August. The curtain rose on the concluding scene of Melbourne's premiership.

He played it in character. Never a parliamentarian, he had neither the will nor the energy to make much of his farewell to the House of Lords. The Tories moved a vote of no confidence in the Government; and the Duke of Wellington attacked Melbourne for changing his mind about the Corn Laws. Looking weary and dispirited, Melbourne rose to make a brief, negligent and flippant reply. Of course he had changed his mind, he said, but so did everybody when circumstances altered; "We are all very much in the habit of taunting one another with having changed our opinions, but the fact is we are always changing our opinions. . . . It is nonsense to proceed with measures which it is impossible can succeed." He was followed by Brougham who took the occasion to pay Melbourne back for turning him out of the Government by making a bitter, malicious and detailed personal onslaught on him. Melbourne seemed a little disturbed; leaning forward he asked one of his colleagues if he thought one particular accusation was in any way justified by the facts. But, whether from lack of heart or from a fundamental indifference, he did not bother to get up and answer Brougham. On 28th August, after they had been defeated in the House of Commons, Melbourne, in a few short sentences, announced the Government's resignation.

Meanwhile, up to the very last minute he had gone on doing everything he could to make things easy for the Queen in the new situation she was about to enter. He suggested some final hints to Peel, through the medium of Anson, as how best to gain her confidence; and to the Prince as how best to increase and maintain it. Don't let him irritate her by talking solemnly *at* her about religion, "She particularly dislikes what Her Majesty terms a *Sunday Face!*" To the Queen herself Melbourne once more, and for the last time, earnestly urged the advantages of tact and discretion. The great thing was to avoid an open conflict with her ministers. If she found she disagreed with them, she had better say that she needed time for further consideration, and not let herself be driven into a corner. For the rest, he made a final effort to remove her prejudice against Peel and the Tories. When the Queen complained that the Tory ministers had looked cross at their first interview with her, Melbourne said that most likely they were only shy and embarrassed; "Strange faces," he explained, "are apt to give the idea of ill humour." He grew suddenly worried lest he had biased her unduly against some of them. "In the course of this correspondence," he wrote off to her, "Lord Melbourne has thought it his duty to Your Majesty to express himself with great freedom upon the characters of many individuals . . . but Lord Melbourne thinks it right to say that he may have spoken upon insufficient grounds, that he may have been mistaken and that the persons in question may turn out to be far better than he has been induced to represent them."

The Queen listened to his words more calmly than in the previous year. She still said that losing him was the saddest event of her life, she still complained that she found Peel's manner disagreeably stiff. But when she and Melbourne met there were none of the passionate protests and emotional storms of May, 1839. She shed tears, but they were the gentle nostalgic tears of one who regrets the irretrievable past but is resigned to accept the inevitable future. Melbourne encouraged her spirit of resignation. This was for his own comfort as well as hers. He recognized the fact that even if the Tories fell, he himself was unlikely to be up to taking office again; and so was determined that for neither of them should his last hours with the Queen leave any needlessly painful memories behind them. He strove studiously to keep the tone of their intercourse as normal and even cheerful as possible. On the last evening he dined at the Palace as Prime Minister he actually managed to appear unusually merry. Not that he repressed sentiment altogether. Melbourne was the last man to cultivate an unnaturally stiff upper lip. He knew what she was going through, he told her, how the expectation of a dreaded event could cast its shadow over every pleasure, how hard it was to concentrate on work with a troubled mind. But, he said, work did dissipate trouble if one persevered with it; and he trusted that when the time came she would find she did not miss him as much as she had feared. He did not think she would because she now had the Prince to advise her. "The Prince understands everything so well," he said, "he has such a clear, able head. . . . When you married him," Melbourne added with a twinkle, "you said that he was perfection, which I thought a little overrated, but I really think now that it is in some degree realized."

For himself he admitted he was going to feel the separation deeply—"It is painful for me," he confessed to her on their last evening together, standing on the terrace in the starlight. "For four years I have seen you daily and liked it better every day." He noticed too, he told her, that he was beginning to wake earlier which, with him, was always a sign of depression and anxiety. All the same she must not worry about him, he slept well until he woke: indeed he was well altogether. The Queen tried to persuade him to accept the Garter as a token of the honour and love in which she held him. Melbourne refused it. This was not from any quixotic disinterested-ness, he hastened to say; if he had been poor and she had offered him a pension, he would have taken it gratefully. But he had always refused honours, and—he hoped this showed no false pride—he would like to keep intact his reputation for refusing them. However, he was delighted to accept a present of some etchings which the Queen sent to him. "They will certainly," he wrote, "recall

QUEEN VICTORIA AND THE PRINCE CONSORT

to recollection a melancholy day but Lord Melbourne hopes and trusts that with the divine blessing it still will hereafter be looked upon with less grief and bitterness of feeling than it must be regarded at present." In these words, while he professes to look forward to happier times, Melbourne does allow his grief to reveal itself a little more explicitly. And in a note on practical matters, written soon after his resignation, he took occasion to declare, though in plain and formal terms, his full sense of what his relation to her meant to him. "Lord Melbourne will ever consider the time during which Your Majesty is good enough to think that he has been of service to Her Majesty the proudest as well as the happiest part of his life."

Thus, quietly, gracefully, composedly, Melbourne took leave of Queen Victoria.

(1)

COMPOSEDLY, TOO, he settled down to the new phase of his life. Poor Lord Melbourne was going to feel the change dreadfully, said the gossips of the town to one another with gloomy relish. What was he going to do with himself? Melbourne seemed determined to show that he could do very well. On the 3rd September, the members of the Carlton Club looked out of the window to see him strolling idly and smiling down to the House of Lords for the first time since his resignation. As he passed them, he moderated his walk to a saunter as though purposely to exhibit his carefree demeanour to his Tory supplanters. He entered the House, too, with an air of easy composure which astonished his fellow peers. In private life he appeared equally cheerful. Indeed some people were shocked at his frivolity. "Lord Melbourne did not appear to advantage," complained the serious-minded Lady John Russell meeting him at Woburn a week or two after his resignation. "He showed little wish for conversation with anybody but seemed trying to banish the thought of his reverse by talking nonsense with some of the ladies."

So far as outward circumstances were concerned indeed, there were considerable compensations in his new form of life. No more State papers, no more Cabinet quarrels, no more speeches in Parliament, except when he felt inclined! Plenty of time for dining out, for lounging at Brooks's, for staying with his friends in their spacious country houses, for musing over French novels and patristic folios in the library at Brocket! Philosophically, Melbourne set to work to take advantage of these new-found opportunities for the life of pleasure. He dressed later than ever—people now found him shaving at half-past five in the evening—he pulled down his theological books from the shelves with the idea of writing a commentary on St. Chrysostom; he paid a special visit to the country in the spring, that he might savour at leisure for the first time for many years, the fresh beauty of bluebells and apple-blossom. He also went out a great deal in society. We hear of him staying with Lord Leicester and the Duke of Bedford and the Palmerstons, and dining often at Holland House and with Mrs. Norton.

For she had begun to come into his life again. She had never completely left it. He felt sufficiently responsible for her woes to keep in touch with her in order to see how she was getting on. It was a very discreet touch though: for the Queen was now on the throne, and not for Caroline Norton or anyone else was Melbourne going to risk compromising his good name in such a way as to harm the Queen. This consideration dominated his relations with Caroline. She wanted to be presented at Court by way of proving her respectability to the world. In principle Melbourne could not object to this, for she had been declared innocent in a court of law. But for him principle had never counted in the balance against hard facts; and he realized perfectly well that Mrs. Norton's reputation was too tarnished for strict persons to think her a proper person to be presented to a Queen who was also an unmarried girl. Melbourne therefore told her that she could not be presented till the Queen had a husband. She submitted, but she did not like it, and she said so. In a series of letters to Melbourne's young nephew, William Cowper, with whom she had made friends, she fulminated in a powerful vein of sarcasm against the injustice of the world and the hypocrisy of the great, in particular, of the Queen, whom she mistakenly considered responsible for her exclusion. "Your uncle has walked over from Storey's Gate to Buckingham Palace and pursues the same course with her as with me. . . . No one talked of my inexperience and yet I did not forbid *my* mother to disturb our interviews, nor believe in *my* mother's misconduct. . . . I have waited because I have accustomed my mind and soul to walk about the world in chains, thinking what your uncle calls his good pleasure might be. If he thinks I can be brought to bear tamely what the Royal Girl considers a fit punishment for me for being her predecessor in the long conversations which take place at her palace, I can't help it."

The tone of these letters is not attractive. Alas,

Caroline Norton was not the sort of woman who is ennobled by suffering; her character had deteriorated under the strain of her troubles. It may be said in her excuse that they were very real troubles. Through no fault of her own she was poor, cold-shouldered by good society and—what added an element of genuine tragedy to her situation—cut off from her children. Too spirited to let herself be crushed, she did her best to keep her flag flying; continued to cut a dash in pearls and black lace, to edit albums and write novels, to give lively dinner parties, to cultivate new friendships with interesting men. But misfortune brought out, in its most unpleasing form, that exhibitionist egotism which was the bane of her nature. For the rest of her life her own wrongs were an obsession with her; and she set up as a sort of professional injured person, theatrically lamenting the unexampled cruelty, with which she had been treated, to every individual she met; and, if she got the opportunity, to the general public as well. She and George Norton wrangled endlessly about money. Provoked by some unusually offensive act on his part she would rush into print or the police court; and for a day or two the newspapers would resound with yet another recapitulation of the dreary sordid history of her marriage. It did her nothing but harm. People might have forgotten the scandal if only Caroline could have kept quiet about it. But keeping quiet was one of the things that Caroline simply could not do. Even Melbourne could not always control her. In 1840 she suddenly embarked on another vain attempt to get custody of her children, and sent a friend to Melbourne to ask him to help her. As usual he was shaving. "So you are going to revive that business," he said, "it's confoundedly disagreeable." "You know, my lord," pleaded the friend, "Mrs. Norton can't live without her children." "Well, well," sighed Melbourne, "it must be done effectively. You must have an affidavit from me. That story was all a damned lie, as you know. Put it into form and I'll swear it."

He had too much heart not to try to help her over her children. Indeed, if it involved no risk of harming the Queen, he was always ready to do what he could for Caroline; gave her money, paid her an occasional quiet visit of friendship, and, once the Queen was safely married, saw to it that she was presented at Court. His kindness had its effect on her. Misfortune, though it had made her tiresome and self-pitying, had not eradicated from her personality its streak of warm, crude, Irish good nature. She still found it natural to respond and to make things up. She did not revere Melbourne as she once had. He was weak and indolent, she told him with affectionate candour, and could be trusted to get out of doing anything unpleasant to himself, if it was possible. But she was fond of him, she knew he meant well, she would try not to worry him more than she thought right. And, in fact, as she was at pains to point out both to him and to others, she did more than once refrain from publicly proclaiming her unspeakable wrongs, in deference to his wishes.

Anyway, now he was out of office and the figure of the Queen no longer stood between them, there was every reason for her to let bygones be bygones. Melbourne was an ailing, ageing man. Remembering what he had

been in the past, she felt a gush of affection and sympathy
for him which showed itself in an energetic wish to help
him. Besides, he was still a social lion who would be a
distinguished ornament to her salon. Accordingly she
asked him frequently to her house, wrote him letters full
of rhapsody and vivacious scoldings and pleasantly daring
jokes, took him to the play and once more began introducing him to coming young men. "What! Do these
young fellows want to know me?" he remarked. "Bring
them by all means." As always, they were charmed by
his attention and entertained by his talk. Melbourne could
not help feeling gratified.

All the same, to a penetrating eye it was apparent that
his new form of life was not the success it might seem
to a stranger. One day, soon after his resignation, Sir
John Campbell, his late Attorney General, went to call
on Melbourne in order to congratulate him on his release
from the cares of office. "I hope you are happy," he said.
"Oh, very happy!" replied Melbourne, and smiled. His
smile, Campbell noticed, was not that of a happy man.
It grew no happier in the succeeding months. There
were several reasons for this. For one thing, Melbourne
found he minded being out of office. This was natural.
Pretty well every man minds losing a position of power
and eminence, if he has held it for any length of time.
We are happy in proportion as we believe ourselves and
our life to be of value; and few people are so disinterested
or so conceited as to trust wholly to their own judgment
in this matter. A Prime Minister moves through life
surrounded by people who treat him as the most important man alive. Even if he does not believe them, he feels

better pleased with himself for their admiration. When he loses power, this suddenly stops. Inevitably he feels flat, chilled, diminished. Melbourne, for all his theoretical detachment, was far too human to be immune from this common weakness of humanity. His sense of the value of his existence dwindled in his own eyes because he perceived it dwindling in the eyes of others; all the more since he could no longer forget himself under the continuous pressure of hard and necessary work. Nor, so he discovered, could he force himself to take up new work. Like an ageing horse he was only able to trot when he was harnessed to the vehicle to which he was accustomed. The projected commentary on St. Chrysostom remained unwritten. He was too old and too tired for it. He was even too tired to read in the way he used to do. Ironically enough, reading had been easy for him when he had other things to do. During the last six years he had astonished people by the way he had managed to keep up with all the new books that came out, French and American as well as English. Now he picked up a new book and turned its leaves over and let it drop from his hand. Indeed, his zestful responsiveness to experience was leaving him, with the vitality of which it was the expression. How could he respond to the beauty of the spring? It only emphasized by contrast the November sadness which brooded over his own spirit. Social life was hardly more heartening. He did enjoy it but nothing like so much as he had. His gaiety had grown a little forced and febrile. That was why some people now complained that he would never talk seriously. He did not dare let himself be serious, he felt his depression would show too much if he did. Moreover, for him the world of London society was a less entertaining place than it once had been. Lord Holland had died at the end of 1840; and, bereft of his genial presence, evenings at Holland House had lost more than half their amenity. He had been Melbourne's oldest and most congenial political friend, Melbourne felt his death as he had never felt that of any other man. As for Mrs. Norton—well, she was a good sort in her way, and he would always be fond of her. But her behaviour during the last years had rubbed off the bloom of her charm for him; he had learnt all too well what a nuisance she could be. She badgered him for money, her passion for self-advertisement embarrassed him, and she was intolerably indiscreet. "She's a passionate, giddy, dangerous, imprudent woman," he confided to Stockmar.

But even if she had been as fascinating as Cleopatra, Melbourne would have extracted little pleasure from her society. Irrevocably his heart was given to another woman; and she was the only one in England he could not see. Here lay the most powerful cause of his low spirits. Old age, fatigue, loss of friends, loss of power— he could have borne them all if life had still been irra- diated by the light of the Queen's presence. Now this was withdrawn. The withdrawal had been a gradual process. His official parting with her had not turned out to be his final parting. The Queen would not allow it to be. Late in October she invited him to the palace. He was so beside himself with joy at seeing her again that he wrote afterwards nervously apologizing, lest his exuberant spirits had betrayed him into talking too much and too heedlessly "which he is conscious they sometimes do." Meanwhile, defying previous warnings, the Queen had gone on writing him letters asking his advice, and Melbourne, forgetful of his former resolutions, had gone on giving it. He was too tired to resist her, and perhaps by now he felt her absence so much that he could not bring himself even to try to. As a matter of fact his advice was extremely circumspect. Now and again he gave his opinion as to the fitness of a candidate for some non-party post; but he avoided all controversial topics of policy and confined himself mainly to making good blood between her and her new ministers. All the same people began to talk, and their talk got to the ears of Baron Stockmar who had hovered on in England as a sort of unofficial confidential adviser to the Prince. He rightly thought that for the Crown to be known as constantly communicating with the Leader of the Opposition was bound to do it great harm. Immediately he took steps to stop it. They were tactless, Teutonic steps. He wrote a long, solemn, scolding memorandum on the subject which he desired Anson to give Melbourne to read. Melbourne's reaction revealed how little his calm exterior corresponded with the grief and agitation which in reality filled his heart, and what a strain it must have been to him to maintain it all through these last months. With changing countenance and compressed lips he read the memorandum twice through. Then, "This is a most decided opinion indeed, quite an apple-pie opinion!" he said acidly. Anson went on to observe that Stockmar thought it a great pity, if Melbourne had meant to go on writing to the Queen, that he should, a day or two before, have publicly attacked the policy of the Government in the House of Lords. This was the last straw. To be lectured like a schoolboy by an officious foreigner, when two months ago he had been Prime Minister of England, was more than Melbourne could stand. For the first time his self-control deserted him. Leaping up from the sofa he began pacing wildly up and down the room, "God Eternal, damn it!" he exclaimed, "flesh and blood cannot stand this. I only spoke upon the defensive . . . I can't be expected to give up my position in the country, neither do I think it is to the Queen's interests that I should." Anson persisted. Did Melbourne honestly think that such correspondence was wise, he asked. With a supreme effort Melbourne pulled himself together. After a long pause, "I certainly cannot think it right," he muttered.

He did not find it so easy to give it up though. The Queen went on writing and he went on answering. A fortnight later, Stockmar returned to the attack. This time, more wisely, he went himself to see Melbourne and pointed out that by persisting in the correspondence, against what he must know to be his own sense of what was wise, he was encouraging the Queen in a course of action that must in the end get her into serious trouble. At his words Melbourne looked distressed, and agitated and guilty. What ought he to do, he asked. Stockmar replied that he should wait till after the Queen's confinement and then write and tell her that for the future he thought it best that all communications on politics between them should cease. Melbourne appeared convinced by his words: and in fact he soon afterwards did tell the Queen that he did not think for the time being he ought to dine at Buckingham Palace. Stockmar sat back in victorious calm. What was his horror two months later to learn that Mrs. Norton of all people was going round London saying she had it on the best authority that the Queen and Melbourne wrote to each other daily and that she consulted him about everything. Stockmar poured out his feelings in another voluminous epistle to Melbourne in which he ended by adjuring him in pained grave terms to be true to his better self, and make the break. Melbourne was still too much upset to bring himself to discuss the matter with Stockmar. He briefly acknowledged the letter without commenting on its contents. But it had done its work. Henceforward his letters contained less and less about politics. Nor did he ever lift a finger to keep his influence over the Queen.

One wishes, for his sake, that he should have been able to carry through the break to the end with the graceful calm with which he had started on it. But the fact that he faltered makes us admire him more; for it reveals what his self-sacrifice cost him. Nor had he faltered for more than an instant: he had recovered himself quickly and completely. So completely that he did not even let himself feel annoyed with the man who had been responsible for his momentary breakdown. He knew Stockmar was in the right. Melbourne was too magnanimous to bear a grudge against an opponent who had proved to be in the right. "He is an excellent and most valuable man," he told the Queen, "one of the coollest and soundest judgments I ever met."

Magnanimity did not save him from paying the full

price for his self-sacrifice. By refusing to advise her politically any longer, Melbourne had broken the last link that kept the Queen in any way dependent on him, stopped up the only remaining channel through which flowed a stream that might keep their relationship a living one. Henceforward their ways lay irretrievably apart. Melbourne minded acutely: all the more because she was so painfully, so tantalizingly, close. It would have been more bearable if she had died or left the country. But she was living within a few streets of him, living the same life exactly as when he was with her. He could visualize her every moment: now she must be riding, now writing her letters, now going into dinner, now consulting with her new Prime Minister.

Once or twice he actually caught a glimpse of her; but in circumstances so different from those of the past that it was almost more unbearable than not seeing her at all. Once in May, 1842, he found himself at a ball where she was present. He missed, through some muddle, his chance of being presented to her. Pathetically afraid lest she should think he had been deliberately uncivil, he wrote off an agitated letter to her. "Lord Melbourne is very sorry indeed and entreats Your Majesty's pardon for his great omission on Monday evening. He was never told that he was to pass before Your Majesty at the beginning; at the same time he admits that it was a piece of blundering stupidity not to find this out for himself. After this he never saw the glimmer of a chance of being able to get near Your Majesty." On another evening in April, 1842, he drove by the Palace. Through the window of the Queen's sitting-room, open to the warm spring air, he caught sight of the familiar pictures and furniture, gleaming in the light of the newly-lit candles. Suddenly the great doors of the Palace were flung open and a small, stately, well-known figure was ushered out to step into a carriage waiting in the court-yard; the Queen was setting out for the opera. But Melbourne was not going with her. In the gathering dusk he drove on alone.

He missed her every hour of the day, missed her more even than he feared he was going to do, and more with every month that passed. The handsome, genial old gentleman, who swore and chuckled and sparklingly conversed at club and dinner table, bore within his breast a starved and aching heart. Gradually the disturbance of his mind began to make its impression on his enfeebled body. His infirmities rapidly grew worse throughout the year. In November he had a stroke. For a day or two people wondered if he was going to die.

(2)

Better if he had! For though Melbourne recovered sufficiently to linger on for six more years, yet the main-spring of his vitality was finally broken and the rest of his life is no more than a sad chronicle of decaying faculties and declining spirits. A brief chronicle too; the records of it are scanty. Already, before he died, the mists of oblivion gathered to hide his departing figure from our view. The outward form of his life did not change much, at least for two years. He divided his time between Brocket and London, with occasional

LORD MELBOURNE in 1844

visits to his friends' country homes and once or twice to
the Queen at Windsor. When in London he dined out
and attended the House of Lords; in the country he read
and meditated. Sometimes he was alone; more often a
relation was with him. It is lucky for the ageing to belong
to a united family. The Lambs throughout their lively
and varied careers had always contrived to remain intimate and devoted to each other as in the long ago days
of Melbourne House. Now the only surviving members
of the family rallied to look after their loved and distinguished elder brother. Fred Lamb, now Lord
Beauvale, had returned to England from his long
diplomatic sojourn abroad in 1842, handsome and
debonair at sixty as at twenty-five, and newly married
to an Austrian young lady nearly forty years younger
than himself, sweet-natured and absorbedly in love with
him. The Beauvales threw themselves into doing what
they could for William. After his stroke they made their
home at Brocket for much of the year. Fred took on the
job of looking into his brother's financial affairs. It was
high time that someone did. Melbourne, when he
succeeded to his title, had been a very rich man. In 1835
he still had a gross income of tweny-one thousand a
year. But he was generous, lavish and careless. He
allowed his servants to cheat him—there were sixteen
of them at South Street, all thievish and drunk, he said—
and out of boredom he neglected to go into his estate
accounts for years together. The result was that by 1842
his income had dwindled by more than a third, and what
was left was so mismanaged that it looked as though it
might diminish to a point where a man, who was living

by the lavish standards demanded from the aristocracy of the day, would find himself actually embarrassed for money. Fred set to work to stop the rot and put things in order. Meanwhile, Melbourne's house as well as his estate needed attention. Since he did not keep his servants up to the mark, they did not run it well; and in the course of years Brocket had acquired that neglected, impersonal, unlived-in look so often seen in single men's residences. Here it was Lady Beauvale who came to his assistance; taking over the domestic arrangements of the establishment and acting as hostess for Melbourne when he had visitors. She also watched over his health. "I would rather have a man about me when I am ill," he had asserted in the days of his strength and of Caroline, "I think it requires strong health to put up with a woman!" He did not think so now. To Lady Beauvale's gentle ministrations he responded with a tender, grateful affection. His sister Emily, too, helped to look after him. She lived part of the year in her old home at Panshanger, only a few miles from Brocket, and was always coming over to see him. So did her youngest son, William Cowper, Mrs. Norton's friend, an amiable youth who combined a fervent Victorian piety with a propensity to fall frequently and romantically in love. He made his uncle his confidant in these delicate matters. Melbourne, touched and entertained by young William's enthusiastic *naiveté*, gave him sympathetic and characteristic advice from the rich stores of his own experience. "My dear William," he writes on one occasion, "I think you are quite right not to engage further in these affairs without the certainty of an adequate provision; and I am

glad that you find a consolation in St. Paul's epistle to
the Corinthians. But you must not run about flirting
with girls and persuading them that you intend to marry,
unless you have the intention. St. Paul would not approve
of this. Indeed, would he like to think his epistles made
the instruments of flirtation?" And again, when William
had at last actually got engaged, "Remember that
happiness is in a calm, settled and satisfied state, and is
totally inconsistent with a frequent change of objects . . .
remember also what I said of happiness, that it lies in the
knowledge of causes of things and in rejection by
yourself of all vain and superstitious terrors."

In these words we hear the accents of the wise, amused
Melbourne who had won the heart of the young Queen.
Indeed, his decline was gradual. Now and again the
mists part to disclose a glimpse of the old Melbourne;
with Mrs. Norton at a performance of a play of Ben
Jonson, for instance—"That it should be dull I had
expected," he was heard exclaiming during the interval,
"but that it should be so damned dull I had not conceived!" or talking to a Maid of Honour when dining
with the Queen, "This dish is damned bad. On ordinary
occasions I should try to leave out the adjuration; but on
this occasion it is not worth while—it is *so* damned bad!"

These flashes, however, were few and far between.
Old acquaintances who met him after 1842 were for the
most part shocked at the change in him. White-headed,
dim-eyed, with stiff gait and dragging leg, he showed no
trace of that exuberant social vitality which had once
been his distinguishing characteristic. Greville watched
him at a house party at Broadlands sitting hour by hour

grave, stern and silent, with an expression "as of a perpetual consciousness of his glory obscured" written on his face, then breaking for a moment into a feeble echo of his old style of conversation, then relapsing once more into silence: in the middle of a dinner at Lord Cottesmore's through which he had sat neither speaking nor, apparently, taking in what was said to him, he suddenly arose and hobbled out of the room. The effort needed for conversation was more than he could manage.

Politically the same process of decline showed itself. Up to the time of his stroke it was not noticeably apparent. Melbourne, though he cannot be said to have exerted himself once he had resigned, continued to play an influential part in the counsels of the Whig Party. He was against the Whigs going in for aggressive opposition, partly out of his own innate conservatism, and still more because he did not want to rouse the Queen's anti-Tory feeling against her new Government. Both at informal meetings of the party leaders and in letters to John Russell he preached the wisdom of doing nothing in particular, with his old incisive vigour. "As we haven't a majority," he said, "we may be allowed to think a little what is best for the country and the world." On the rare occasions, too, that he summed up the energy to speak in the House of Lords, he could still be at his old independent-minded best. One speech in particular, during a Corn Law debate in February, 1842, was memorable. "Though I am ready to consider any measure for the alleviation of distress," he said, "I can never hold that the cause can be prevented by changes in the constitution or by changing the persons who administer public affairs. I am opposed to this, for if the existence of national distress is looked on as a reason for organic change in the constitution or in the individuals who compose the Government, there is an end of all stability in public affairs. In every state of the country, I fear it will not be difficult to make out such a case of poverty and suffering as may support an argument for great and immediate alterations. We have lived lately in a time of great change and many strong measures. It is supposed that these measures have produced disappointment, that Catholic emancipation has not ended in the tranquillity that was expected from it, that the Reform Bill has not improved the condition of people at large; and that those who recommended these measures do not enjoy with the country the same popularity that they formerly did. How this may be I know not. But I do know that, if there is disappointment, it does not arise from the vicious principle or the ill-working of those measures themselves, but from the wild, unfounded, exaggerated expectations of their effects which were indulged in and anticipated. A man does not know himself, nor is he a safe judge of his own conduct. But I believe myself never to have contributed to the raising of these wild and illusory hopes." In these words Melbourne states more fully and forcibly than anywhere else the reasons determining his ambiguous attitude to that great general reforming movement which had been the dominating feature of political history throughout his active career as a statesman. They may stand, indeed, for his political apologia.

For his political swan-song too. He made no important

speech during the following months; and after his stroke he could not. He rose from his bed changed politically as much as socially. He still wrote to his colleagues about affairs and occasionally attended their meetings. But the letters, traced painfully out by his semi-paralysed hand, were illegible and rambling. And he sat through the meetings, for the most part, slumped in his chair in a dazed apathy, unable it seemed to take in what was going on round him. Growingly he lost grip, lived in the past, seemed incapable of grasping what was happening in the world.

The change in him could not fail to make its impression on his colleagues. They were too fond of him not to listen deferentially and courteously whenever he spoke; but naturally they paid less and less attention to his opinions. The world in general noticed this; and followed their lead. Gone were the days of Melbourne's dressing-room levées with queues of people following one another up the stairs to ask him favours and regale him with gossip while he shaved. Whole afternoons passed now without a knock resounding on the front door of South Street. Melbourne minded. Well acquainted with Vanity Fair though he was, he was too incurably sensitive not to be hurt when he was brought thus face to face with the selfish fickleness of its natives. Besides, he needed company to keep up his flagging spirits. An old friend found him one afternoon alone and gloomy in his library. "I am glad," he exclaimed "you have come. I have sat here watching that timepiece and heard it strike four times without seeing the face of a human being; and, had it struck the fifth, I feel I could

not have borne it!" More unreasonably, he felt wounded
and surprised that his colleagues consulted him less than
they had. For it was one of the most distressing symptoms
of his decline that he failed to realize it. At the time
of his resignation he was well aware that he was not likely
to be up to taking office again. Not so after his stroke.
Early in 1844 it looked as if the Tories might be about to
fall. One evening Melbourne was dining at the Palmerstons': "I was kept up half the night," he announced to
the embarrassment of the company, "thinking, suppose
that I was sent for to Windsor, what advice should I give
the Queen: and it kept me long awake!"

As a matter of fact, by this time there was no question
of his being fit for active work of any kind. Living in
London at all was getting too much for him: during the
next two years he spent more and more time down at
Brocket. There, day after day, he would sit, an unopened
book on his knee, gazing out of the window or at the fire,
sunk in an apathetic melancholy. No wonder! In the
quiet of the country he was forced inescapably to contemplate his true situation, to face the fact that he was
now old and infirm and on the shelf, with nothing to
look forward to except death. He would be heard
mournfully murmuring over to himself some lines from
Samson Agonistes:

"So much I feel my genial spirits droop,
My hopes all flat. Nature within me seems
In all her functions weary of herself.
My race of glory run, and race of shame.
And I shall shortly be with those that rest."

His friends and relations did what they could to cheer him up. Lord and Lady Beauvale hovered round; Lady Palmerston drove over from Panshanger; Mrs. Norton wrote regularly; now and again a visitor from the outside world—an old friend like Lady Holland or one of Mrs. Norton's clever young men—came down to spend a night. Melbourne could still respond to these efforts to entertain him. He sat up till well after his ordinary bedtime talking and listening to the visitors; and he dismayed innocent, Victorian Lady Beauvale by the way he chuckled over the spicier passages in Mrs. Norton's letters. But these wafts of a brighter mood evaporated with the occasion that stirred them; all too soon he was plunged back into melancholy once more.

For in him the sadness ordinarily attendant on old age was reinforced by peculiar reasons for suffering. Amid much that was dimming and fading one memory remained painfully fresh; the memory of the Queen. People noticed that his eyes filled with tears every time her name was mentioned: if he was unwell, it could even produce a sort of hysterical outburst. He missed her more than ever, when there was so little to distract his mind from his sense of her loss. For he had lost her finally and completely now. After 1841 the relationship was a dead one. Melbourne made pathetic efforts to keep it going. He was always writing to her; gentle, gossipy letters, lit up from time to time by a faint glint of his old characteristic self. Let her not buy objects merely for their historical interest, he urges—"What is the value of Cardinal Wolsey's cap? A Cardinal's cap is no great

wonder!"—or he counsels her about the education of the
child Prince—"Be not over-solicitous about education . . .
it may mould and direct the character but it rarely alters
it." Alas, his letters did not evoke the response he yearned
for. He would wait for the arrival of the post trembling
with hope. More often than not it brought him nothing.
The Queen did not write as frequently as he did. In his
weakened state he could not restrain himself from gently
upbraiding her for her neglect; he had begun to think
Her Majesty's silence rather long, he told her wistfully.
The Queen apologized. But she wrote no more often
than before. Melbourne had to accustom himself to
hearing from her only occasionally; and though these
occasions were now easily the happiest moments of his
life, yet the letters themselves were not what they once
had been. No longer did she write to pour out her
feelings, but filled up the page as best she might with
mild family news and conventional words of sympathy
and encouragement. "The change from progress to
decadence is a very hard and disagreeable trial," he replies
to her apologetically, "Lord Melbourne has been reading
Cicero on old age, a very pretty treatise, but he does not
find much consolation in it. It is certainly, as Your
Majesty says, wrong to repine at everything, still it is
difficult not to do so." Once or twice his longing for her
betrays itself in a brief, understated, poignant phrase.
"Lord Melbourne cannot say otherwise but that he
continually misses and regrets the time when he had
daily confidential communication with Your Majesty."

Their rare meetings did nothing to soothe him; short,
stiff interchanges in company, utterly unlike the leisurely

intercourse of the past. There is a distressing account of a visit to Chatsworth in the winter of 1843. Melbourne had arrived as excited as a child at the prospect of seeing the Queen again. And then she never saw him alone or talked to him for more than a few minutes; even at dinner she soon turned to the other side. Oblivious of the people round him, the old man sat, his face working with the unconcealed anguish of his disappointment. The Queen's conduct on this occasion seems to have been due to gaucherie, not lack of heart. She was flustered to see how he had changed and frightened of tiring him. Indeed, considering the limitations of her character and situation, she treated Melbourne after his fall as well as anyone could reasonably expect. She never forgot that she owed him a great deal, and sought conscientiously to discharge her debt: wrote to him when she had time, sent him presents, invited him for an occasional visit; and when she heard he was embarrassed for money, she lent him a considerable sum to tide him over his difficulties. All the same, it must be admitted that she was not the sort of woman who knew best how to soften the hard pang of parting. Her egotism and her honesty alike forbade it. She could not put herself in his place nor enter imaginatively into his feelings; and it had never been possible for her to pretend to a sentiment she did not feel. For Melbourne she now felt very little. Though the Queen could love intensely, she was only capable of loving one person at a time. The Prince had now completely replaced Melbourne in her affections; so much so that she somehow felt she had been disloyal in ever having been so fond of Melbourne at all. "Reading this again," she notes in 1842, after looking back at some entry of two years before in her diary, "I cannot forbear remarking what an artificial sort of happiness *mine* was *then*, and what a blessing it is I have now in my beloved Husband *real* and solid happiness, which no Politics, no worldly reverses *can* change; it could not have lasted long, as it was then, for after all, kind and excellent as Lord M. is, and kind as he was to (me), it was but in Society that I had amusement, and I was only living on that superficial resource, which I *then fancied* was happiness! Thank God! for *me* and others, this is changed, and I *know what* REAL happiness is."

She never stopped to think what was real happiness to Melbourne. But, as a matter of fact, even if she had, it would have made little difference to him. Not the Queen, but the nature of human existence, was responsible for his sorrow. For what he minded was the fact of separation, and this was inevitable. An old man at the end of his life's journey, and a young girl just setting out on hers, what bond could hold them together?—especially when the girl happened to be Queen of England and newly married to a man of her own age whom she passionately loved. For a short time their ways had crossed. Now, with hopeless, regretful eyes, he watched her figure grow small and disappear over the horizon.

The trouble was that she had grown to be the only thing that made life worth living to him. Here we come to the crucial, central, incurable cause of his melancholy, a cause that finds its origin far back in the dim beginnings of his history. For all that it had been so packed and brilliant, Melbourne's had been an unfulfilled life. He was born with a strong, subtle intelligence, always restlessly searching to discover some ultimate truth and significance in human existence. But his search had been frustrated by the congenital, fundamental division in his nature. Never had he been able to reconcile the sceptical realism of his judgment with those ideal aspirations, which alone commanded the enthusiasm of his heart. Indeed he had long ago given up trying to do so; and, resigning himself to accept the fact that he would never be sure of the ultimate value of anything, he had surrendered himself in a spirit of cheerful ironical detachment, to such immediate satisfactions as life offered to him; to the pleasures of society and the interest and excitement of great affairs. So long as he was vigorous and zestful, this policy had worked well enough. Now it did not do so any more. He had neither the spirit to enjoy society nor the strength to take part in public affairs. This would not have mattered so much if he had not been solitary, for, along with his intellect, nature had endowed him with an intensely affectionate heart that might have enabled him to forget his own troubles in the interests and happiness of others whom he loved. But, once youth is past, such a heart can only find complete and continuing fulfilment in family life, in the close stable relationship that a man has with wife and children. Here Melbourne had been cruelly treated by fate. Born to be a husband and father, he found himself, through no fault of his own, when near on seventy, a childless widower; well liked by many, but needed by none.

In face of this situation, all his age-old, carefully

constructed defences crumbled. What good was a hedonistic philosophy, however intelligently conceived, when the power to enjoy was failing. What strength could he find in his detachment? Detachment can only strengthen the spirit if it is a positive detachment founded on a sense of some timeless and absolute reality, immune from the accident of mortal existence; whereas Melbourne's was negative, sustained by nothing firmer than an instinctive response to the call of the passing hour. Against the injurious onset of time, age and death, the human soul is fortified by two things only, faith and love. Melbourne had no one who depended on his love, nor had he ever been able to find ground on which to build a sure faith. During these last years he met the Archbishop of Canterbury who spoke to him of the help given by prayer. "Yes?" queried Melbourne, "but who is one to pray to and what is one to pray for?" After many changes of fortune the life-long battle between his sanguine temperament and his questioning destructive intellect had ended in his temperament's decisive defeat. At last he was forced to feel, as well as to think, that life was a vain and empty dream. A grey sense of the insubstantiality and fleetingness of things human possessed his spirit. "The fire is out," he muttered to himself as he sat gazing before him at vacancy. "The fire is out."

In a bitter-sweet mood of recollection, he mused on the time when it was still alight. His mind tended, as the eventless rural days succeeded one another, more and more to dwell in the past. It was natural that it should at Brocket. The chintz-curtained bedrooms, the gilded, elegant saloon, the leather-scented quiet of the library, the park with its grassy vistas and the swans sweeping down on thunderous wing to settle in the river reeds —all these were heavy with memories for him, memories stretching back as far as he could remember at all. Not a phase of his earlier life but was connected with Brocket. There on his holidays from school, he had romped and ridden with Pen and Fred and "that little devil Emily"; there he had argued and laughed with Lady Melbourne; there he had learnt to study and to meditate; within these walls had been enacted much of the long drawn-out ironical tragedy of his marriage, from its rapturous, troubled honeymoon, to the muted pathos of Caroline's last days. He spoke of her sometimes, and also of his mother. The most important figures in his life had always been women, these two pre-eminently. As he brooded on the past, it was their ghosts who stole forth most often to stand beside his chair. With them came another's, whom he had loved perhaps more tenderly than either. She was not dead, though as irrecoverably lost to him as if she were. At the thought of her, visions of youth and childhood vanished; Brocket faded as Windsor rose before his mental eye; and once more the tears gathered to prick his eyelids and trickle down his withered cheeks.

In 1846 an event took place which roused him from his reveries once again to make an active appearance on the contemporary political scene. Peel changed the declared opinions of a lifetime and came out against the Corn Laws. By so doing his split his Party. If the Whigs chose to ally themselves with the infuriated right wing of the Tories, they had a chance of turning the Government out. It would be an unscrupulous act on their part to do so, for up till then they had been in favour of modifying the Corn Laws themselves. Oppositions, however, like turning Governments out, and the Whig leaders were tempted. They held a meeting to discuss the subject. Melbourne struggled up to London to attend it. The arguments veered this way and that; suddenly, and for the first time that day, his voice, now slow and halting, made itself heard. "My Lords," he said, "it's a damn thing that Peel should have repealed the duty on foreign corn. But he has done it and the consequences are that you will all have to vote for it." He had gone to the heart of the matter. Whatever the immediate political advantage, there was no doubt that the Whigs would be disastrously discredited if they voted for the Ultra-Tories. After Melbourne had spoken, no one had the effrontery to suggest that they should do so. For the last time the flame of his energies had flickered up to exhibit a flash of his old penetrating shrewdness. It was not bright enough, however, to persuade his colleagues into thinking him once again fit for office. Alas, Melbourne still did not realize this. The Tory Government fell: and buoyed up by his passionate desire to return to the Queen, he hoped that he might be offered, if not the premiership, at least some less onerous office like that of Lord Privy Seal. Hopefully he waited. Then came a letter from the Queen tactfully explaining that she had not called upon his services because she thought his health would not stand the strain. Melbourne wrote back assuring her that of course and as always she was right. But for a short time at any rate he was acutely disappointed.

His friends noticed it. For it was another effect of his disintegration that he found it harder and harder to hide his feelings. The old characteristic urbanity of demeanour would be suddenly broken by outbursts of nervous agitation. In the same year he was dining one evening at Windsor: the conversation turned on Peel's *volte-face*. This had shocked Melbourne very much: to throw over party and loyal colleagues for the sake of a doctrine, and an economic doctrine at that, was the last sort of thing with which he could sympathize. "Ma'am, it's a damn dishonest act," he burst out. At once amused and embarrassed by his violence, the Queen laughed and tried to change the subject. But Melbourne was by now too upset to be diverted from his course even by the Queen herself. The company sat awkward and silent as, confusedly and frantically, he continued to rail against Peel and his anti-Corn Law activities.

Back at Brocket he at last resigned himself to accept the fact that his day was done. But resignation did not mean tranquillity of spirit. Melbourne never attained the famed serenity of old age. Few people do. Serenity implies an ability to rise above trouble, whereas age and weakness generally make people more susceptible to it. Certainly Melbourne was. He had been born with a high-strung, sensitive, vulnerable temperament, but he had early learnt to control it by the exercise of a cool, sensible judgment. Now his power of judgment was decaying along with his other faculties. He, once so conspicuous for his robust indifference to petty causes of

annoyance, became an easy prey to fits of worry about
ills, trifling or imaginary. Sometimes he fancied for no
reason that a friend had turned against him; sometimes
he was seized with a sudden fear that he was ruined;
sometimes—and this was the strangest of all in him—
he worried about his reputation. A newspaper would
quote, slightly inaccurately, some public utterance of his.
With trembling, laborious hand he wrote off asking
that it might be immediately corrected. In 1848 it
somehow came out that in 1832 Tom Young had written
a letter from the Home Office to the leader of the
Birmingham League encouraging them to raise an
insurrection if reform broke down. This revelation
should not have distressed Melbourne much. Young
had written the letter without his knowledge; and,
anyway, who cared about 1832 now? But Melbourne
was so upset, lest in some way he should be held responsible, that for a day or two he was actually ill.

It would be a mistake, however, to think of this final
phase of Melbourne's earthly existence as all trouble and
gloom. There was more of twilight than black darkness
about it. If old age led him to worry easily, it also made
him forget his worries soon; and much of the time he
did not worry at all. His attacks of acute depression,
too, seem to have grown rarer as his vital forces weakened.
Strangers who came to Brocket found Lord Melbourne
a genial, tranquil old gentleman. And a very agreeable
one as well. He spent most of the day in his bedroom,
but if a visitor came to stay, he would bestir himself to
come down to dinner; and afterwards for an hour or two
the company would be treated to a display—faint and

fatigued, no doubt, in comparison with those that had dazzled society in his heyday, but still delightful—of his racy, whimsical, accomplished conversational art.

So two years slipped by. Then in November, 1848, he was suddenly taken dangerously ill. After two days racked by convulsive fits, he gradually became unconscious. Lady Palmerston, coming into his room on 24th November to see how he was, found him sleeping. In the pale light of the autumn day, his countenance, still beautiful in spite of the ravages that time and suffering had wrought upon it, wore an extraordinary look of contentment and resignation and peace. He lay for thirty-six hours more, with the life silently ebbing away within him. Then, at six o'clock on the following evening, he gave a long, soft sigh, and died. A few days later his body was borne through the leafless Hertfordshire lanes to be buried quietly near Caroline's in the neighbouring country churchyard of Hatfield.

The proper formalities were observed. Palmerston wrote announcing the sad news to the Queen; the Queen sent her condolences to Lady Palmerston; and a lengthy, if unenthusiastic, estimate of Melbourne's character and achievements appeared in *The Times*. But, in fact, his death made little stir. The world was changing fast in the nineteenth century. And, though he was only sixty-nine when he died, he had outlived his time.

LIST OF AUTHORITIES

The Windsor Papers.
The Panshanger Papers.
The Broadlands Papers.
The Howick Papers.
The Holland House Papers.
The Bowood Papers.
The Lamb Papers, in the possession of the Dowager Lady
    Salisbury.
The Hatherton Papers.

ACLAND, ALICE. Caroline Norton.

AIRLIE, MABELL COUNTESS OF. Lady Palmerston and Her
    Times.

ASPINALL, ARTHUR. Lord Brougham and the Whig Party.

BROUGHAM, HENRY, 1ST BARON. His Life and Times,
    written by himself.

BROUGHTON, LORD. Recollections of a Long Life.

CAMPBELL, LORD. Life of.

CLARK, G. K. Peel and the Conservative Party, 1832–1841.

CARLYLE, THOMAS. Letters.

CRABITÈS, PIERRE. Victoria's Guardian Angel. A Study
    of Baron Stockmar.

CRAWFORD. Victoria, Queen and Ruler.

COLE, G. D. H. History of Trade Unionism.

COLE, G. D. H. Life of William Cobbett.

COLE, G. D. H. Life of Robert Owen.

CREEVEY PAPERS.

CRESTON, DORMER. The Youthful Queen Victoria.

DARWIN, EMMA. A Century of Family Letters.

DISRAELI. Coningsby.

DISRAELI. Sybil.

DUNCKLEY, HENRY. Lord Melbourne.

EDEN, EMILY. Letters.

FONBLANQUE, E. Life and Letters of Albany Fonblanque.

FULFORD, ROGER. George IV.

FULFORD, ROGER. Royal Dukes.

FULFORD, ROGER. Life of the Prince Consort.

GERARD, FRANCES. Some Fair Hibernians.

GRANVILLE, HARRIET, COUNTESS. Letters of, 1810-1845.

GREVILLE MEMOIRS.

GUEDALLA, PHILIP. Palmerston.

GUIZOT, G. F. Memoirs.

HALEVY, ELIE. History of the English People in the Nineteenth Century. 1815-1830.

HAMMOND, J. L. The Village Labourer, 1760-1832.

HAMMOND, J. L. The Town Labourer.

HAYDON, BENJAMIN. Diaries of.

HAYWARD, ABRAHAM. Sketches of Eminent Statesmen and Writers.

ILCHESTER, EARL OF. Home of the Hollands, 1605-1820.

ILCHESTER, EARL OF. Chronicles of Holland House, 1820-1900.

JERDAN, WILLIAM. Autobiography.

JOYCE, MICHAEL. My Friend H.

KEBBEL, T. E. Life of the Earl of Derby.

KEMBLE, FANNY. Records of a Girlhood.

LE MARCHANT. Memoirs of Viscount Althorp.

LIEVEN, PRINCESS. Letters of.

LYTTELTON, SARAH SPENCER, LADY. Correspondence.

LIST OF AUTHORITIES

MACAULAY, LORD. Critical and Historical Essays.

MALMESBURY, LORD. Memoirs.

MARTIN, SIR THEODORE. Life of the Prince Consort.

MARTINEAU, HARRIET. Autobiography.

MAUROIS, ANDRÉ. Disraeli.

MELBOURNE, LORD. Letters and Papers, edited by Lloyd Sanders.

MONYPENNY AND BUCKLE. The Life of Disraeli.

MOORE, THOMAS. Memoirs, journal and correspondence.

NEW, C. W. Lord Durham, a biography.

NEWMAN, BERTRAM. Lord Melbourne.

NORTON, CAROLINE. English Laws for Women.

PERKINS, J. Life of Mrs. Norton.

PRESTIGE, G. L. Life of Charles Gore.

QUENNELL, PETER. Byron: the Years of Fame.

REID, S. J. The Life and Letters of the 1st Earl of Durham, 1792-1840.

RUSSELL, G. W. E. Collections and Recollections.

RUSSELL, LORD JOHN. Early Correspondence.

SANDERS, LLOYD, C. The Holland House Circle.

SMITH, SIDNEY. Letters and Works.

STANHOPE, 5TH EARL. Conversations with Wellington.

STOCKMAR, BARON. Memoirs.

STRACHEY, LYTTON. Queen Victoria.

TOLPUDDLE, The Martyrs of, 1834-1934.

TORRENS, W. M. Life of Lord Melbourne.

TREVELYAN, G. M. British History in the Nineteenth Century.

TREVELYAN, G. M. Lord Grey of the Reform Bill.

TREVELYAN, G. O. Life and Letters of Macaulay.

VICTORIA, QUEEN. Letters.

LIST OF AUTHORITIES

VICTORIA, QUEEN. The Girlhood of, edited by Benson and Esher.

VICTORIA, QUEEN. The Correspondence of, edited by Viscount Esher.

WALLAS, G. The Life of Francis Place.

WALPOLE, SPENCER. History of England from the conclusion of the great war in 1815.

WALPOLE, SPENCER. Life and Letters of Lord John Russell.

WEBSTER, G. K. The Foreign Policy of Palmerston, 1830–1841.

WHATELY, E. J. Life and Correspondence of Archbishop Whately.

WILBERFORCE, R. I. Life of William Wilberforce.

INDEX

Adelaide, Queen, 112

Agricultural labourers' revolt (1830), *see* Labourers

Agriculture workers and trades unions, 101, 103

Aides-de-camps, sashes for, 195, 196

Ainsworth, Harrison, 155

Alava, Don Migual di, 193, 194

Albert of Coburg, Prince (later Prince Consort), visits England (1839), 265–6; marriage to Queen Victoria decided on, 266–7; questions of his precedence and income, 267–9; Queen's efforts to keep him out of politics, 270, 293–4; Queen chooses his Household, 270–1; relations with M., 270–4, 192–3; Queen quotes his views to M., 272–3; marriage to Queen (1840), 275–6; and Palmerston's foreign policy, 288; trained by M. for his future responsibilities, 292–5; replaces M. in the affections of the Queen, 324–5; mentioned, 298, 300, 310–11

Althorp, Lord, *see* Spencer, Lord

Anabaptists, 145

Anson, George, 270, 271, 293, 295, 296, 298, 310–11

Arnold, Dr., 141

Art, State patronage of, 89–90

Ascot, demonstration against the Queen, 255

Attwood, Thomas, 32, 49, 55

Auckland, Lord, 60, 151

Ballot, secret, 129, 192, 234, 254, 291

Bank Bill, 84, 87

Baring, Lady Augusta, 69

Beauclerk, Lord Amelius, 195, 196

Beauvale, Lady, 316, 322

Beauvale, Lord (earlier Frederick Lamb) (brother), 14, 35, 55, 86, 165, 166, 280, 315–6, 322, 328

Bedford, Duke of, 135–6, 286, 303

Bentham, Jeremy, 124, 147

Birmingham riots (1839), 279

Boswell, James, Queen Victoria compared with, 186

Branden, Lady, 30–1, 68, 71, 152

Branden, Lord, 30–1

Brighton, 190, 215

Bristol riots (1831), 48–9

Broadlands, 317

Brocket Hall, 3, 151, 208, 211, 249, 303, 314–6, 321, 327–31

Brooks's Club, 40, 43, 78, 133, 186, 250, 303

Brougham, Lord, supports Reform Bill, 47–8; character sketch, 81–4; M.'s attitude to, 86–7; and Irish Coercion Act, 107–8, 109; rage at not being made Prime Minister; tour of Scotland, 116–7; William IV's dislike of, 119; gives *The Times* news of Government's dismissal (1834), 119; M. excludes

INDEX

Brougham, Lord (*cont.*):
from Government (1835), 124–6; opposes Government in debates, 192, 229; and Durham's mission to Canada, 229–30; personal attack on M., 297–8; mentioned, 20, 78, 110, 149, 192, 285

Buckingham Palace, 186, 190, 208, 215, 249, 275, 304

Byron, Lord, 208–9

Callcott, Sir A., 90

Cambridge, Duchess of, 214

Campbell, Sir John, 162–4, 307

Canada, 192; rebellion (1838), 224–6; Durham's mission to, 226–33

Canning, George, 17, 20, 22, 26, 133

Canningite-Tories, 2, 17, 19–22, 26–8, 32, 34, 74

Capital punishment, 40, 42

Carlton Club, 302

Carlyle, Thomas, 18

Cary, H. F., 137

Catholic emancipation, 22–4, 32, 35, 106, 108, 319

Chalmers, Dr. Thomas, 145

Charing Cross Library, 46

Chartist Movement, 279

Chatsworth, 324

Children and the Factory Acts, 95–6

Church-going, M.'s views on, 189, 261–2

Church of England, proposed reforms, 74, 144; finance, 127; M. and ecclesiastical appointments 137–44; control of education, 279

Church of Scotland, 144–5

Civil List pensions, 136–7

Clare, Lord, 25

Clarendon, Lord, 284, 285, 292

Clarke, Sir James, 217, 218

Clarkson, Thomas, 140

Clergy, incomes of the 144

Cobbett, William, 32, 33

Conroy, Sir John, 178–82, 201–3, 214, 217, 219, 256

Corn Laws, repeal of the, 74, 234–6, 252, 279, 290–2, 296–7, 318, 328–30

Cornwall, Duchy of, 221

Coronation of Queen Victoria (1838), 191, 198, 212

Cottesmore, Lord, 218

Court, etiquette tightened up, 197, 214; Peel suggests changes in Queen Victoria's Household, 239–40; Queen refuses consent, 241; Queen chooses Prince Albert's Household, 270–1; compromise over Queen's Ladies, 295–6

Cowley, Lord and Lady, 195, 196

Cowper, Emily Lady (sister), *see* Palmerston, Lady

Cowper, Spencer, 263

Cowper, William, 304, 316–7

Crabbe, George, 15

Creevey, Thomas, 169, 185

Crime, schemes for checking, 92

Croker, J. W., 120

Denison, Mr., 95

Derby riots (1831), 48

Devonshire, Duke of, 45, 155

Devonshire House, 187

Dickens, Charles, *Oliver Twist*, 15, 44; *Pickwick Papers*, 162
Disraeli, Benjamin, 53, 66, 182, 191
Dissenters, 145
Dorset labourers' trial, *see* Tolpuddle
Douro, Lord, 189
Downing Street, M.'s refusal to live in, 133
Drink, control of sale, 92
Druids, 56
Dudley, Lord, 27–28
Duncannon, Lord, 134
Durham, Lord, and Reform Bill, 51; character sketch, 80–1; missions to Russia, 81, 124; resigns from Government (1833), 84, 107; M.'s dislike of, 86; and the Irish question, 107; intrigues with Duchess of Kent, 177; M. rejects proposals to readmit him to Government, 222; mission to Canada (1838), 226–33; mentioned, 78, 149, 257
East Retford disfranchisement, 27–9
Eden, Emily, 60–2, 65, 70, 88, 117, 119, 151–2
Education, M.'s attitude to, 129–30; proposed reform, 234; Bill (1839), 278–9
Egypt, 284
Elizabeth, Queen, 207
Ellice, Edward, 68
Ernest of Coburg, Prince, 265
Eton College, 191, 208
Europe, in 1834, 114; in 1840, 280–3

Factory Acts, 84, 95–6
"Finality Jack", *see* Russell, Lord John
Fitzgibbon, Mr., 25
Fluke (groom), 163
Foreign affairs, M.'s attitude to, 280–9, 290
Fox, Charles, 89
France, Revolution (1789), 33, 38, 101, 114; July Revolution (1830), 32; and British support of Turkey, 284–9
Francis I of France, 247
Garter, Order of the, 6; M. refuses, 137, 300
General elections (1831), 47; (1835), 120; (1841), 297
George III, 189, 207
George IV, 17, 22, 26, 32, 35, 97, 187
Germany, Queen Victoria's first visit to, 175; M.'s opinion of Germans, 206
Gladstone, William Ewart, 182
Glenelg, Lord, 148, 149, 223, 225, 233, 234
Goa, Island of, 281–2
Goderich, Lord, 26
Goldsmith, Mr., 135
Gore, Mrs., 196, 197
Grand National Consolidated Trade Union, 99
Grantley, Lord, 63
Great Seal, Brougham plays "hunt the thimble" with, 116–7
Greville, Charles, 36, 53, 54, 60, 85, 111, 112, 117, 258, 317–8
Grey, Lady, 185

INDEX

Grey, Lord, leader of the Whigs, 20; efforts to gain support of Canningites, 34–5; and Reform Bill, 47; and trade unions, 49; and creation of peers, 51; character sketch, 66; and Irish question, 107–8; resigns, 108–10; mentioned, 52, 121, 124, 134, 192

Grey Government (1830–1834), 34, 75–84; resigns, 108–10

Guizot, G. F., 285

Hampden, Dr. R. D., 142–3

Hastings, Lord, 218, 219

Hastings, Lady Flora, 178, 217–220, 236, 255–7

Haydon, Benjamin, 88–90, 147

Hayward, Abraham, 111

Hazlitt, William, 89

Head, Sir Francis, 225–6

Heneage, Mr. and Mrs., 69

Henry VIII, 206

Hertford, Lord, 167

Hill, Rowland, 278

Historical painting and State patronage, 89–90

Hobhouse, J. C., 223

Holland, Lady, 29, 135, 197, 236, 261, 288, 289, 322

Holland, Lord, diary cited, 120; and honours, 135; and Palmerston's foreign policy, 283, 284, 285; threatens to resign, 287; repeats Cabinet secrets at parties, 288–9; death, 309

Holland House, 35, 88, 117, 147, 187, 250, 288, 303, 309

Honours, M. and, 6, 134–7, 300

House of Lords, Reform Bill rejected, 47–8; proposed creation of peers to force Reform Bill through, 51, 54, 127; proposed reform, 74; decoration, 90; Bills held up or thrown out, 122, 127, 130, 132, 169, 257; hostile to the Government, 150, 221; M. only moderately successful in, 134; M.'s attendances after his resignation, 302, 318

Household, Royal, see Court

Houses of Parliament, burnt down (1834), 117–8

Howick, Lord, 193, 223, 233, 237, 253, 276, 279

Howick Hall, 76, 84, 108

Hunt, Henry, 44

Hunt, Leigh, 137

Huskisson, William, 27, 28, 34

Ingestre, Lady Sarah, 255

Inverness, Duchess of, 79

Ireland, M. as Chief Secretary, 18, 22–6; M.'s attitude to, 114, 131–2; Catholic emancipation, 22–4, 32, 35, 106, 108; Church, 22–4, 113, 120, 121, 131–2, 224; Coercion Act, 35, 107, 128; conditions in (1827), 22; Corporation Bill, 224; Grey Government's policy, 106–9; Parliament and the Irish, 121, 122, 233; Poor law, 224; Secret societies, 22; Tithes, 24, 127, 224; Unwritten pact with O'Connell, 131

Irvingite Sect, 188

Jamaica, 192, 238, 252, 254

James, Mrs., 136

Jews, civil disabilities, 92

Johnson, Dr. Samuel, 204

340

INDEX

Keats, John, 89

Kensington Palace, 171, 176, 178

Kent, Duchess of, 149, 175–81, 199–204, 214, 217–8, 256, 269

Knowles, Sheridan, 137, 197

Labourers' revolt (1830), 32, 38–9, 40–5, 50–1

Laissez-faire, M.'s belief in, 94, 100

Lamb, Augustus (son), 29, 67–8, 168

Lamb, Lady Caroline (wife of second Viscount Melbourne), 2, 29, 69, 70, 173, 183, 198, 208–9, 328, 332

Lamb, Emily (sister), see Palmerston, Lady

Lamb, Frederick (brother), see Beauvale, Lord

Lamb, George (brother), 46, 95–6

Lamb, Peniston (brother), 328

Lamb, William, see Melbourne, second Viscount

Lansdowne, Lady, 195

Lansdowne, Lord, 26, 110, 113, 195

Lansdowne House, 35

Laure, Mademoiselle, 209

Lehzen, Baroness, 176, 178, 200, 203, 217

Leicester, Lord, 303

Leopold, King of the Belgians, 177–8, 214, 265, 269, 288, 289

Liberals, 20, 44, 114–5, 271

Lichfield, Lord, 278

Lieven, Princess, 184, 200

Literary Gazette, 29

Littleton, E. J., 108, 141

Liverpool, Lord, 17

Louis Philippe, King, 289

Lyndhurst, Lord, 188

Macaulay, T. B., 44, 276

Malmesbury, Lord, 152

Marriage, civil, legalizing of, 144

Martineau, Harriet, 44

Mehemet Ali, 284–9

Melbourne, first Viscount (father), death (1828), 29–30

Melbourne, second Viscount (earlier William Lamb) (*see also* under names of persons and subjects throughout index), death of eldest brother, 1; Chief Secretary for Ireland in Canning Government (1827), 17–18, 22; suports Canningite-Tories, 21; visits Ireland (1827), 22–26; joins Wellington Government (1828), 26, 35; resigns (1828), 28–8; succeeds as Viscount Melbourne (1828), 29–30; Lord Branden's case against (1829), 30–1; joins Grey Government (1830), 34; Home Secretary during labourers' revolt, 36–9, 41–8; growing reputation as statesman, 44; action to repress disorders (1830), 49–50; friendship for Emily Eden, 60–2; friendship for Mrs. Norton, 62, 66–72, 152, 155–65; relations with members of Grey Government, 85–7; dealings with William IV, 97–8; Prime Minister (1834), 110–11,

INDEX

Melbourne, 2nd Viscount (*cont.*):
112–8; Government dismissed,
119–20; again Prime Minister
(1835), 120–1; choice of Ministers, 123–6; refuses to move
to Downing Street, 133;
urged to accept Garter, 137;
Mr. Norton's case against,
(1836), 155–65; considers
resigning, 161–2; acquitted,
164; death of only son (1836),
168; visits Queen Victoria on
her accession, 171–2; personal
relationship with Queen, 172–
173, 181–212, 215–6, 324–5;
Queen's recording of his remarks, 188–9, 192; at Queen's
Coronation (1838), 191, 212;
remarks on characters of
public men, 192–3; political
and social tutor to Queen,
192–6, 204–8; stiffens Court
etiquette, 197; and the Duchess of Kent, 201–4; affected on
meeting Lady Byron, 208–9;
the affair of Lady Flora
Hastings, 217–20, 255; clings
to office, 222, 237; deterioration in health, 236; resigns as
Prime Minister (1839), 237–9;
distressing interview with
Queen, 238–9; returns to
office, 244–5; further decline
in health, 249–52; anxiety for
Queen's reputation, 255–7;
persuades Queen to visit Lady
Flora Hastings, 256; worried
about Queen's political reputation, 257–8; accused by
Queen of neglecting her,

260–1; ill-health, 260, 264,
288; and Queen's decision to
marry, 266–9; relations with
Prince Albert, 270–4, 292–3;
attends Queen's marriage
(1840), 275; final private interview with Queen, 275; reluctant to give up office, 278, 280,
281, 286; trains Prince Albert
for future responsibilities, 292–
295; prepares Queen for his
leaving office, 292, 295–6,
298; resigns as Prime Minister
(1841), 290, 296–8; takes leave
of Queen, 299–301; again
refuses the Garter, 300; finds
compensations at first in private life, 302–3; not happy
out of office, 307–10; invitation to the Palace, 309–10;
Queen continues to corre-
spond with, 310–2; refuses to
advise Queen politically, 312–
313; stroke (Nov. 1842), 314;
income from estate dwindles
315–6; decline in last years,
314–32; meeting with Queen
at Chatsworth (1843), 324;
Queen's treatment of him
after his fall, 324–5; loneliness
in his last years, 326–8; last
illness and death (1848),
332
Melbourne Government, First,
(1834), 110–20
Melbourne Government, Second
(1835–1841), 120–7, 132–3,
147–9, 168–70, 221–4, 233–4;
resigns (1839), 237–9; returns
to office, 244–5; difficulties,

342

INDEX

Melbourne Govt. Second (*cont.*):
252–3, 276; resigns (1841),
290, 296–8
Melbourne House, 27, 30, 43,
208, 315
Middle classes, 21, 99, 100, 115,
116, 130
Mill, John Stuart, 18
Milton, John, quoted, 147, 321
Montrose, Duchess of, 255
Moore, Tom, 88
Mozart, 205
Municipal Corporations, refor-
mation of, 127, 130
Napier, Col. W. F. P., 137
Napoleonic Wars, 2, 18
Newman, John Henry, 140
Newport riots (1839), 279
Nonconformists, and Govern-
ment posts, 27; and universities, 129
Nore mutiny (1799), 101
Normal schools, 194, 195
Normanby, Lord, 258
Norton, Augusta, 67
Norton, Mrs. Caroline, M.'s
friendship for, 31, 62, 66–72,
110, 117, 121, 152–3; her history, 63–6; pamphlet on English Laws for Women, 71;
relations with her husband,
152–5; husband's suit for
divorce, naming M., 155–65;
separated from her children,
156, 305–6, effect of the trial,
165–6; correspondence with
M., 167–8, 322; M. resumes
friendship, 303–17; desire to
be presented at Court, 304;
presented, 306; character

deteriorates, 305–6; indiscre-
tions, 309, 312
Norton, George, 62–4, 66–7, 69,
71, 153–67, 305
Nottingham Castle, destroyed
(1891), 48
O'Connell, Daniel, 22, 106, 108,
113, 114, 131, 169, 221
Ossulston, Lord, 69, 71
Owen, Robert, 99, 276–7
Oxford University, Regius Professorship of Divinity, 142
Paget family, 130
Palmerston, Lady (earlier Emily
Lamb and Lady Cowper)
(sister), 14, 17, 61, 165, 283,
316, 322, 328, 332
Palmerston, Lord, joins Canning
Government, 17; resigns, 27–
28; M.'s attitude to, 114–6, 124,
283; policy, 114–6; M.
appoints to Foreign Office,
124; rash and unmanageable,
149, 223, 253, 288; foreign
policy, 280–9, 290; intriguing
with Tories, 292; M.'s meetings with, 303, 321; announces
M.'s death to Queen, 332
Panshanger, 61, 70, 316, 322
Parliamentary reform, *see*
Reform
Patronage, M. and, 134–44
Peel, Sir Robert, and East Retford disfranchisement, 27;
Minority Government (1834),
120; M.'s relations with, 123,
127, 150, 170, 253; Queen's
attitude towards, 182, 195,
239–44, 257–8, 268, 298–9;
interview with Queen, 239–

Peel, Sir Robert (*cont.*):
240; suggests changes in Royal Household, 239–44; declines office as Prime Minister, 244; compromise on Royal Household question, 295–6; takes office (1841), 298; supports repeal of Corn Laws, 328–9, 330
Peers, proposed creation of to force Reform Bill, 51, 54, 127
Pitt, William, 207
Place, Francis, 46–7, 50
Political Unions, 49, 51
Poor law, 84, 95, 254
Portugal, 35, 192, 281
Post, penny, 278
Prime Minister, M.'s views of duties, 133
Privy Council, 171–2
Pusey, Dr., 138, 140, 142, 144
Racine, 204–5
"Radical Jack": *see* Durham, Lord
Radicals, and Parliamentary reform, 74, 75, 224; William IV and, 113; perpetual threat to Government, 121–2, 149–150, 169, 221, 233, 276; M. and, 124, 128; efforts to win confidence of, 234; and Jamaica trouble, 238; Queen and, 257; mentioned, 223, 227, 280
Raphael, 9
Reform, Parliamentary, proposed, 19–21; M.'s attitude to, 20–1, 37–8, 52, 54, 129, 224, 235, 319; agitation for (1830), 32–5; Grey Government pledged to introduce, 34; Bill before Parliament, 47–8;

thrown out by Lords, 48; rioting, 48–9; proposed creation of peers to force Bill through Lords, 51, 54, 127; proposed modification of Bill, 51, 54; Bill passes (1832), 54–5; England after passing of Bill, 73–6, 319; William IV and, 96–7; working-class and the Bill, 99; Russell and the "final limit", 224
Reynolds, Sir Joshua, 89
Richmond Park, 191
Rogers, Samuel, 82
Roman Catholic Church, M. and, 10, 145, 146, 147
Rotten Boroughs, 54
Royal Commissions, 124
Russell, Lady John, 302
Russell, Lord John, character sketch, 78–80; in Grey Government, 84; M. and, 86, 88, 192; and Tolpuddle labourers, 105; and Irish question, 107, 113–4, 118, 131–2; William IV's dislike of, 118–9, 148; advocates creation of peers, 127–8; and Reform Bill, 129, 224; resignation threats, 149, 170, 233, 253, 287; and ballot question, 192; against compromise with Tories, 223; Queen and, 237, 259; and Chartists, 279; and Palmerston, 283; advocates compromise with France, 286, 289; M.'s letters to, 318; mentioned, 108, 110, 135–6, 139, 150, 235, 251, 252, 271, 297
Russell, William, 136

INDEX

Russia, Durham's missions to, 81, 124; and Turkey, 284, 285

Russia, Grand Duke of, 264

St. Chrysostom, M.'s projected commentary on, 303, 308

Scotland, Brougham's visit to, 116–7

Scott, Walter, 194–5

Sebastiani, M., 193

Secret ballot, see Ballot

Sefton, Lord, 169

Senior, Nassau, 100

Shakespeare, M.'s appreciation of, 56–7, 205

Shelley, P. B., 89

Sheridan, R. B., 62, 63, 64

Sheridan family, 70, 153–4, 167

Slave trade, 9–10, 234, 282

Smallholdings, 94

Smith, Sidney, 79–80, 141

Social reform, 94, 96

South Street, Mayfair, 30, 53, 57, 60, 66, 71, 133, 155, 315, 320

Spencer, Lord (earlier Lord Althorp), character sketch, 76–8; in Grey Government, 81, 84; and Irish question, 107, 108; William IV and, 110; succeeds as Lord Spencer, 118; M. and, 124; declines Canadian mission, 226; advocates compromise with France, 286

Stael, Madame de, 207

Stanhope, Lord, 70

Stanley, Lord (earlier Edward Stanley), 78, 81, 84, 86, 107, 121

Stockmar, Baron, 265, 309, 310–2

Storey's Gate, 62, 65, 165, 304

Suffield, Lord, 94–5

Sussex, Duke of, 195, 196, 267, 269

Sutherland, Duchess of, 79, 208, 214

Thiers, L. A., 285, 289

Thirlwall, Dr., 139

Thynne, Lord Edward, 69

Times, The, 117, 119, 169, 332

Tithes, 33, 144

Tolpuddle labourers, trial of 101–6, 277

Tories, against Parliamentary reform, 34; and action against revolution, 44; unpopularity, 75, 87; gaining in power, 110, 120, 221; suggested Tory-Whig coalition, 113, 121; obstructive to the Government, 122, 131, 150, 276; Whig Government's compromise with, 223, 252–3; and Durham's ordinance, 230; popularity growing, 233; Queen Victoria's dislike of, 246, 257–8, 268, 270, 298–9; and Prince Albert's precedence, 268; Palmerston intrigues with, 292; M. tries to remove Queen's prejudice against, 298–9

Trades Unions, 38–9, 42, 49, 92, 99–106, 236

Transportation, 40, 43, 102

Trelawny, E. J., 155

Turkey, 282, 284–9

Turton, Thomas, 227–30

Ultra-Tories, 17, 19–20, 329
Universities, religious tests at, 129, 144
Vaughan, Miss, 154
Victoria, Queen, accession (1837), 171–2; M.'s personal relationship with, 172–3, 181–212, 215–6; childhood and upbringing, 175–80; difficulties with her mother after her accession, 150–1, 199–204, 214; recording of M.'s remarks, 188–9; opens Parliament, 191; Coronation (1838), 191, 198, 212; M. responsible for her political education and her social tutor, 192–6, 204–8; concern about social morality, 196–7; consults M. on religious dogma, 197–9; confidence in M., 204; tightens up Court etiquette, 214; desires M. to be near her, 215–6; affair of Lady Flora Hastings causes unpopularity, 217–20; fear of losing M. as Prime Minister, 237; interview with M. after his resignation (1839), 238–9; Peel suggests changes in Royal Household, 239–40; attitude to Peel, 239–41; refuses to change Court Ladies, 241–4; persuades M. to return to office, 242–5; M. resumes dining with, 246–8; M.'s gifts of flowers, 249; hostility to her in high society, 255; demonstration against at Ascot, 255; visits the dying Lady Flora Hastings, 256; mother becomes more friendly towards, 256; M.'s anxiety for her good name, 255–7; M. worried about her political reputation, 257–8; attitude to the Tories, 257–8, 270, 298; touchiness about her royal rights, 258–9; accuses M. of neglecting her, 260–1; and M.'s religious tone 261–3; meets Prince Albert of Coburg, 265–6; decides on marriage, 266–7; effects of her decision, 267–9; efforts to keep Albert out of politics, 270, 293–4; chooses Albert's Household, 270–1; marriage (1840), 275–6; final private interview with M., 275–6; intervenes in dispute between England and France, 288–9; M. prepares her for his leaving office, 292, 295–6, 298; signs of Albert's influence, 294–5; compromise with Peel over dismissal of Ladies, 295–6; takes leave of M., 299–300; offers M. the Garter, 300; gift of etchings to M., 300; invites M. to Palace, 309–10; continues to correspond with M., 310–12; M. refuses to advise politically, 312–3; M. visits at Windsor, 315; corresponds less frequently with M., 323; meets M. at Chatsworth (1843), 324; treatment of M. after his fall, 324–5; fails to recall M. to office (1846), 329–330; hears of M.'s death, 332

INDEX

Voltaire, quoted, 111
Wakefield, Gibbon, 227–30
Warburton, Henry, 278
Ward, J. W., *see* Dudley, Lord
"Waverers, The", 52, 53, 78
Wellesley, Lord, 25, 107, 108, 109, 124, 125
Wellington, Duke of, refuses to serve under Canning (1827), 17; Prime Minister (1828), 26–7; and East Retford question, 27–8; loses supporters, 32–3, 34; attitude to Parliamentary reform, 33–4, 73; fall of Government (1830), 34; relations with M., 35, 96, 98, 162, 212; William IV anxious for him to take office, 118; M.'s opinion of, 192–3; and Lady Flora Hastings affair, 219; supports disallowance of Durham's ordinance, 230; M. recommends for office (1839), 239; advises Queen to send for Peel, 239; consulted by Peel on Queen's Ladies' question, 241–2; relations with Queen, 242, 257; invited to Queen's wedding, 274; M. wins promise of support, 287; attacks M. on Corn Laws issue, 297; mentioned, 96
Westhorpe, Mr., 25
Whately, Archbishop, 9
Whigs, M.'s attitude to, 2, 253, 318; supporters of Canning, 17; resign from Wellington Government (1828), 26; leaders friendly to M., 35; and parliamentary reform, 38, 47,

54, 74; increased majority at general election (1831), 47; Durham's influence on, 81–2; support sought on Irish question, 108; position on Grey's resignation, 110; coalition with Tories suggested (1834), 113; division in Party, 121; further reforms introduced, 127; and running of local affairs, 130–1; and Church of Rome, 146; William IV's attitude to, 148; fears of effect of possible fall of Whigs (1837), 170; effect of Queen's accession, 220; declining popularity, 233, 243; middle way policy, 252; Queen's attitude to, 296–7; and Corn Laws, 328–9
Wilberforce, William, 139, 194, 195
William IV, fears of revolutionary forces, 42, 49, 97–8; dissolves Parliament (1831), 47; character sketch, 96–8; M.'s relations with, 97–8; dislike of the Whigs, 110, 148; asks M. to form Ministry (1834), 110–111; suggests Tory-Whig coalition, 113; dislike of Brougham, 116; M. resigns; suggests Wellington for office, 118–9; against second Melbourne Government, 121, 148; urges M. to accept Garter, 137; and Dr. Hampden, 142; rudeness and ill-temper, 148–9; attitude to Duchess of Kent, 149, 176–179, 201–2; advises M. against

347

INDEX

William IV (*cont*.):
resignation at time of Norton
divorce suit, 161–2; moodiness
with his Ministers, 169–70;
and Princess Victoria, 176–9;
M.'s concern that he should see
a clergyman when dying, 147;

death (1837), 171
Windsor Castle, 173, 190, 197,
258, 260, 315
Windsor Park, 191, 248
Wordsworth, William, 210
Young, Tom, 45, 46, 47, 50, 92,
111, 331